Surviving Myself

Surviving
M Y S E L F

Jennifer O'Neill

WILLIAM MORROW AND COMPANY, INC.

NEW YORK

To Cheri

acknowledgments

$\mathscr{I}$ DECIDED to write *Surviving Myself* at the prompting of my children. I thank Aimee for her courage and insight, Reis for his selfless support and honesty, Cooper for understanding my long hours at work and his hugs of encouragement. Thank you, Mom and Dad, for your staunch support, candid reviews, and permission to share your private lives with the public . . . And to my husband, Mervin, for your uplifting words in the midst of momentary fears. To the Chrisagises, my second family, thank you for your prayers, hard work, and notes of purpose and focus. To my mentor of the written word, H. Jackson Brown, thanks for the guiding light. And Melissa and Cindy, you are two exceptional ladies. Tom Reich—my appreciation for being my friend without exception. Your integrity, humor, ethics, and intellect have been a cornerstone in my adult life. You have single-handedly proven that trust in another is possible in today's world.

As this is my first book, finding the quintessential publisher for *Surviving Myself* was of great concern to me, but the moment I spoke with Betty Kelly, editor in chief of William Morrow, I knew I was home. Betty, I appreciate your craftsmanship, candor, and above all, your unique sensibilities amidst razor-sharp competition. And thank you for your matchmaking skills, pairing me with Guy Kettelhack as the editor of *Surviving Myself*—a real professional, he performed beyond your accolades and my expectations. As well,

I've gained a dear friend along with his overviews and insights. It's true what they say about a good editor . . . Guy, I couldn't have done it without you.

But first and foremost, I thank God for His grace, guidance, protection, and unconditional love. I ask for His blessings on this book and His wisdom to guide my stewardship in His name.

TAKING THE HURDLES

THERE is a laughter so deep within us that at times it cannot be contained. There is singing that comes from our very souls. There are record-breaking Olympic moments, births, springtimes, and lovemaking . . . And sometimes there is a unique ballet that happens between animal and man; a melding of muscle, mind, and spirit that identifies two as one. That's what it feels like to jump a fence in perfect harmony with your horse. That's why I love the sport so much. It is unlike any other; it's not a sport of machines such as racing cars, it's not a strategy team sport like football or baseball, and it's not an individual sport such as running or diving. It requires a marriage between an animal that weighs at least ten times more than you, has moods, physical limitations, and a mind to win or not. Mutual rhythm, respect, and heart make a special horse-and-rider team, and if you've ever known that even for a moment, you can't help but want more.

But sometimes it's hard to find rhythm, respect, and heart in everyday life. Like the elusive chord that turns a mediocre song into a classic. And then, sometimes, there are only sour notes. Sharing that feeling of union with a horse tells me about what real love and faith can feel like, what they may mean and what they might do. But in my life, that freedom has been hard-won. *Summer of '42* . . . What a blessing to have been part of that film, to have had it introduce me to the world. I knew how to portray the pain and isolation of Dorothy, the character I played, because I had already experienced so much pain and isolation in my own life. Maybe not so different from that other Dorothy . . . the one who whirled up in a tornado and landed somewhere very strange and far away. I've had my Oz, and my Kansas, too. And I've nearly been killed by all sorts of flying monkeys and wicked witches. It took so long to learn what Dorothy—and Jennifer—had to learn: that the answer to life was found in such a simple place. I didn't need tornadoes and crashing houses to teach it to me. I just had to look into my own heart. But that's getting ahead of myself. What comes to mind right now is the beginning. A silly memory: a pair of shoes . . . not exactly ruby slippers.

Surviving Myself

one

PINK SUEDE SHOES

HEY were pink suede shoes—and they were mine. As much as I wished it wasn't so, there they were, in all their ugliness, tied with a double knot to my nine-year-old "Flintstone-shaped" feet. The shoes seemed to have taken on a life of their own just to taunt me. When I wasn't wearing them, they dominated my closet like a hungry dog on the prowl, seeming to growl at me late at night. Sometimes I stared at them from a safe distance, trying to figure out the fastest way I could wear them out. Even though I had been the owner of these shoes for just a few short days, I was sure they'd been sent to destroy me.

I felt so insecure as a child, the chameleon in me would take on other people's quirks and accents in hopes of fitting in. I just wanted to be liked. I was already struggling with the addiction that would afflict me for most of my life. My core desire wasn't drugs, alcohol, or sex, but it was just as insatiable. What I was addicted to was simply, my *need* to be loved. Of course, all of us want that, but when we don't receive affirmation of ourselves as children, it can set in motion a frantic search for love as we become adults. At least that was my experience. It was as if I had a hole in my heart that would not be filled and an aggressive personality that absolutely would not give up. The patterns of my life started to form in my ninth year.

My family lived in a wood-frame house set back not too far

from a road in New Rochelle, New York. Although the houses were close together, we had some privacy, and each home was built in a different style. To distinguish ours, Mom and Dad poured a pink cement patio and built an enormous stone "cookout" into the hill. No one else in the neighborhood had anything like it. An older girl named Jan lived in a house behind ours, in a much more expensive area up the hill. I was in the third grade, she was in fourth. I wanted to be her friend as badly as I wanted a pet. The animal issue was not open for discussion with Mom and Dad, so I decided to plant a rock garden and find a friend. Jan was it. She had long braided black hair, I had short tufts. She had all the dolls, clothes, and pets; I had a vivid imagination. On top of that, boys liked her and she knew it. (Boys were about as interesting to me as a stubbed toe. Besides, they reminded me of my brother.)

Still, I wanted to be just like Jan. After all, she was the most popular girl I had ever run into. She must have been doing something right to be so loved by her parents that she was allowed her very own dog *and* cat *and* dollhouse *and* bows braided into her hair at breakfast every morning . . . *and* penny loafers!

Jan walked on the outsides of her feet, which wore down the heels of her brown, shiny loafers, crowned by two Indian-head pennies her grandfather had given her for her birthday. But the fact that she was pigeon-toed was unimportant to me. What counted was, she was cool and I wanted to be cool, too. (I have entertained the notion that my bowed legs did not come from riding horses or family genes, but from trying to walk like Jan.)

She also bit her nails to the quick, something I noticed when we played jacks. Since she was perfect and I needed to be, I began chewing away at my fingertips with a vengeance: stumps for nails was the look for me. I could actually incorporate this bad habit into my life without anyone's permission because they were my nails and I could do what I wanted to them, right? *Wrong.* Mom caught me biting and polishing one of my stubs and immediately nixed my mission with Tabasco sauce. But I didn't care; all I really wanted were some penny loafers.

I waited impatiently for Mom to get around to taking me shopping; my chance came sooner than I calculated. Mom and Dad were having one of their famous parties that coming Saturday, and so, as it happened, Mom needed a new dress. Well, she didn't really *need* one, but she "deserved" one because she'd recently lost a lot of weight, looked grand, and just had to show herself off. No question about it, I was born to two fabulous-looking, volatile parents. Mom and Dad were also Mr. and Mrs. Revolving Charge . . . Bloomingdale's owns a big chunk of what would have been their net worth.

I loved it when Mom and I went shopping together. We didn't do it often, and we didn't go on sprees, but it was just about the only time we spent alone together. Once inside the dressing room, I'd attend to her like a handmaiden, sorting, zipping, pulling at her hem. What was the most fun was being sent out into the store unaccompanied to find my mom another size or color of outfit. I was very efficient. Mom would always ask what I thought as she verbally tore herself to shreds in the three-way mirror . . . a strange habit of hers, especially since she was awesome looking. I'd tell her how pretty she was, even though I knew she didn't really listen to me. The fact that she even asked what I thought thrilled me. Mom is the most secure-insecure person I've ever known.

On this shopping day before her big party, she felt pretty good about herself, so I figured the timing was right to pop my question. "Mom, can I get some new shoes? Mine are all worn-out." I scrunched my toes to the breaking point, throwing my feet out at odd angles, which only made my sneakers look lopsided rather than old. Mom glanced down at my feet and actually seemed amused as she nodded yes. I was shocked. I hoped then and there that she'd stay thin for the rest of her life—she was such a misery when she gained weight.

Unfortunately, her good mood didn't end up saving the day. Although I saw—from five counters away—the exact penny loafers I wanted, waited an eon or two while the elderly salesman retrieved a pair and then jammed them on my feet, they turned out to be woefully too small. My mother was adamant at first. "Jen, your feet look like sausages!" But somehow I convinced her the shoes were just comfortably snug. Until, after paying for them, she saw me limping in agony off the store escalator. She took me back to the shoe department, where she discovered that the sock on my right foot was soaked in blood. The manufacturer had left a stray nail jammed between the sole and the side of the shoe and it had stabbed deeply into my foot.

After going through two handkerchiefs to mop up the mess, the salesman nervously offered us a free pair of shoes in compensation for my damaged toe. I quickly sorted through everything available in my size—sneakers, sandals, rubber slippers, even a pair of silk ballet toe shoes (which Mom insisted were not appropriate for everyday wear; neither were pink suede shoes, as I was to find out).

But when I first saw them, I fell in love: Elvis had blue suede shoes, I had pink . . . and I had the floor at my parents' Saturday bash. I spun like a top and leaped through the air—I was talented. The dancing made me happy, applause made me feel safe. I was a big hit and my shoes grabbed their own share of attention from the crowd. I couldn't wait to show them off to everyone at school on Monday.

But Monday was a disaster. In my classroom, kids pointed at my pink feet and laughed. When I tried to sit on them, my teacher told me to sit up straight. Everyone laughed again. When I tried to hold my feet up under the desk to hide the offensive footwear, the teacher told me to take a walk to the principal's office. My eyes fell in embarrassment. What I thought would jump-start my way to instant popularity ended up only tightening the noose around my already doomed campaign to win friends. The worst part was, my potential older-best-girlfriend with the braids chose not to be seen with me around the school yard as long as I was shod in "those things." I felt nauseated the entire day until school let out and I walked home alone.

Jan did, however, grace me with her glorious presence that next Tuesday afternoon before her riding lesson. Riding lessons! I already knew at age nine that it was dangerous to pine for something so entirely out of the realm of my possibilities. Penny loafers were one thing, but a *horse* . . . For me that was the most hopeless of all my dreams. My parents made their feelings very clear: "Jennifer, you are not getting riding lessons, a pony, or even a horseshoe, so don't bring the subject up again." I learned to face *some* facts early on.

One day while Jan and I were playing hopscotch in front of the house, my dad pulled into the driveway. I was surprised to see him home so early, and more surprised to see that he was alone. An unprecedented plan started to formulate in my miniature mind. I was going to attempt my first serious stab at the famous wrap-daddy-around-your-finger school of behavior, get whatever this little girl wanted, play the bat-your-eyes-and-whine scenario I had seen Jan pull on her father countless times. You know, the innate girl-thing that is supposed to be practiced on fathers and then refined on husbands. The beauty of this moment was that my mom wasn't around; I wouldn't have a prayer if she had been. Dad basically didn't know I was alive when Mom was anywhere nearby, which was almost always.

As I approached my father, with Jan right behind me for moral support, I stated my request for a new pair of shoes. I wiggled, I whined, I did everything I had been coached to do, and more that somehow just came naturally: I "feminine wiled" him with a vengeance.

Since Dad listened without responding right off, I thought I had it made. This wishful thinking inspired me to lay it on even thicker, especially when my friend surreptitiously gave me the thumbs-up sign. After I had used up every dramatic trick in the book, I shut up and waited for the magic answer. "Of course you can have a pair of new shoes, sweetheart. It doesn't matter that you just chose those pink ones. Tell you what, I'll take you down right now and you can pick out whatever you want," I imagined Dad saying. "Not only that," he continued in my fantasy, "why don't I take you over to the stables afterward and we'll get some horses and go for a nice long ride together." Oh, boy!

I was lost in my fantasy when, out of nowhere, Dad smacked me across the bottom so hard it knocked me into the bushes. I bounced off the hedge, then pulled myself up, shaking. My heart was pounding so loudly, I could barely hear my father say, "Jennifer, don't you ever try and pull that nonsense again! I happen to know you asked your mother this morning if you could have some new shoes. She said no. You wanted those pink things and you will wear them till they're worn out. Now go to your room and stay there until I get an apology." Before I could respond, he grabbed me by the arm and escorted me into the house. I turned to say something to Jan as I vanished, but the storm door slammed between us. I was just able to catch a glimpse of her standing there like a wooden Indian, fear frozen across her face. She never talked to me again. I felt like a very bad girl . . . very ashamed. Sometimes it's easier not to remember.

t w o

MAIN INGREDIENTS

M Y father, Oscar Delgado O'Neill Jr., was born in San Juan, Puerto Rico. Although Dad has his biases—actually, he could give Archie Bunker some competition in the prejudice department—he is proud of his birth land, his pride based not on the romanticized vision of a *West Side Story*, but rather on his hard-nosed you-can-make-the-best-of-whatever-you're-given view of life. That belief made the real-life hero "Oscar the Ace" into an amiable prisoner of World War II. His mother's highbrow Spanish heritage and the fact that her ancestors were one of Puerto Rico's founding families proved Dad's family tree had roots buried deep in the history books. His ancestors were pioneers—pioneers, by the way, who hauled legions of servants with them down the trail. Add to the mix my grandfather, Oscar Delgado O'Neill Sr., a truly dynamic presence as an entrepreneur and visionary, and *boom,* a dynasty of O'Neills is born.

Dad insists he had a spectacularly loving upbringing. If so, I remain curious as to the origin of his intermittent, deep-running anger and the cutting sarcasm he unleashes more often than not at cocktail hour. Maybe it's just the nature of the alcohol beast to overpower our basic good natures. On the other hand, maybe all good behavior is learned behavior: just watch how toddlers instinctively grab for toys and then smack each other with them. Since the memory of a drinker is selective at best, I think it might be helpful to impose a rule on all of us who like to partake in the infamous cocktail hour: all portions of the evening must be video-taped for future reference and for the protection of the innocent. I was chatting with Mom and Dad the other day about my comment on Dad's "deep-running anger and cutting sarcasm." He responded with a chuckle: "Jen, just say it's a personality trait of mine." Between the lines, my dad also sports unswayable integrity, a tender heart, and an infectious sense of humor. He is a good man.

When my grandfather courted my grandmother, he was rejected straightaway by her family as a renegade. But one did not say no to Oscar Sr. (known as "Pae" to us), so he picked up all of the four feet eleven inches of my grandmother Ada and whisked her off to a frontier land called Brazil. Clearly, petulance is a family trait. Perhaps a more colorful example of the "O'Neill" bulldog genes is depicted on our family crest. It tells the story of our ancestor, seafaring Captain Neil, who ordered his hand to be chopped off by a sword and thrown onto the approaching Irish shore. You see, his adversary's boat was beating Neil's to the promised land and whoever arrived on shore first would be crowned king. I'm not sure I would have made such a sacrifice for a crown. I'm also not sure whether my ancestor's was an act of bravery or of stupidity . . . Maybe we O'Neills are all just a bunch of nuts.

As a kid, I thought Pae (pronounced "Pie") was a perfect name for my moon-faced grandfather, but I also felt that if honesty was to be the policy in handing out nicknames, Ada should have been called "Pencil Head" (she bore an uncanny resemblance to Woody Woodpecker). No one else seemed to make the connection, though, and I was told not to be rude. Boy, who makes up the rules about rudeness?

Being an innovative businessman, Pae raised his family with all the very best money could buy. This included a top-notch, Stateside education for both my father and his brother, Lee, born eleven months apart. Travel and knowledge added fuel to my dad's fiery temperament, which causes him to insist on always being the center of attention. At age eighty, he continues to demand that billing and to this day, Mom and Dad "bossa-nova" their way to center stage at any and all gatherings.

For the most part, Mom takes a backseat to "The Ace" publicly, but only as long as the evening lasts; alone with him, she is clearly the dominant figure. One of the many things I've always loved about my dad is the pleasure and pride he takes in his brother Lee's Yale education, compared with his own single year at Colgate University. No jealousy there: Dad was a good brother—and son, for that matter. Although my uncle eventually died of a broken heart and too much to drink, he had a great impact on all of us.

Fifty-four years since Dad winged his way to his destined rendezvous with my mother by order of World War II, my parents' relationship continues to resemble something out of a romance novel. My parents are also like the little-girl-with-the-curl: when they are good, they're very very good, and when they are bad . . . well, you know.

As the seventh daughter of a seventh daughter, Irene Freda Lillian Pope (Mom to me) was born in London to a poor but close-knit family. Despite wartime constraints, which precluded any hopes of a real ongoing education, she remains one of the most intrinsically bright people I have ever met, with an elegance about her that can only be compared with royalty. She also ranks high in her ability to gun down a relationship if it doesn't fulfill her requirements, and if you cross her in any way, there is absolutely no possibility of redress. In short, it's her way or the highway.

Mom was a diligent housekeeper, and dinner was always on the table—meat, potatoes, and vegetables—and it was always more than tasty. Mom insists on quality regardless of whatever financial volleyball she and Dad were playing at a given time. "Buy the best, even if you have to charge it," she's always said. "If you buy the cheap cut, it just shrivels up in a river of fat."

My brother Mike and I were born sixteen months apart and were a heck of a cute team till we were about ten years old. The slow but constant deterioration of our relationship leaves me sad to this day. I never had a sister, and truth be known, I had a brother only for those very early years. I was thinking the other day, *What's the most important thing in life that we have no choice in? . . . Our immediate family*, an inner voice quickly replied.

For business purposes, Mom and Dad moved from glamorous Rio de Janeiro, where I was born (an exotic fact I later loved to repeat; somehow it conferred a special status on me). Although I was less than a year old, and not a syllable of Portuguese had formed on my lips, Latin rhythm managed to infiltrate my baby bones. We lived on a "starter" family budget in Detroit, Michigan, for five years and then moved "uptown" to the suburbs of New York City—nothing fancy, but closer to everything that was.

Winters in New Rochelle offered a good share of snow days when school was closed. We lived down the street from a big lake, which provided us with everything from sunny summer fishing to winter-white ice skating. I did not participate in the fishing escapades. It was painfully clear to me that when my brother caught the "sunnies," they were pleading with me to help them escape their excruciating death. Due to what I already felt was my unique connection with the nonhuman world, I concluded that all those who insist that fish don't suffer should have a jagged hook laced through their lips, be dragged to the shore for sport, then hurled up onto the ground while their lungs slowly burn up. Then let them say it doesn't hurt. Starting as early as I can remember, I couldn't stand to see any animal in pain—fish, cat, dog, horse, even insects.

There's nothing like being loved. It's better than food and Christmas. Some of the grandest shows of affection I ever received from Mom happened after days of ice skating on our frozen lake. Trudging home, I'd stumble along behind my brother as fast as my little ice-block feet could carry me. I was convinced for years that my toes never grew to a normal length because of those frozen ice-capades (when I'm feeling melodramatic, I still claim that frostbite is the reason for the smallness of my feet).

Charting a wobbly path through the winter wonderland, Mike and I would finally arrive before the vision of Mom standing guard behind our frosted front door. Her breath formed mist on the glass, her smile was warm and inviting. We piled into the house, depositing what seemed like half the world's snow on the rug, and she didn't even care. Mom helped us unwrap the layers of scarves, socks, and rolls of plastic inside our boots and mittens. Then came the best part. She would sprawl on the couch, opening her arms like a foldout card to my brother and me in an invitation to snuggle up, and in an access of maternal self-sacrifice, she would put our frozen feet under her bare armpits for instant thawing action of the nth degree. She didn't even flinch from the cold intrusion. No hot tub, blazing fire, or hot chocolate could top this memorable method of warming and the feeling of being cared for that came with it.

When we were very little, Dad's special time with Mike and me was to pile us into the shower with him for what was known as the "scrub." He'd throw us in the air, catching us under the spray that cascaded over us like a healing waterfall. Mom and Dad were never very playful with us kids, but shower time with Dad meant we could squeal, squirt, and splash our way through what I normally considered to be one of the bigger chores in life. Of course, for modesty's sake, the good-time showers stopped when Mike and I were about ten, and unfortunately were never replaced with any other kind of special time with our dad.

I was still nine and sporting a runny nose when I had a "Polaroid experience" (my term for an image I can't get rid of). It was raining and cold, but not full-fledged winter yet. I was alone, on my way home from school, when I came upon a man standing near the lake with his dog. He appeared in the half-light of dusk, his body made ethereal by the layers of fog that rolled about him. Nothing moved until his eyes snared mine with a look that caught all of my attention. I had been taught about "strangers," but had never actually run into one. And besides, this stranger had a dog. The man smiled at me as he started to walk away; the dog wagged his tail, which to me was a clear invitation to come closer. The pup looked to be well fed, which made me happy, because the man seemed less than cared for. He had a long, scruffy beard and un-combed hair that stuck out at odd angles. Still, I wanted to pet the dog, whose tail now looked like a propeller gone wild.

"Is he friendly?" I said as I stepped forward.

"Sure." The words slipped out between the man's mustache and his grin.

Goody, I thought. As I approached, the man's battered coat suddenly opened with the swishing flair of Dracula's cape; moments later his zipper was down and he was exposing himself to me. He had an expression on his face, a look I have seen more than once in my life . . . a look I'll never get used to no matter how many times I run into it. I bolted, racing so fast I knew my feet weren't touching the ground. So fast that when I finally looked over my shoulder, the man had disappeared in the mist. But even though he was gone, he owned a hidden part of me from then on like a scar that marks an incision point.

Mom called the police when I told her about the incident. There were no sirens, no guns drawn, nothing "policelike" about these men in blue. They just seemed kind of fat and one of them, I recall, had hair growing out of his ears. The other one chewed his gum with his mouth open, and surprisingly, Mom didn't even comment on his bad manners. They drove us down to the lake to identify the man, but he was gone. They told Mom some other policemen had already taken him away and only the dog remained, tied to a stop sign. I was numb, barely able to hear the echo behind my head. It was one of the police officers asking me, "Is that the dog that was with the man?" I looked into the dog's eyes. His tail was still, his head low, his demeanor defeated. He was crying—a long slow whimper. The pup finally looked at me, his eyes shifting. Light brown circles marked his eyebrows, which seemed to tele-graph his thoughts with great accuracy. He didn't know anything about the right or wrong of what that man had done. The guy was just his owner . . . his life . . . and I had ruined it.

Mom and the policeman kept saying I'd done the right thing, that the dog would be taken care of and the man needed help. But it didn't matter; I knew I shouldn't have told. Betrayal can provide such a treacherous foothold for guilt. In this instance I had no sense of guilt about the man; he did something bad, I knew that much. And he scared me. But I betrayed the *dog* and it was something I was not going to get over. Maybe it would have been different if I just could have talked Mom into letting me take the dog home, but remember, *that* subject was closed.

I was growing up. I could tell because I was thinking about sitting up straight at the dinner table without being told and sometimes I was worried about whether my skirt was straight or my slip was showing. I remember a trip to Manhattan with my father, mother, and brother. We had lunch at a very nice white-linen-napkin restaurant. While I was taking in the room, I was conscious of holding a pose that would have challenged Audrey Hepburn for princess-like perfection. Conversely, my brother was bored, only perking up when our Shirley Temples piled a mile high with cherries were placed before us like sacrificial offerings. Mike guzzled his down in a shot while I sipped mine, as was only proper for an up-and-coming young lady soon to take on the whole of New York and its surrounding suburbs with her blooming womanhood . . . I was ready.

I was certain that all eyes were on me as I excused myself from the table to go to the powder room. Even better—Mom slipped me a dollar to give the attendant. As if that weren't enough, I floated my way across the entire restaurant both coming and going, convinced I had the makings of a runway model. As I returned to the table, I locked eyes with Mike, who was seated across from me, in a request for him to stand as Dad was doing in my honor. Mike just looked at me like I was mentally impaired. Finally Dad nudged him to get up. Mike slowly rose to his feet, his pursed lips expressing his annoyance at my disturbing his single-minded attack on the sweet rolls. It was a triumphant moment, which, unfortunately, was short-lived, for as the waiter pulled my chair out to assist me, I merely noticed his act of gallantry. Holding Mike's gaze, I smiled and began my descent, thinking my chair was where I had left it. I remember Michael's image vanishing behind the table as I fell to the floor, my legs flying straight up and over my head. My brother laughed till he cried, the waiter fluttered about me with apologies, and although everyone else tried to sympathize between giggles, I knew it would take a good fifty years for me to recover my dignity . . . Maybe a hundred years would have been a more realistic estimate.

three

CHANGING OF THE GUARD

M Y family moved to Wilton, Connecticut, as I was entering fourth grade. I don't know why changing schools at ages nine and fourteen almost buried me; kids do it all the time. I've never considered myself a wimp, but both occasions represented great losses in my life. The Wilton move marked the beginning of my brother's vanishing act, and although he made, so to speak, a slow-motion departure, I missed what he could and should have been to me.

Taking us farther out into the country and representing a longer commute for my dad and more isolation for Mom, this move to Wilton was an act of self-sacrifice on my parents' part for the benefit of my brother and me. Education was of paramount importance to them and the schools in Connecticut were superior in every way to those we had been attending.

Connecticut was a cliquey place. Most of the kids in my new class had lived there all their lives and it would require the rest of mine before they would consider letting me join their "inner circle." Actually, I moved away well before I got as much as a toe in the door. As devastating as my pink shoes had been to my childhood forays on popularity, so was the "blue dress" on my near-adolescent efforts. Although Mom and I decided that my new dress was perfect for the first day of school, we might as well have decided I should wear pedal pushers to the White House. Connecticut was all about long blond hair, plaid shirts, monogrammed sweaters, and blue jeans. My dress had a full skirt, with white lace on the trim, and the moment I stepped on the school bus, I got everyone's attention—for all the wrong reasons. Realizing that my short hair was not flowing in the breeze and my ankle socks were falling over my Mary Jane shoes, I experienced a flush that lasted the entire day. For me, a "flush" is a blush that won't quit. Some kids actually pointed at me like I was a rare beast at the zoo.

Later that day, when I spotted my brother down the school hall, he seemed to be fitting in a little better than I; then again, *he* wasn't wearing my blue dress. The girls in his class had ponytails, went to dancing school, and were "built," according to Mike. This latter observation opened up an avenue of torture Michael promptly seized upon, launching a campaign of almost daily reminders that I was flat-chested. Unfortunately, the fact that he had flat feet didn't seem to faze him in the slightest when I used it for a counterattack. I should have known that in the matter of self-esteem, archlessness for guys is nothing compared with booblessness for girls. In those days, remember, Barbie dolls defined the perfect form and Veronica and Archie comic strips set the fashion and the dialogue.

Mom had a best friend named Elinore C. Lee. She was twenty years Mom's senior, Dad's aunt by marriage as well as both Mike's and my godmother. She was also a partner in the dental and hospital supply business that my grandfather Pae owned and Dad and Lee ran from their Rockefeller Center office in New York City. Elle had a small apartment on Fifty-fourth Street and Fifth Avenue that remained in our family for over forty-five years. It was there that I began my courtship with the piano. I loved to visit Elle. She would actually sit and listen to my musical compositions (if you could call them that) with undivided attention—it was such a special time for me.

Elle was Mom's greatest supporter, and it was her idea that Mom accompany Dad on one of his longer business trips and that Elle stay with Mike and me in Wilton. This suggestion was perceptive on Elle's part, since Mom seemed to be having an increasingly difficult time with all of Dad's traveling for business. To put it simply, Mom had always suffered from mood swings, and lately they'd been increasing, especially the ones that occurred on a monthly basis. I believe Mom must have been a legitimate sufferer of PMS, which, thankfully, we know more about now than we did back then. I swore as a young girl that whatever this thing was that happened to my mother once a month, which made her flat-out mean, emotional, and volatile, was not going to affect me the same way. Now I have much more empathy for her extended times without Dad while raising two kids and her bouts with runaway hormones.

Mom's friendship with Elle was an example of that special bond only two women can have—and the only bond like this she had, since Mom otherwise seemed interested and involved only with my father. Dad's male bonding occurred with men he met in his business career and occasional tennis and golf outings, but since Mom didn't work or participate in sports, golf and tennis were merely tolerated by her and never encouraged. Mom did share at home in all of Dad's business decisions and was an extremely effective partner by her support with business entertaining.

As youngsters, Mike and I went to church with our parents for a short period of time; later on they just drove us to Sunday school and picked us up following services. As preteens, we were given the choice of whether or not we wanted to attend church on Sundays, and of course we preferred just to play all day. Mom prayed every morning. I know because we weren't allowed to go into her bedroom during those ten or so minutes. Dad crossed his fingers, claimed thirteen as his lucky number every time he passed St. Patrick's Cathedral on Fifth Avenue, and said Mom took care of the praying in the family. I figured that was the way it worked when you were married. Everyone plays the part they're best at.

We had some friends who ate fish every Friday. They were Catholics and they made Mike and me happy to be connected to a less formal, less restrictive religion by attending the Episcopal church. I have always had great reverence for God, but didn't have a clue as to who Jesus Christ was or, for that matter, what "saving grace" was all about. As far as I knew then, unconditional love was something you could get only from a dog or cat, and a "relationship" was about who was in charge and who followed. Love was something that needed to be earned and self-esteem was already a foreign concept to me, as my insecurities were on the rise. Right or wrong had more to do with getting caught than it should, and the feeling of being protected was becoming a memory. In other words, at that point in my life, it seemed true solace was something I'd have to find somewhere other than in church.

Elle was doing her sacrificial duty as sitter to Mike and me while our parents were off on their six-week business trip. She was a devoted, soft-spoken Christian woman, Mike and I were wild Indians free from Mom and Dad's discipline. But despite our heathen behavior, she was able to impart wisdom and direction. Elle's approach was so unique, I finally asked her straight out why she didn't yell or get mad, and why she was so nice. She smiled before she answered, "God."

As a little girl, I knew my nose was crafted perfectly to fit next to my dad's when we exchanged butterfly kisses, but by age ten I had no idea if we fit anymore since I was discouraged by Mom from sitting on his lap. The one-on-one moments with my father stopped, and from then on, any warm, "fuzzy" feelings for me centered around family-group activities like getting the high sign from Mom to tune in the TV for all of us to watch *The Wonderful World of Disney* hosted by Tinker Bell or *The Honeymooners* with Jackie Gleason.

When my parents were off to a party, chicken potpies or fried chicken TV dinners were the menu, and the sport for Mike and me was to see how much past our bedtime we could stay up without getting caught. One night we were on our tenth argument of the evening about who was going to pick what show we were going to watch when car lights flashed across the picture window downstairs. This was our warning signal that Mom and Dad were home from their evening out and we had only two minutes and fifty-three seconds to cover our tracks.

Although Mom and Dad ran hot and cold depending on their

moods, they were always good sports and this night was one of those occasions that would test their humor. As it turned out, the car lights weren't from Mom and Dad's car, but rather from Bud and Peta, their best friends, who snuck into our house (scaring my brother and me out of our wits) and proceeded to inflate a huge, high-altitude balloon that totally filled my parents' bedroom. It was an anniversary gag. When Mom and Dad arrived shortly thereafter and were accosted by the raging weather balloon, we all laughed well into the morning.

However funny some moments were, there were others around the same period of time that could only be called grim. Mom started to express her displeasures, shall we say, more *vividly*. "Go to hell," "drop dead," and "I want a divorce" seemed to represent the gist of her feelings. It is frightening for children to hear those words on a fairly regular basis, but Mike and I cautiously began to view our mother's outbursts as all frustrated talk and no action. One thing that helped us keep her explosive nature in perspective was that not once, under any circumstances, did we ever hear our father say or even intimate that he wanted a divorce from Mom. I do respect him so for that. Mom never left because she absolutely adores my father, and despite her bluster, she was, and is, totally devoted to him. By her own admission, Dad makes her feel completely secure as a woman. However loud and frightening my mother's tantrums, I learned to trust that my parents really did love each other, which gave me a basic model for commitment between a man and a woman, even if it was one I would often find hard to emulate.

Mom grew up in a family where there was no closeness whatsoever between her parents; her mother's focus was totally on her children to the exclusion of her husband. My mother was determined not to repeat that pattern in her marriage, and so the pendulum swung to the other extreme: she focused mainly on Dad. In doing so, the message I received as a kid about marriage and relationship was one-sided, especially when it came to how children fit into the mix. To put it simply, Mom and Dad showed virtually no interest in Mike's or my interests, not only because they did not relate to them, but because they were each other's top priority. No matter how grown up I wanted to be as a child, I was still a little girl who needed to be heard and feel important to her parents. And when their love for each other seemed to leave no room for me, I felt abandoned. I had to get over my "need" for them before I could begin to appreciate my parents as individuals instead of just missing them—that process took me well into adulthood.

But until then, I was determined to get my share of Mom and Dad the only way I felt I could. I'd earn it. Maybe if I got straight A's in school, they would know how special I was. Dancing, spinning, twirling, and leaping across the floor during their parties had been well received for several years, but obviously, as I got older, I needed an infusion of new material. Besides, other kids in school received five dollars for every A on their report cards; maybe if I was perfect, I could get a cat, or even a dog.

Mrs. Leone was the name of my sixth-grade teacher, and aside from Elle, her supportiveness made the biggest impact on my young life. My straight-A plan was set, but the problem was, I couldn't spell. I was sporting all A's and only one infuriating B in spelling as the year was coming to an end. Despite the embarrassment I suffered at every spelling bee, which I regularly entered for extra credit, I still couldn't spell. In fact, Mrs. Leone told me she thought I would never be a good speller, but she finally gave me my A because she knew how much it meant to me and how hard I had tried.

I had another ally in my "straight-A/be-cherished/get-a-pet plan"—my uncle Lee's wife. She helped talk Mom and Dad into letting me have one of her kittens to take home as an outdoor cat. The "outdoor" part felt like getting a present you really couldn't have (if your pet isn't allowed to come in the house, is it really yours?). But I was willing to take any form of a pet under any condition.

My aunt and uncle lived in a nifty house in nearby New Canaan, with more land than we had. Next door was a real mansion, with llamas that spit at you over the fence; I know because I sneaked over to talk to them once and soon realized that all cute-looking things aren't necessarily well mannered. (I was to spend a good portion of my life confirming that discovery at the hands of various men I have known.) My aunt gardened, was tanned, had lots and lots of animals, and was *way* cool—that is, until she was caught cheating on my uncle.

I never did get any money for my straight A's, by the way. Dad said I shouldn't get paid for doing my best. It didn't matter, though; my kitten was better than millions in the bank to me. We named it Groucho because it had a gray mustache and because my aunt swore it was a male after holding "him" by the scruff of the neck and inspecting his equipment. Her expertise was questioned after Groucho delivered several litters of kittens. But Groucho's sex didn't matter to me; as far as I was concerned, she was the best feline on the face of the earth. Rain or shine, she was always waiting at the bus stop when I got home from school and she would come instantly when I called her, just like a dog. I finally had a pet and I was the happiest I could ever remember being.

Mike and I walked to the top of our hill to catch the bus for school along windy and mysterious roads and woods primed for adventure. Dad had bought one of the first houses built in the neighborhood; the others followed like the invasion of the pod people. In 1959, our house cost $24,000, which seemed like a good deal since we had a couple of acres and lived in a "nice" town. Wilton hadn't been developed as much as New Canaan or Westport, but it was still considered an upscale woodsy area. In keeping with their style, Mom and Dad immediately erected a stone-and-wood fence in the front of the house and an enormous rock patio in the back for entertaining. There was split-rail fencing by the driveway that formed a perfect paddock area for the horse that I was never going to get.

One of my parents' favorite things to do was to go out to dinner. It's occurred to me lately that if going out for drinks and food had been my "sport" of choice as a kid, my parents would have attended every one of my "games." Mike and I were invited to go with them most of the time, and on the way home in the car, we'd sing songs like "Sixteen Tons" by Ernie Ford and some of "that new guy's" hits . . . Elvis Presley. Apparently this was when I was told I should shut up because I couldn't carry a tune. Having blocked that experience from my memory, I have to take my brother's words for it. (Mike mentioned that story to me at the time I signed a record deal in 1975. The fact is, when I get nervous and I try to sing, I sound very much like a goat; perhaps that insecurity is a direct result of my less-than-appreciated crooning as a kid . . . ?) After three or four songs in the car, we'd all imagine Groucho holding court in the garage where she lived and where she was routinely courted by several howling male cats and one neutered wannabe named Mr. Tulip. We pictured Groucho as the sexiest thing to come along in fur, luring her male suitors to her side by wearing bikini undies and a set of three bras.

On occasion, my parents also liked to go to the movies. This was considered a special treat that Mike and I were allowed to partake of provided we were well behaved. That meant absolutely, unequivocally *no talking* once we were inside the theater; otherwise we were banished to the car. Silence was quite a task for us since, like most kids, our sibling exchange consisted of a constant stream of poking, making fun, or arguing.

Only a few days had passed since Dad's most recent round of discipline was indelibly ingrained in Mike's and my brains. Its point of origin was Mike's burst of independence, which had been directed at Mom. When Dad came home and learned of my brother's behavior, his response was swift. He picked Mike up with a single, outstretched hand and lifted him by the top of his jacket, pinning him against the dining-room wall. Dad explained to my brother in short, simple sentences that disrespect would not be tolerated, *ever*! I believed him and I wasn't even the one hanging from the wall. (The only other time I saw Mike's face so red occurred in New Rochelle, when all the kids were playing war and they caught and hung my brother upside down for being a traitor. I escaped and ran to get Mom, who cut him down and scattered the kids with a vengeance; she was in her "lioness" mode.) And here Mike was with another red face, suspended at arm's length. It was surely the most astounding display of strength I had ever witnessed, and although Dad didn't hurt my brother, he did make a lasting impression—don't mess with Dad.

The wall-pinning incident was a fresh memory when we entered the movie theater, so, needless to say, Mike and I were on our very best behavior. As the lights dimmed, an enormous hulk of a man moved down the row of seats directly in front of us. I hoped he wouldn't sit near me since the back of his head would block out most of the screen. Glancing at Mike, whose feet were resting on the turned-up seat in front of him, I could tell he was holding the seat in a folded position so as to dissuade the man from choosing it. I grinned, impressed with my brother's quick thinking, and at first it seemed the strategy was working. The man swept across the row before us like a slow-moving tugboat, but then suddenly shifted back, depositing himself directly in front of Mike—right where Mike's feet were before he had a chance to pull them out. Mike shot straight up in pain, his feet now bent at right angles under the man's immense weight. He started to scream when Dad, oblivious of my brother's predicament, threw him a look of warning. Mike melted down, his feet still hopelessly smashed as he began to plead, "Sir . . . sir," in a pathetic voice, "excuse me . . . sir?" Mike tapped the man on the shoulder— getting zero response. What was worse, I couldn't do anything but watch him writhe in pain, as I, too, felt the force of Dad's eagle eye. Just when all seemed lost and my brother's permanent deformity appeared certain, the man leaned over to grab his soda. Mike's feet popped out, now fashioned into an S shape and surely flattened for life.

For all my fond memories of childhood with my brother, there was also a lot of hurt and anger between us. Recently I realized that my then-evolving "search-for-love addiction" was born not only of my inability as a child to inspire more interest from my parents, but was also a result of my brother's combative attitude toward me. Mom, Dad, and Mike made up my entire family, and in the absence of positive dialogue among us, I got the message that "Jennifer" must be the problem, especially from my brother. You see, most brothers I knew protected and adored their sisters

. . . at least when they weren't squabbling. There was some of that for Mike and me when we were very young, but from the time I was ten years old, sibling rivalry slowly choked the life out of us and left me with a defensive approach to relationships with males. As a child I felt that if I wasn't lovable enough to warrant encouragement and respect from my own brother—and I certainly didn't feel like the apple of my dad's eye—as far as I was concerned, I was already a failure. Mike began to tear me down at every turn, was argumentative, mean, and insisted I was evil at the core. I can remember only one time that he came to my defense and only one supportive letter he wrote to me as an adult. And to this day, his usual reaction is combative if I disagree with him or his theories. There was little applause from my brother for any of my accomplishments, only criticism of either my motives or my methods. Before I hit my teens, life already felt like an emotional battlefield and Mike and I went on separately like soldiers fighting different wars.

four

OUT OF THE NEST

*L*ATE in my eleventh year, it was Mike's and my turn to take a trip to spend the summer in Rio de Janeiro with my grandparents, Pae and Ada. Ever the sport, Elle was accompanying us on what promised to be a memorable chapter of our childhoods.

My grandparents' town house in Rio looked to me like a movie set, spanning an entire city block, with huge stone walls protecting its perimeter. Wood paneling, crystal and china, a formal dining room, and priceless art and antiques created the opulent atmosphere. Their country club was the only decent place to get ice cream, since Brazilian milk was watery at best. On the other hand, the bananas were the smallest and sweetest I ever had the pleasure of sinking my teeth into. In my "What I did last summer" report for school the following fall, I wrote about the thick jungle foliage, the fierce Copacabana Beach undertow that threatened to sweep me away on a regular basis, the brown-skinned people spouting their foreign tongue accentuated by broad physical gestures, eating squab (which made me sick when I found out that squab was pigeon), and being attended to by servants for the first time.

Elle and I shared a room, which very nearly cost her her life. As nifty as Elle was in every imaginable way, she wasn't a pretty woman and she snored. The pretty part didn't matter in the slightest to me. In fact, I was kind of happy she wasn't pretty, because if she'd looked like my mom, she would for sure be married and she wouldn't have the time or inclination to be my best buddy. As it was, she listened to my dreams and played cards for hours. Her snoring was the only glitch in a nearly perfect package.

As I remember this time, I suspect that in my subconscious, the stage for my ongoing battle was being set; scare tactics by way of recurring nightmares, unidentified patterns of fear, and deep unrest grew within me. Since I was nine the star of my nightmares had been an enormous gorilla that ravaged the neighborhood in search of its ultimate victim . . . me. The beast terrified me for years, perhaps because I always sensed myself on the verge of being attacked; I had already taken on the habit of walking in my sleep when I was particularly excited (or if I drank too much Coca-Cola before bedtime). It was on one of those occasions that I saved Elle's life; at least that's how I like to remember the event.

I was on my way back to bed after having walked into a wall— fresh scratches down my forehead, nose, and chin bore witness to my rude awakening. Though the room was expansive, my late night movements were made difficult by an obstacle course of heavy, brocade-covered furniture looming before me. I was barely awake enough to notice that Elle wasn't snoring as she lay in her bed. In fact, she wasn't making any sound at all . . . or moving at all, for that matter. I squinted in the shadowed room, searching for some source of electric light. I finally made my way to Elle's bedside, which was illuminated by a sliver of moonlight. She was inert. Upon closer inspection, I noticed that something was wrong with her mouth. Actually, it looked like she had no mouth! I considered my options—running, screaming into the night for help, or turning on the reading lamp for a better look . . . Was she dead? . . . Had creatures from Planet Z stolen her lips? I opted for a grab at the light. Once I could see better, it took a couple of moments for me to figure out what was wrong with Elle's face; a dozen or so skin-colored Band-Aids had been smashed across her mouth. I whispered her name but she didn't respond. Ever so slowly, I secured a corner of the main Band-Aid and let it rip; I had to save her from what I was convinced was imminent suffocation. She screamed, I jumped, she grabbed at her mouth as if she could contain the excruciating pain with her hand, I screamed because she screamed, and soon everyone in the household arrived like the cavalry, sure we were being murdered. When I held out the Band-Aid to show my grandparents the cause of my concern, I saw that Elle's mustache had been ripped off her upper lip during the removal process! I opted for a separate bedroom for the rest of the trip, considering that Elle could flat-out die from trying to keep me company. To make me feel better, she said that she was thrilled with her free wax job . . .

Half our time was spent in Rio and half in a place called Teresópolis, an area where my grandparents' country home rested in the mountains about two and a half hours from town. The trip there took us through back roads that revealed the extremes of South American economics; in Brazil, you were either very rich or very poor and there was and still is no middle class. Everything my grandfather did displayed extravagance, style, and abandon; he literally cut off the top of a mountain and built a magnificent home to satisfy his urge for adventure. Further, to appeal to his wife, Ada, he constructed an exact half-size replica of the main house small enough for my grandmother (who was less than five feet tall) to enjoy. On my visit, I loved to play in the "doll" house, appointed with tiny plates and forks and furniture just my size.

My grandfather traveled extensively for his various businesses, which included banking and the creation of a new city to be called Brasilia. Since he was away so much of the time, he made sure that Ada was entertained by hiring a "companion" for her. This woman became part of the O'Neill family, even meriting her own home, which Pae built on a neighboring mountaintop in Teresópolis. As the years went by, the closeness of Ada and her companion became cause for scandal among the adults, although Mike and I were not privy to the various less-than-conservative activities of some of our family elders until we were much older. Ada played the piano beautifully ("Danny Boy" was her favorite song) and she let me borrow her riding boots and breeches that summer since I was exactly her size. A glass of Scotch was a permanent fixture in my grandfather's hand, although I never saw him or my grandmother out of control from drinking. Still, alcohol keeps its own set of scorecards; Pae died in his early sixties of cirrhosis of the liver, Ada a little later from a heart attack. Pae had a saying: "Whoever doesn't like me, it's his own damn fault," he'd proclaim with some bluster, a mysterious gleam in his eye betraying the leprechaun in him. I wish I had known all my grandparents better. I never met Mom's dad; he was already dead when I was born. Mom's mom, Emmy, was from London and spent only a little time with us in Wilton. I remember she was nice and soft-spoken, with long gray hair that she wore in a bun and false teeth that she took out at night.

During that summer in Brazil I couldn't wait for my visits to Teresópolis because my grandparents had a horse named Neilsa and a mule named Miguel that they kept in a barn behind the kennels. Neilsa was black, with a star under her forelock and a look of the wind about her. Although she was in foal, she was still sleek and fast, holding herself in good form from her Thoroughbred breeding. Miguel, however, was thick, slow, gray, and stubborn. Pae had a method to all his madnesses, and although at the time I thought his rules about riding were unfair, in hindsight, they served me well: the deal was that as soon as I could take Miguel out by myself for at least a two-hour ride in the mountains, I would be allowed to ride Neilsa. I was on a mission.

It took me three weekends to accomplish the task, and even then, I had to cheat a bit. I managed to bribe the mule with hidden carrots and apples as we rode down to the bottom of the long driveway. Disappearing from view from the main house, I dismounted the giant antenna-eared beast and gave him some treats, then let him graze on the grassy slopes until it was time to go back. Returning in triumph, I claimed I'd had a wild and woolly ride for the past several hours, and was finally allowed to take the mare out for a spin.

Neilsa was better than I ever dreamed; fast as lightning, we tore through the jungle and conquered the mountaintops as my love for horses grew. Even better, I would come home after riding all day and recount my escapades to an interested family gathered at the dinner table. What a treat! Surely I was dreaming. I was having so much fun, I was determined to talk my grandparents and parents into letting me come back the next summer to visit Neilsa and her foal, but that wasn't in the cards. Not long after I returned to Connecticut, I received a letter from Ada saying Neilsa had died giving birth. It didn't matter what everyone said to the contrary, I was sure I'd killed the mare from riding her too hard. No question, out of all the horses I've lost over the years, Neilsa was the toughest blow . . . a blow that was to set the stage for my first deep depression.

Even though, at twelve, I displayed the fastest time in the long-distance run for the entire junior and senior Wilton High School classes, I still couldn't make much headway in the popularity sweepstakes. President Kennedy was on a physical-fitness kick, and although in my mind I carved myself out as a surefire Olympic hopeful, when I tried out for cheerleading, I was rejected because I couldn't do a split. Foiled again, I figured that I would keep plugging away at trying to get a horse, a desire which I had finally allowed to resurface in me as an absolute obsession.

And then came a glimmer of hope. I discovered a dilapidated, half-starved horse named Montgomery in the backyard of a house a few miles from where I lived. After striking up long conversations with the horse over the fence, I finally gathered up the nerve to talk to his owner. I proposed a business deal; I would feed, clean, and care for "Monty" as long as the horse was mine to ride. We cut the deal on the spot. Actually I should have called the humane society on this guy for animal abuse, but then my only chance of having a horse would have been lost in paperwork.

Mom and Dad were convinced that my love for horses was just a passing fancy, "a phase I was going through." They never had a clue about the depth of my connection with animals in general because it wasn't anything that interested them. Nor have they ever been the least bit motivated to learn anything about the sport of horses. Thirty years later we all had a good laugh when Mom and Dad came to live with me at my Malibu horse farm; Dad looked over the sea of horses forty head strong and observed, "Well, Jen, I guess it wasn't a phase." Dare I say, it's nice to finally be recognized.

During the Monty episode, what I lacked in practical horse knowledge, I made up for in enthusiasm. For the next year I ran back and forth every day before and after school to take care of this horse. Monty's story was sad and unfortunately all too common; he was the product of a divorce. The little girl he had been bought for moved away with her mother, leaving a disinterested, single father in charge of the animal's well-being. When I first found Montgomery, his coat was "molty" and multicolored from malnutrition. His hooves were so long he would trip over them, and to be honest, his personality left most everything to be desired. I couldn't blame him; who puts on their best smile while they're being abused? Every time I think of Monty, I think about a cartoon I once saw in a magazine. A horse was lying on a psychiatrist's couch. Observing his equine patient, the doctor remarked, "Why the long face?"

Starving, Monty had adopted the habit of escaping his paddock at night and ravaging a neighbor's flower beds. His owner was threatening to give him away if his plunderings didn't cease. I was sure the horse was being let out after dark by someone determined to ruin my life, since Monty was way too lazy and too weak ever to consider jumping out of the barn area on his own. My parents finally granted me permission to stand vigil one evening to uncover what was really going on, and frankly, I was humbled by this horse's ingenuity. Monty was contained by a four-foot-high, three-rail fence that formed his paddock area. I never bothered to hook up the bottom rail after riding him because it offered no deterrent from escape, so low was it to the ground (or so I'd thought). Thankfully, the moonlight revealed just enough detail of Monty's activities for me to finally solve the mystery. The horse sashayed over to the part of the fence where only two rails were up. He then proceeded to reposition himself no less than four times before appearing satisfied with his stance. Suddenly he buckled at the knees, lay down, *rolled under the fence,* and got up on the other side.

Pleased with himself, he gave a little shake and moved off into the night in search of flowers and green grass. Had he miscalculated even slightly, he would have been trapped under the fence, perhaps fatally. Don't let anyone ever tell you that horses aren't bright. Monty and I were joined at the hip for the next two years—I kept him fat and he learned to jump . . . sort of.

While some of the worst things that have ever happened to me in my life, either by my own hand or someone else's, involved alcohol, most of the purely delightful times involved horses—not counting all of the crashes and broken bones, of course. I was to learn that everything in life has its price.

five

EARLY LOVES

*I*T took me an average of twenty-five minutes to get from my house to Monty's barn. On paved roads, it would have been at least an hour's run, but I discovered various short-cuts that carved a path more directly to my object of desire. The route took me to the end of our neighborhood, which then suddenly exploded into a vast opening, a quarry that transformed the manicured green lawns of suburbia into a wild land of adventure and imagination. As if inspired by a blank page, I colored in details and directed grand dialogues among imaginary friends using the rocky slopes as a backdrop. It was during one of my twice-daily passes by the quarry that I suddenly saw what I thought to be a mirage. Squinting toward a back-lit image, I swore I saw Neilsa, my black mare from Brazil, in the midst of a slow-motion "rear" while pawing the bottom of the sky as if she could climb her way to heaven. But there was something different about this image compared with my average daydream . . . This one was real!

Not only that, someone was riding the black horse, and that someone was a guy wearing blue jeans—no shoes and no shirt. His hair matched the horse's mane—thick, dark, and flowing. He appeared to be an extension of the animal instead of just a passenger, and it became instantly clear to me that the Lone Ranger had nothing on this guy. Spinning out of a turn, his steed raced down the carved mass of rock and proceeded to bound into the water below with great abandon.

"Hi," he said from a slight distance. (How did he get from the water to my side so fast?) I suddenly thought that maybe I was standing there with my mouth hanging open, looking like a total moron. "Hi," I answered managing to shut my mouth at the conclusion of my muttered word. I was a runaway train stalled at the station and I had just fallen in love at first sight.

I tried to remember that I was only thirteen and I hadn't even talked my mom into buying me a Grow-bra yet. Sure, by then I had managed to find a girlfriend in my class whom I spent a lot of time with, but she wasn't one of the "in" crowd, so it didn't really count. Oh, and there was the time the kids in the neighborhood played spin the bottle and I got smacked on the face with a pair of lips—everyone called it a kiss. But the bottom-line truth was, I was tall and skinny, I was riding a borrowed flea-bitten horse, and the girl next door had just had a dance party I hadn't been invited to . . . Next door! Now, what kind of chance was I going to have with a guy who must be older because he had beard stubble and chest hair that ran like a river into the tops of his jeans and, most important, he had an amazing black horse.

His name was David. He was a senior at my school, and to me, he shot the moon. To the rest of the high school he was just a nerd who liked horses and was short. Clearly we were looking through different binoculars. If first crushes are bittersweet, they are more bitter than sweet, since happy endings are as rare as a balanced checkbook. Unaware of life's odds and percentages as I stood at the quarry that day, I decided that I was going to get to know this boy better. Of course, none of my womanly "equipment" was in place, and as usual, I was ahead of myself. It's amazing the hours and hours we pine, plot, and wish our way into situations, and when at long last we find ourselves there, we don't know what to do. Even my imagination could not have come up with such a perfect match: boy meets girl and they ride off on his horse, double bareback, into the sunset.

Although more likely a result of excruciating shyness on David's part than lack of interest in me, I translated his aloofness as rejection. That was such a familiar feeling for me. The lengths to which I went to ensure regular rendezvous by the quarry with him could fill volumes. I thought I was finally making some headway, but my fantasy quickly blew up when one afternoon I saw him riding—double bareback—with the flaxen-haired "other" Jennifer. What made matters worse, she was "stacked," a senior in school, and at the top of every boy's hit list. Now, no one had ever told me that a girl's catalog of charms did not ensure a real loving or lasting relationship. No one had made sure I felt what every young girl should feel about herself—special, valued, a gift to be honored and respected. I was having trouble with the rules. Sure, I'd heard all about "good girls and bad girls," "appropriate and inappropriate behavior," but as a teenager, I knew nothing about being a prize in the eyes of the one who truly loves you . . . In short, I knew nothing about self-esteem. All I knew was that in those days, Jennifer was a very unusual name and I had the misfortune to run into the only other Jennifer in my school and she just happened to be well endowed, sought after, and living within a hundred-mile radius of me. I was shattered . . . This was war.

I'm sure Mom was confused about why we were at the store buying me a bra a few days later. She couldn't see any need for one, but she finally acquiesced after I bombarded her with a stream of rationales. Besides, she was going shopping anyway. Once home and armed with my "over-the-shoulder boulder-holder" contraption, I snuck into the bathroom and stuffed the stretchy material full of Kleenex . . . *Wow* . . . What a difference a little paper can make. I flew out the door, down the block, across the quarry, up the hill to Monty's, tacked him up, and galloped back down to the quarry in what felt like less than a minute. I made such extraordinary time that my hair was blown back slick and my nostrils felt permanently flared. My timing was perfect. David was just trotting down the trail on his way to Jennifer's when I caught up with him. Trying to look casual, I asked if he wanted to take the horses swimming— all the while sticking my chest out to show off my newly procured shape. He must have taken notice because he immediately said yes. I guess that's what "stopping someone in their tracks" means. I surely liked this newfound power, noting then and there how easily boys are led astray, especially by poised young ladies who know how to stuff their bras.

The sun shimmered across the quarry. I felt like I had been "beamed" someplace soft, warm, and gentle as the water rose around David and me. Our horses were swimming effortlessly, their thrust creating a wake that vanished off to our sides in rhythmic ripples. Then he touched me . . . his hand turning my shoulder toward him . . . his face coming closer to mine . . . He was going to kiss me . . . he was—wait, what's wrong? Why did he turn away? He changed, the mood changed, his horse changed direction. He was swimming to shore. I heard David yell something about having to go home to do some homework, and then he was gone before I could even make it to land. Monty finally hurled himself out of the water like a beached whale, his sides heaving from the strain of the swim.

David had already disappeared over the hill when I felt the light wind across my chest. I looked down to see if my blouse had come undone, and sure enough, three out of five buttons were ripped away. Soaked, my shirt clung to me like a second skin, bearing evidence of a gross deformity planted right there on my chest: my new Grow-bra had become crooked, one side exploding with shapely tissue, the other side flat as a pancake. My head whipped around so fast to check the water, I almost flung myself off the back of my horse—and *boom*, there it was, proof of my humiliation. Tangible evidence of stupidity beyond a reasonable doubt. I was caught in a lie that floated on the surface of the otherwise clean, sparkling quarry. Kleenex was everywhere. My right boob had washed out from under me like a cloud blown out to sea.

No words could describe my embarrassment. I never saw David again, except at a distance at school, when I would invariably hide till he was gone. As far as my confidence and self-esteem went, "went" was the operative word: critically damaged, both were spiraling downward at a rapid pace.

Back at home, after Groucho had delivered several more litters of kittens and Mom and Dad had lost countless nights of sleep due to howling feline courtship rituals, I was told I could finally get a dog, but the cat had to go. Spaying and neutering must have been the best-kept secrets around because that option was never brought up for Groucho. I convinced myself that my cat would find a better home once she was brought to the pound. She'd adopt new owners who would let her come into the house, sprawl on the couch, and sleep in their bed. After all, she deserved that much; she was the best cat in creation. The truth is, all I could think about was what I wanted and so I deserted my cat, no two ways about it. All my life I've been told by a therapist here, a friend there, that the cat would have been given away as an inconvenience to my parents no matter what I did or said at the time. Also, that I was a kid and my parents shouldn't have forced me to make such a decision, but in my heart, I knew I was wrong. I was responsible. To this day, the choice I made back then causes me pain. No matter how many experiences I've had with lame, "useless" horses or older pets whose care is difficult, I've never betrayed an animal since Groucho. In fact, I've gone to the other extreme; I am the proud owner of the oldest, sickest animals on the face of the earth and I have the vet bills to prove it. Still, what I did to my cat remains a deep scar, one of those ugly footholds guilt gains as it tortures you throughout your life.

Meanwhile, my brother was going through his own torture over being sent away to boarding school at fourteen. It was not until many years later that he expressed how much he resented this decision. Mike was less than a diligent student; in fact, he was rather lazy and disorganized. There was and is no question that he's exceptionally bright, but as a kid he was unmotivated, argumentative, and yes, we all said Mike should be a lawyer when he grew up.

Dad had adored every second he spent at prep school and both he and Mom stretched themselves way beyond their financial means to offer the same advantage to Mike. I had also been slated to attend boarding school at some later date, but since Mike was the elder, he was first to go. It was thought best by my parents and the school that my brother repeat a grade since his previous work left something to be desired. I could be wrong, but I think he absolutely hated that move. I was able to postpone my own leaving home because my grades were still in the straight-A category. Certainly I was not any smarter than Mike; I just had better study habits and perhaps a greater need to be recognized by Mom and Dad . . . You see, Mike was the "lovable" child, I was the "organized" one. I'm not sure those labels were of much help to either of us in the long run.

It's interesting how people's perceptions can differ so radically about the very same memory. As an adult, my brother has made no bones about expressing his intense feelings on the school issue; he interpreted Mom and Dad's decision to send him away to boarding school as a wish not to have him around at home. From my parents' point of view, they couldn't have done a more loving and sacrificial service for my brother.

I was thirteen and a few months when I finally got to own my very first dog. I called her Mandy, which is what I wished I had been named, especially after the Jennifer/David fiasco. Mandy was a yellow Lab mix, not as squarely built as a purebred, but just as good as "Old Yeller" any day of the week. She lived outside, invaded the garbage on rare occasions, and after six months committed only one unforgivable sin: she ate the liver pâté off the table at one of my parents' parties. She did chase cars once in a while, but she and I had had some serious discussions about the perils of strangers and the dangers of car tires. I was confident that she was under control. Six months with Mandy felt like a lifetime of happiness for me. She was worth every bit of the wait, and when she'd come along riding with me, I was surrounded by my two best loves; the world was a perfect place as far as I was concerned . . . Finally.

The first ominous feeling came when the school bus creaked its way to my stop: Mandy was nowhere to be seen, and that was beyond unusual. As fast as my mind started racing, I couldn't seem to get my legs in gear. But as I stumbled and ran to my driveway, I knew I didn't want to go any farther. Mom was standing by the car door with a look on her face I had never seen before. What came with this new expression was silence: it seemed my mother was at a loss for words. But she really didn't need to say anything, did she? Not when I saw Mandy lying in the back of the car, not moving . . . not jumping up and running out to greet me . . . not bouncing around in circles chasing her tail so I would give her a treat . . . not howling and leaping straight up in the air, so her ears would stand out like a pair of sails. Not anything but lying there . . . dead . . . I *told* her about cars . . . I told her, but she didn't listen. I went with Mom to the vet to have my dog buried and then I went home and cried till my face looked like someone else's. I figured I abandoned Groucho, so Mandy left me. What else did I expect?

What I didn't expect was what happened a few weeks later. Mom took me to the grocery store, where they were selling mixed black Lab puppies for twenty-five dollars, and she let me buy one. I decided to call her Mandy . . . again. Actually, I decided Mandy had never really left. My yellow dog was so special, she could change color and size like Tabitha on *Bewitched*. Mandy had just opted to be black instead of yellow from then on. Kind of like changing clothes, that's all . . . Cool.

It was quieter around the house now that Mike was away at school. Sometimes I would talk to him anyway, even if he wasn't there. I remember the time just before he left for Westminster when Monty threw me on a barbed-wire fence, slicing open my back. I was wearing a white blouse and I knew the red blood pouring out of the cut would have been the last straw for Mom if she saw it. She had already warned me that she wouldn't let me ride anymore if I didn't stop demolishing myself on a regular basis. But today I lucked out; Mom had gone shopping and only Mike was home. I begged for him to throw some Band-Aids across the slash on my back and help me clean up all the blood. He finally agreed, but not before demanding his choice of TV shows for the next month as a bribe. He said he was just being practical. Incidents like that made me wonder why I missed him, but still I did. Besides, I'm sure I had my own mean streak.

At thirteen, my focus started to change as I faced some hard facts, facts I couldn't ignore any longer. Getting any kind of esteem-building support from Mom, Dad, or Mike wasn't happening, but with the onset of puberty, other avenues suddenly seemed to open to me. Thoughts of falling in love, getting married, and having my own children and family began slowly to replace all those failed attempts to win acceptance in my family. Surely I wouldn't always be reliant on my parents or brother as my only sources of comfort. In keeping with my penchant for persistence, I decided to look outside my immediate family for a long-overdue taste of unconditional love . . . As it turned out, I was on a mission without a compass.

Dad believed maintaining control of moving vehicles was of paramount importance whether you were a girl or a boy, so he taught me how to drive when I was fourteen. I never felt less valued because I was a girl, and it seemed I was well plugged into my "male side" as far as talents and strengths went. For instance, if someone had to hold the train tickets, Mom and Dad gave them to me instead of Mike since he tended to misplace things. I'm sure that didn't make Mike feel great, but after all, we had to get to our destination, didn't we? Being in charge began to feel natural for me; I had an intense drive and often felt that if I didn't take care of things, they wouldn't get done at all. (*Not* a good balance to take into marriage, by the way.) There was never any envy in Dad's frequently voiced statement that he wished his father could have seen how much success I enjoyed as I grew up, "You outearned your grandfather . . . That's something," Dad would say. An oft-used quote of my father's is "There's nothing worse than mediocrity." I happen to agree, but only when you haven't done your best. To me, someone's best is never mediocre. The fact was, Dad was always tough on me. I'm sure he'd say that his theme of "it's never good enough" was meant as a way of encouraging the best in me, but I have to admit that I almost always interpreted these words as criticism.

Although I continued to be a well-behaved, well-mannered girl on the surface, it was as if something within me was slowly breaking away from my old mold. I developed an adventurous side that surprised even me, and while I remained painfully shy and insecure, parts of my life began taking quite a dramatic turn.

six

GATHERING SPEED

*D*ESPITE all the crashing and burning I endured on Montgomery the horse, and the humiliation I suffered at the pony-club shows, where I never had the right clothes, tack, instruction, or friends, I refused to give up on my *National Velvet* dream. I was determined to be a good rider, and thankfully I had some natural talent because as far as advantages went, talent was all I had. The only thing that held a candle in my mind to hooved flight was, if you will, wheeled flight, and over my life I managed to get in at least as much trouble in a car as I did in the saddle.

In my second year as a teenager, I was riding with a ponyclubber one afternoon along the "miracle mile." This was a stretch of road where there was an abundance of sand used for traction during Connecticut snowstorms and then deposited in ribbons along the roadside—perfect footing for racing horses at breakneck speed. The girl I was riding with had a strutting, gleaming, fire-on-ice-gray pony and I felt both honored and stupid to be in her presence.

As it happened, her dad was driving down the same road we had just entered from a side path. He screeched to a halt in his convertible sports car to greet his daughter and then acknowledged me. There it was again—that "daddy-daughter thing." He had a gleam in his eye as he winked at his little girl and shouted, "Let's race!" Without warning, she tore off down the road, sand spraying in my face like a Sahara insult. Being left in the dust somehow inspired in me one of the first and strongest attacks of competition I have ever experienced. Even Montgomery seemed to feel it as he rose to the occasion in a surprising show of spirit. We raced after the pony, taking the lead before half the stretch was behind us. I remember a brief moment of eye contact with the father as I sped past his daughter. His look was a mix of annoyance and amazement, and when we all pulled up at the crossroads, he commented: "Pretty damn good for a bucket of bolts"—referring to my heaving, sweaty horse—"twenty-two and a half mph." Before his daughter could pout about her loss, he consoled her. "Sweetheart, her horse is twice the size of your pony. She had the advantage." I thought it was cool he was trying to cheer her up. And suddenly, *poof,* he was gone, and then so was she, down the next shortcut home. *Twenty-two and a half mph* . . . I was glad I beat her, and for that moment I thought of Monty as a super-horse.

Not only did that stretch of road called the "miracle mile" offer me my first big win, but it provided the location for just about the happiest day I ever spent with my dad. It was one of those very rare occasions when we were alone in the car driving back from New Canaan. I couldn't resist telling him about my incredible race with the pony. I was talking so fast, Dad pulled the car off the road, instructing me to slow my speech and refrain from saying "you know" every other word. I immediately stopped talking, sure that was what he preferred, but he just waited, nodding for me to continue. I couldn't believe it. He actually sat there and listened to my entire rendition of the event. When I finally finished, he smiled, the end of his nose tipping down like a wilting flower. And then the most extraordinary thing happened: he got out of the car, walked around to the passenger's side, got back in, and told me to "move over and drive." I was just fourteen and barely made the pedals, but I managed the stretch in the best "Gumby" tradition. Although Dad was overwhelming as he barked orders, I knew I was doing a good job and he was pleased with my performance in the end. That recognition has been a treasured part of me ever since. It makes me think of an unforgettable dessert I've just devoured—for a few moments I'm glad for the taste and then the yearning for it starts all over again. It seems lasting satisfaction remains an unattainable goal for a glutton.

A few weeks later, Mom and Dad left in Dad's station car to go downtown to vote. It was all but dark outside and I was feeling restless. Out of the blue, I decided I just had to go for a drive on my own in Mom's Buick. Mind you, I had driven with Dad less than a handful of times. I wasn't under the influence of peer pressure or anything else, it was just this expanding wild side of mine that encouraged the spin. After all, Mom and Dad would be gone for at least an hour. The keys were in the Buick and I was off on down the road before I even thought twice. The escapade still boggles my mind, since I was clear and sincere about the importance of not disobeying my parents. Short of a few "normal" departures from obedience, I had never done anything downright rebellious . . . And there I was, whizzing along, making up for lost time.

The road was narrower than I remembered, dark and winding, with fall leaves that swirled and then stuck to the windshield of the car like nasty little beings determined to block my view. I had just come to the brilliant conclusion that I was in way over my head and started to look for a place to turn around when suddenly my eyes were struck by the sight of oncoming headlights. I panicked! The road barely accommodated *my* car, how was I ever going to be able to pass this wall of light barreling toward me? I sat up tall, stretching my body without losing contact with the pedals. Shaking all over, my hands fumbled about the steering wheel in search for some reassurance. As the headlights filled my vision, I swerved and closed my eyes in preparation for impact. This was the first time in my life I felt the unforgettable escort of angels hovering over me as the other car passed by without incident. But it did not pass without leaving my parents' faces embossed on my brain. It was Dad's car I had almost sideswiped. *I had just passed Mom and Dad on the road and there was no way I could possibly beat them home!*

Finally able to pull over, I parked for a long time and contemplated my future as my breath formed a film of steam on the car windows. I decided I *had* no future and that I might as well go home and face the music. I wrote something stupid on the foggy windshield and then erased it, watching my words vanish in a smear of water drops. Catching a glimpse of my face in the rear-view mirror, I saw tears running down my cheeks like the water on the window.

Take all the times I've been plunked inside a dentist's office, steeling myself for a shot of Novocain, multiply that fear by one billion, and that's what I felt that night sitting in my Mom's Buick by the side of the road. Running away did occur to me for a brief instant, but in my heart I knew that wasn't a real option. Unfortunately, that option seems to be all too real to kids today, the street swallowing them up, their hearts broken, their spirits squashed, their bodies abused, and their lives sometimes snuffed out as they flounder through a netherworld unfit for our enemies, let alone our children.

But back then, *I* was the kid. As I gingerly finessed Mom's car down the driveway of our house, the headlights shone on my dad, alone in the middle of the front lawn, standing his ground like a sentry. I remember thinking for an instant that I hated my father's certainty that I would come home and not run away into the night. My increasingly dramatic personality was beginning to let itself be known. Since then, there have been endless times when I wished I hadn't been so transparent . . . so blatantly wrong both in motive and act.

There I was, the dog coming home with her tail between her legs, remorseful because I already knew that the lecture I was about to receive was well deserved. I felt fear sweep over me. But then, as I carefully put the car in park and waited for the first indications of my father's wrath to manifest themselves, I got the feeling that *he* was waiting for *me* to make the first move. So I ventured forth and stood before him like a lamb leading itself to slaughter. But he didn't yell—didn't threaten—didn't punish. Dad actually took the time to explain to me in detail how dangerous my actions were, how much I worried Mom and him, and how I was never, ever to "pull such a stunt again." What got my attention more than any of his words was the hint of a smile I could see on his face. It was about as close to that "daddy-daughter thing" as I had ever come, and it was far more meaningful to me than not getting into deep trouble. I knew that inside, my dad was impressed by my "chutz-pah"—or at least that I hadn't crashed the car. Maybe he was actually plugged into me enough to know that I was scared out of my wits and I really didn't require a full-fledged, fire-and-brimstone sermon. In short, I skated for once in my life—I knew it, he knew it. It was the second-best moment I ever had with my dad.

Just as my life seemed to be taking a turn for the better, everything fell apart. Granted, I hadn't achieved "popular" status at school with either the boys or the girls, but I did have access to a horse. And although I still missed my cat Groucho, I did have Mandy the magic dog that turned from yellow to black. And although I hadn't gotten my period yet, I did have a Grow-bra. And even though I missed my brother, at least he wasn't there to tease me all the time about how I didn't need that poor excuse for a bra. And of course there was my straight-A stature. Things were going along pretty darn well . . . until *the decision.*

From my parents' point of view, Dad had commuted to work too long on that "lousy, stinking train" and Mom had suffered the seclusion of country living till she was about to "lose her mind." She needed a fix of city living before divorce became more than just a repetitive threat. After all, "Mike was away at school and Jennifer was all but grown up." I was fourteen when Mom and Dad decided that they were selling our house and moving into New York City. All the move meant to me at first was that I would lose my horse, that Monty was doomed to join Groucho the cat in the graveyard of my heart. But just when I thought life couldn't come in a meaner package, my parents hit me with the big one: my dog, Mandy, was not included in our journey. Bottom line, Mom said that an apartment in New York City was no place for a dog, so Mandy had to be given away. I tried to tell her that an apartment in New York City was no place for *me,* but my opinions held no importance. In fact, there was no aspect of the move that was up for discussion, according to my parents. Although I begged heroically about letting me at least keep my dog, my mom and dad didn't hear a word I said or feel a tear I cried. They completely ignored that to me, my world was crashing . . . But they couldn't have known, right? They would have done something about it if they had known, wouldn't they? Have you ever felt time fly by yet remain at a standstill? The next few months felt that way to me.

I had never noticed how rotten my dog's teeth were until I began taking her door-to-door trying to find a home for her before the big move. The deadline was closing in, and although Mandy was under a year old, she'd been born with no enamel on her teeth, which left her with rows of rotting incisors for a smile. On top of that, she had a horrific case of halitosis, and despite my certainty that she was an absolute miracle dog, there were no takers. I bathed her, lectured her about her manners, warned her of the infamous "animal pound" where they put unwanted pets to "sleep." I was out of control: no one was good enough for my dog and yet my dog didn't seem to be good enough for anyone else. I told Mandy I knew how she felt. As always, she comforted me, licking me all over and wagging her body in a display of affection. I was incredibly sad.

It was a Saturday afternoon at the end of a winter-gray day. Dad was ensconced in his corner chair, which faced the second-story landing. Newspapers were scattered at his feet, and a book lay in his lap. I had heard his voice through my bedroom door, and since his words were muffled by the distance, I assumed he had called me. But Dad hadn't called for me. He was in the midst of filling out my application to the Dalton Girls' School in New York City and was actually yelling a question to Mom, who was somewhere upstairs. As I opened my door, I heard him ask her if I had grown any pubic hair yet. I don't know if Mom answered the question, especially since she didn't know the answer. After all, we didn't talk about such things. I was beyond horrified that absolute strangers at some school had the audacity to ask such a question. What business was it of theirs? And how could my dad even have read such a question about me, let alone yell it around the house!

The impending move to New York City was like a tidal wave gathering force and power. What made matters worse was that I felt so estranged from my parents as well as from anyone on the face of the earth. I have no memory of where my aunt Elle was during that period. My fears turned to desperation as I made my daily rounds trying to place my dog, say good-bye to my horse, and imagine what could possibly lie ahead for someone like me in a cement metropolis. Floods of emotion led to depression as I tried to make sense of what was going on. And the big day kept drawing closer . . .

I was in my bedroom that afternoon. My brother's room was next to mine at the end of the hall and the bathroom was just across from us next to the balcony leading downstairs. Prior to Mike's departure for prep school, it was a part of everyday life for Mike and me to zip from our bedrooms to the bathroom in towels, T-shirts, or underwear, since most of the time we were too lazy to find our bathrobes. As always, that day I was in a hurry, so I yelled out to Dad, who was sitting in his living-room chair reading, "Don't look!" I leaped across the hall to the bathroom, covering my underweared self with my hands, arms, and a twist of motion. As I sailed through the air, I happened to look down toward Dad. He was staring up at me, laughing. It was such a mean thing to do. Instead of respecting my shyness, he was laughing at me. In retrospect, I don't think what he was doing was at all lascivious, but I do know that it was extremely damaging to me as a young girl. I felt like a joke as I lay on the bathroom floor in a ball of embarrassment and anger.

There have been times of pain, both physical and emotional, that seem to be fashioned expressly for me; no one could understand or fix them, and no one wanted to. One of the earliest of these times involved a pain in my legs that was so severe, Mom actually took me to see several different doctors. Their answer simply was, "She's experiencing growing pains." As far as I was concerned, that was a ridiculous explanation. I was tough. The pain I was feeling was outrageous, and if that was normal, no one would make it to adulthood because it simply hurt too much. That round with the doctors made it even more difficult for me to get my parents to take anything that hurt me seriously. The leg pain stopped me physically, but what was coming up was an emotional crisis that almost ended my life's story in act one.

seven

CRASH COURSE

IT was Easter Sunday. The day presented itself in storybook fashion, the sun brilliantly shining, bathing the spring flowers in warmth and encouragement. To me, Easter meant eggs, bunnies, and family gatherings. Going to church to celebrate the holiday was all about buying a new hat and outfit. According to my kid calendar, Easter was basically a school break early in the year. The truth is, had I possessed more than a superficial understanding of the significance of Easter, I wouldn't have made the choice I did on that spring day in 1962. But this year I was all twisted up in my sorrow, anger, and hormones. I let myself be overwhelmed by circumstances that seemed insurmountable and hopeless. I did not have an unswayable sense of self-worth and value . . . I was lost and I had lost hope.

There was no family gathering to speak of that Easter, but someone took pictures of Mom, Dad, my dog Mandy, and me in the backyard. I wore a white button-down shirt with blue slacks that weren't intended to be cut as pedal pushers, but they looked that way since my legs were so long they stuck out six inches from the hem. It was hard to pose with Mandy for the photos. What was the point? Were we going for the picture of the week of things loved and lost?

And then I found myself in Mom's bathroom with the voices in my head that had been haunting me on and off since my gorilla nightmare arrived, the voices that directed me when I walked in my sleep. *Go on, get it over with,* they echoed. *Then they'll be sorry for hurting you so much. Go on, show them how mean they are. You're never going to get your own horse now. They'll never come to see you ride, they never have before. They're going to take your dog away just like they took your cat away. See if your dad will laugh at you now. See if Mike will make fun of you. See how sorry your mother will be when you're really gone. You, Mandy, and Groucho will all be together . . . Go on . . . Go on . . .*

I grabbed Mom's sleeping pills from the medicine cabinet and never looked back. It was as if I had been programmed and there wasn't a moment's hesitation from that point on, only relief that I wasn't going to "feel" anymore. I downed the whole bottle of pills once I made it to my own bathroom for privacy. Although I took the medicine quickly, I did watch myself in the mirror swallow each and every pill. I hated myself, my life, my hair, my body, my parents. I truly didn't want to go on without my horse and my dog, who were my only real friends. As I looked into my eyes in the mirror, I decided that I needed to be with Mandy when I died. I was already feeling woozy, so I had to hurry before anyone saw me acting strangely. I had to make it outside while I could still walk . . .

Mandy was lying on her back by the front fence, her legs extended heavenward, the folds of her snout falling to the ground like a pile of pancakes on a plate. Although she was lost in sunning herself, she still made the effort to get up and greet me; Mandy was such a good dog. I was getting weaker and it was an amazing relief just to lie down in the grass and let the sun keep me warm. Just to lie down next to my dog. I knew I would be safe, because Mandy would always protect me. At least I could count on her. Everything was going to be okay now . . . Everything was going to be okay . . .

The pain in my legs had returned and I seemed to be stuck in a new nightmare. In those days I didn't know how to wake myself up during a bad dream and force the invasion of negativity back into its ugly, dark corner. I was somewhere between life and death when I realized my mission to expire had not been accomplished. As I felt more and more of my body come back to life, I became convinced that I didn't want to be where I was returning. My heart was breaking and my mind was objecting to the coma my body had survived.

This time the pain in my legs wasn't due to "growing pains"; it was a result of the intravenous needles stuck everywhere from my thighs to my arms. I was in a hospital room. My throat was sore from the tube that pumped my stomach, a catheter had been inserted for urine, which caused me astonishing embarrassment when some male doctor finally pulled the covers back and removed it. Later I was told by the doctor who was trying to comfort me as I was coming back to consciousness that I had been screaming hysterically that I hated my mother. I hated her and I never wanted to see her again! The doctor wanted me to talk to him about all that, but I couldn't . . . I didn't want to talk to anyone . . . I didn't want to be there.

Had I had my wits about me, I wouldn't have dared to express my feelings about my mom so vocally, but under the artificially liberating influence of sedatives, truth flooded forth. Unfortunately, I would pay dearly for this outburst. I was still legally and emotionally under my mother's control and she had heard all of the venom I screamed about her down the hospital corridor. When Mom and Dad came to see me, Mom was particularly distant and tense. I knew I'd better find a way to explain and dismiss my screaming statements as quickly as I could. She was very unhappy, and one did *not* make Mom unhappy or else . . . All I could say over and over was that I was sorry, but I could see that this was getting me nowhere. Only one thing changed during the entire ordeal—I finally got my period. I've always laughed at the thought that it took a near-death experience to shock my body into womanhood.

Sometime later another doctor, a psychiatrist, showed up. Apparently, according to state law, when a minor attempts suicide, the parents are required to have the child evaluated by a "shrink." My parents had made their feelings about therapy very clear to me over the years; in a nutshell, they were adamant nonbelievers. I figured I had made enough trouble for everybody and the last thing I needed to do was put my parents in a position of having to talk to a doctor on an ongoing basis about what was really happening at home. They would hate that. Additionally, to hold my parents responsible for paying for the therapy with all their plans for their future life in New York City would be unthinkable. They were under enough strain having committed to pay for Mike's private school and now mine, once we'd moved. I begged my parents not to make me see the psychiatrist, but the law was clear.

My mind was swimming as I sat up in the hospital bed staring past that psychiatrist person. He seemed gentle and at first I found myself really wanting to talk to him, especially about my dog, the animal pound, and my fears. But then I remembered that no matter what I did at that point, I was going to have to go home and face my parents. I couldn't deny that I hoped somehow Mom and Dad would forgive me and change their mind at least about letting me keep my dog. I say their "mind" instead of minds because they always seemed to be of one mind; talking to them felt like running into a brick wall. I had lived with my parents long enough to know how strict they were, but maybe, just maybe, they realized now how seriously upset I was and how much I needed them to understand me.

Of course, I never dared to say any of that to the doctor. After a long while and a wall of silence on my part, he finally said I could be released from the hospital, but he wanted me in his office in a few days to see how I was doing. *How I was doing?* Couldn't he see I was doing swimmingly? Just your average teenager having a nervous breakdown, that's all. Going home was like being assigned a berth on the lowest level of the *Titanic*.

And suddenly, there I was back in Wilton, sitting in our living room facing my parents. Not much was said that first night other than I'd better get some rest for school the next day. I decided the best thing to do at that point was shut up and comply. But the thought of going back to school terrified me; and that fear was not unfounded. It was worse than I even imagined. As soon as I hit the school bus, everyone was whispering and pointing at me. I actually had a taste of what a handicapped child must face, but in my case, I was just having a hard chapter in my life—a handicapped child has a lifetime of hard moments to deal with.

Since we were going to move anyway, I wondered why my parents made me go back to school. Didn't they realize it would give everyone a chance to take one last jab at me? Maybe they did it to teach me a lesson? What lesson? Maybe they just didn't have a clue how hard it was going to be on me? I was hoping it was just another oversight on their part.

The next meeting I had with my parents made everything pretty clear. They were still angry as they sat on the couch like bookends. Mom spoke first, and when she finished, there was nothing else to say. "Jennifer, your father and I have discussed what you have done at length, and we've decided that nothing has changed. We are still moving to Manhattan, you will finish school here, and your dog will be given away. I'm sure you understand that your father and I can't possibly let you get away with such a stunt." She concluded by staring me down . . . and then there was just silence, a silence that created the loudest noise I had ever heard in my head.

Of course I took care of the psychiatrist thing when we met at the doctor's office. I knew just what to say to make that problem go away. I knew just what they all wanted to hear. I told both the doctor and my parents how "sorry I was. I never meant to kill myself. I was just acting like a brat and I was wrong. Yes, I was upset about my dog and horse, but taking the pills was only about being angry and of course I understood that the animals had to go and I had to move." I apologized with the perfect mixture of remorse and awareness. I was good . . . Boy, I was smart and I was good.

We moved late that summer to Eighty-first Street and First Avenue in New York City. I was told my dog went to live on a farm somewhere, and I never saw Monty again. I was accepted at Dalton, one of the toughest schools in the country, and although I appeared to be "back on track," I was really an accident waiting to happen. You see, nothing had really been dealt with. Nothing was ever really understood, forgiven, communicated, grieved, and healed—it all just lay dormant, waiting for the next explosion, and while the voices still had privileged access to the deepest recesses of my mind, my heart shut down for any new business.

I was in mourning. Given my perspective and lack of enthusiasm, New York City was big, loud, dirty, and crowded. It held no magic for me, no excitement, no potential. There would be times, later in my life, when I embraced Manhattan as the most exhilarating place on earth, but not at that point. I was radically uncomfortable in my new, all-girls school, brimming mostly with wealthy Jewish kids who had gone there since kindergarten; yet again, a tight-knit group for me to contend with from the outside looking in.

I did find one friend right off, probably because misery loves company and she and I had a lot in common. Her name was Alice Parnassus. She was a zaftig Greek, even taller than I, absolutely beautiful, and a ton of fun. I met her on entrance-exam day and we were close from then on. It seemed like we were about the only non-Jewish girls in our class, so we used to refer to each other as "O'Neillawitz" and "Parnassusbaum." This was not meant in any derogatory manner, just a mocking acknowledgment of our minority status. I had one other friend, Carolyn, who was a grade ahead of me at Dalton. She was a short, wiry girl with fabulous long red hair and freckles. Actually, Carolyn and I had more in common than Dalton. We had met in New Canaan at an art class we attended one summer. Carolyn and I also became immediate friends, probably because she knew no other kids as she was in the country only for the summers and weekends. I was still stuck in my Connecticut outcast mode, so we seemed a good support team for each other.

Not long after we crossed paths, I was invited to keep Carolyn company on a trip up the Maine coast on her parents' yacht. Aside from becoming seasick and spewing blueberry pie all over the side of their gleaming vessel as we approached our first night at dock, I handled myself admirably in the midst of all the grandeur. (Thanks, Mom, for all the lessons on manners and proper speech.)

Life at the Dalton School turned out to be better than I expected; I found myself overcoming my resentment and being stimulated in ways I never imagined. Dalton, for example, invited anthropologist Margaret Mead to speak at a Friday assembly, offered advanced college-level classes and dance study on a close-to-professional level, and had a string of inspiring teachers. And although I continued to be depressed on and off, I allowed myself to succumb to the educational challenge the school presented. I also began to regroup and plot a strategy to get myself a horse, one way or another. I have to admit, one of the few things I've always really liked about myself is that I never give up . . . *never*. And what a journey that little personality trait has taken me on. My "looking for love addiction" was about to be unleashed full force.

Once I decided I wasn't going to expire from sadness, I started to seek out opportunities to feel better; I found one right downstairs in apartment 12B. Actually, the first time we met was in the elevator, and we were immediately drawn to each other. His name was Sebastian and he inspired a feeling in me of being totally protected and adored. I knew we both couldn't wait to see each other every day. Sebastian filled that part of my heart that had shut down. Just the two of us walking down the street together caused passersby to regard us with respect, and it didn't take long before we were inseparable.

Sebastian, I should tell you, was the first German shepherd I'd ever become friends with, and from then on I've felt that shepherds were just about the best all-around breed of dog anyone could own. Years later, I finally bought a female shepherd named Bête, who was at my side for fifteen years (she saved me from harm on two occasions). Beyond Bête, I worked with many German shepherds while I ran Point of View, my protection-training kennel.

Sebastian's owner encouraged our relationship—not surprisingly, since I ended up being the dog's full-time no-charge walker. I was hoping Mom and Dad would see that a dog in the city was really no problem if they're walked and cared for regularly, but my parents never made the connection. Besides, I knew Mandy was already someone else's girl by then.

The neighbors in the apartment next to ours were two men who happened to work in advertising, and through them, my career was about to be born. These guys had heard at least a million times my various plots and plans to earn money to buy a horse of my own: O'Neill's Diligent Daily Dog-Walking Service, Dirt Cheap Baby-sitting All Hours, and Apartment Cleaning for the Careless were just a few of my schemes. My neighbors kindly listened to me and then suggested modeling. I looked at them like they had three heads. Modeling was not only the last thing on my mind, I was sure I'd never qualify. In my opinion I was a mess. Okay, I was tall and from time to time my parents' friends commented on my "bedroom eyes" and "willowy body" but to me, I was geeky-tall, not pretty, and the only blooming I seemed to do was as a wallflower. Outcasts don't appear in commercials or get featured on magazine covers . . . do they?

My neighbors booked me on a little modeling job in *Hairdo* magazine and, with those photos, sent me to the Ford Modeling Agency for the once-over. The biggest shock to me was the first meeting at Ford's, where, after being reviewed from head to toe, I was told that I needed to *lose* weight. I always felt I was giving Popeye's Olive Oyl a run for her money, and here I was having to drop some weight before I could formally make the roster. Although I was instantly mourning the loss of my chocolate-chip-cookie snacks at school, I was excited about being accepted by Ford right off and presented my modeling plans to Mom and Dad in my most convincing fashion. My grades were still top-notch and I was doing everything I was supposed to do (other than battling the mess in my bedroom). Mom and Dad really didn't have any reason to say no. I might add, my parents never once urged me to work. We were, however, about to stumble over some differences in money management, but aside from that, Mom and Dad were the opposite of the pushy showbiz-type parents so many young performers have to suffer.

As I began my "career," I wondered what everyone was thinking. Not a single part of me was slightly comfortable standing in front of a camera. On the other hand, the thought that I could buy my own horse at the end of this tunnel of discomfort was all the encouragement I needed. At the agency, Eileen planned for me to starve off some pounds before the school year ended and then spend the summer testing and making the rounds to see if I really had what it took to model in New York City—more important, if I had what it took to be a "Ford model." Although the odds were a million to one, Eileen nonetheless seemed fascinated with me. To her, I was a unique mixture of Audrey Hepburn, Katharine Hepburn, and Rita Hayworth. I could look fifteen or thirty with a simple makeup change, and I apparently exuded a mysterious quality that, along with my vulnerability, would become my trademark. But all this hyperbole eluded me; I was left with no more sense of who I was or what impact I had on others than I had when I first walked into the agency. My world was changing faster than I was and I would be required to play a lot of catch-up that sometimes I just couldn't handle.

Mike was going to be home from boarding school for the summer and planned to caddy at the New Canaan Country Club to earn money. It was decided that our family would spend the summer at my uncle's in Connecticut and that I would commute to Manhattan with my dad while I tried to establish my career. It was 1963; I was fifteen years old. I admit, for an instant I felt sorry for myself; I'd have to work all summer in the grimy city while most of the girls at my school vacationed in Europe or the Hamptons, but then I thought, don't be stupid. Those options weren't open to me whether I modeled or not, and it wasn't long before my prospects made all the sweat worthwhile. Besides, hard work never put me off.

eight

BREAKING THE ICE

VERYTHING was suddenly moving faster than would prove good for me, especially my newfound interest in boys, the appearance of which could be compared only to a wildcat gusher.

Carolyn and I discovered a small restaurant about fifteen blocks from Dalton that made fantastic cheeseburgers, although, to be honest, its real allure was not its food. It was run by a guy named Brian who just happened to be the best-looking man I had ever seen. I say "man" because he was in his late twenties and that meant he was a grown-up as far as I was concerned. I also say he had absolutely no business messing around with me at age fifteen, even if I did look quite a bit older. I'm sure I lied to him about my age, but he knew I went to Dalton and his interest in finding out the truth about me played a very distant second to his lust.

After many afternoons of flirting, he finally asked me out for dinner and a movie. The problem was, our date was set for a school night and there was no way my parents would agree to it, especially with Brian. My father would have drawn and quartered him on sight. But I was determined not to miss this opportunity, so I figured the best thing to do was to tell Mom and Dad I was spending the night at Carolyn's. When I look back at all the times my parents wouldn't let me go on sleepovers as a kid, I wished they had said no this time. The fact that I had never really pulled anything devious before (except the car incident) gave my parents a false sense of security about my alleged whereabouts and intent. After all, I was a good girl, right?

My favorite movie at that time was *Breakfast at Tiffany's* and I imagined I was about to embark on a Holly Golightly adventure. Dinner was at Brian's restaurant with candlelight and my very first drink, a rum concoction called a Zombie (and for good reason). After one and a half Zombies sweetened with fruit, *I* was the zombie. I stared into Brian's eyes like a lovesick sap and tried to act casual as my words slipped off my tongue and fell into my salad plate. I decided I needed some coffee before we left for the movies; the last thing I wanted to do was throw up all over the table—or worse, all over Brian. I was getting attention from this man and I liked it. He seemed like such a gentleman, making me feel pretty and desirable—new experiences for me. Chasing David on his horse with my bra stuffed with Kleenex seemed a distant, silly memory . . . I was totally convinced that this was the real thing.

The movie we saw was called *David and Lisa,* which was about two mentally disturbed but very compelling teenagers. Good choice on Brian's part. It created a perfect mood for him to put his arm around me, and when he touched my shoulder, I felt a shiver go right through me. Before I knew it, we were outside looking for a cab. Suddenly the evening was over; I couldn't have imagined a better time.

In the taxi, Brian asked if we could make a quick stop at his apartment to pick something up to take back to his restaurant. He took my hand in his and held it a moment before I nodded yes. After all, it was just for a second; he knew I had to get back to Carolyn's before ten.

Brian apartment was a third-floor walk-up in a brownstone. The overhead lights cast stripes down the hall as we entered, the sound of our steps ringing loud in the hushed stairwell. It took him what seemed forever to unlock his front door, and he paused a long time before venturing into his abode. I remember thinking, *Wow, what a tentative way to approach your own apartment.* It wouldn't be long before I understood why.

On the right of the entrance was a small bathroom that led to the compact kitchen and miniature studio apartment. It was clean and well decorated with strong colors accenting modern design. I sat on the couch as Brian rummaged in the kitchen. He returned with some drinks in a pair of thick goblets. I didn't want to look like a stupid kid, which of course I was, so I returned his toast and took a small sip. This wasn't a sweet, tasty bombshell in a pretty package; this drink was regular old vile vodka on the rocks.

Brian sat next to me on the couch, and for the first time I felt a sickening discomfort. He kissed me, at first softly, and then with mounting force. My hand was locked around my drink, which I extended outward so I wouldn't spill it all over us. But then I began to feel like I was suffocating and what started out as a pleasant experience quickly turned into an onslaught. His hands were everywhere, ripping at my clothes as they searched my body. When I pulled away, he quickly jerked back off me and stood at attention. For an instant I was confused and then it became all too clear. Out of nowhere, standing in front of us was a screaming, hysterical blond woman spewing rage in some Scandinavian-sounding language. I just sat there, frozen to the couch, watching her viciously hit and kick Brian . . . And then she was on me! She grabbed my glass out of my hand, stood only inches from me, hurled words of profanity, and then threw the glass with all her might at my face. My right hand shot up in protection as the goblet literally shattered before my eyes. Blood was instantly everywhere. The glass broke the bones in my hand and severed all its main arteries, which pumped out rivers of red to the rhythm of my heartbeat.

At the sight of my blood, Brian finally found the strength to pick the woman up, slam her into the bathroom, and lock the door. She yelled and pounded the entire time it took for the police and ambulance to arrive. Leaning against the wall, a sensation overtook me as if I were having an out-of-body experience while I was questioned by the police. When asked if I wanted to press charges, I remember thinking *I'm* the one who's in trouble here. I had already soaked blood into five bath towels when I told the police all I wanted to do was go home. That's when the police let the woman out of the bathroom, and then stood by, helpless, as she physically attacked me *again*. She came down the hall so fast, no one could stop her. Now ranting in English, she called me every swear word and synonym for "whore" ever invented. Before anyone could respond, she punched me in the face . . . twice. Finally the police pulled her off just as I was about to lose my mind, and that's when I finally started to cry. I couldn't stop. I had just been brutalized by a lunatic and she really scared me; her rage was terrifying.

Brian went in the ambulance with me to Bellevue Hospital. Let me tell you firsthand—never go to Bellevue Hospital if you can possibly help it. We sat in the emergency room for five hours before anyone would even review my case, and I looked like I had been through a war, so you can imagine the condition of the people ahead of me. Brian never said one word; he just stared at the wall, his right foot tapping the ground nervously.

When the doctor finally called me in, I realized the nightmare had only begun. He was an Asian man who explained everything he was doing, including *not* giving me anything for the pain. He just kept talking about his experiences in the Korean War and how pain was just a state of mind as he sewed my veins together. My mind had to go somewhere else because everything that had happened, and was still happening, and was going to happen when I got home, was just too much for me to consider.

Brian was less than useless; his concerns seemed split between what waited for him back in his apartment and what I might and could do to him as a result of the evening's turn of events. The truth was, I never thought of blaming him, but he didn't know that. I did hear him tell the police I was fifteen and that he was a friend of my family. When asked, I corroborated his story out of fear, and that was that, he wasn't charged with any misdoing. The amazing thing is, despite all that had happened, I still cared about what Brian thought of me. Obviously, I was a case of lower-than-low self-esteem, and I believe that was when another pattern of my life was established: the worse you treat Jennifer, the faster she'll run back for more . . . I thought that was all I deserved.

By the time I got to Carolyn's it was almost daylight. She just stood there in her pajamas with her mouth hanging open while I told her what happened. Her eyes widened with every sorry detail. I was exhausted from the pain and the still-vivid memories of my date. The physical damage to my hand would be lifelong in its effects, but what would prove far more damaging remained hidden—once again, never discussed, grieved, or healed. I told my parents that I'd slipped and fallen on the ice after school and cut my hand. They bought it, or at least they never cross-examined me about my story. It didn't really feel like I had gotten away with anything.

When the school year finally ended, I had shed my designated pounds and was ready to launch myself into a new world, a world that would permanently transform my life. The prospect of modeling made me more than a little nervous; my shyness hung around me like an overcoat. Still, I was determined to get my horse by the end of the summer, no matter what fears were weighing me down. Alice told me there was a "buzz" going around Dalton about my modeling for Ford. Unfortunately, the rumor only distanced me from the other girls and I felt more ostracized than ever. Alice said they were jealous, but I figured they just didn't like me, that's all. Between bouts with my recurring nightmares hosted by Mr. Gorilla, I did have occasional flights of fancy about becoming the next female sensation to grace the silver screen and the fashion magazines, but those images were short-lived. The programming of my psyche was set in stone, and I was already a slave to my constant fears.

The Ford Modeling Agency was a fashion-magazine mecca that beckoned pilgrims from all over the world, and Eileen Ford was the goal of their pilgrimages. She ran her empire with ruthless competitiveness and a fiercely protective attitude about her "girls." Some of the models my age who were imported from Europe actually lived with Eileen and her husband Jerry until they came of age. Although there was a lot of money to be made, especially for a fifteen-year-old, modeling was not the high-profile, superstar-making business it is today. Models who are currently at the top of the heap are also international celebrities who hobnob with the film- and music-business megastars. In the early sixties, a model was assumed to be a bit of an airhead with little but looks to recommend her . . . And if you had an interest in acting in those days, you *never* admitted you were a model. The general consensus was that models could barely walk and talk at the same time, let alone act.

And so the summer commute and pavement pounding commenced. As I built my portfolio, I was sent to meet anywhere from six to eight photographers a day at locations all around Manhattan. It was a hot, grimy task with strong, built-in possibilities for rejection. In the beginning I worked with a few different photographers who were well scrutinized by the agency and approved by Eileen as safe and professional. In the world of legitimate modeling, the model usually does not pay for the test sessions. The photographers need to work on their own books and the girls need new or first pictures, so the sessions become fair trade. As with all budding businesses, you work hard and wait for your first break. Mine came relatively quickly.

There I was, delivered by the magic word of my Ford booking agent into the hands of a professional photographer. The music was so loud in the reception area of the studio, I stood by the elevator door for a good ten minutes waiting for someone to notice I had arrived for my shoot. Other than the *Hairdo* magazine job I'd done—which felt more like the *Perils of Pauline* at a beauty salon than anything else—I was actually on my first booking. Well, not really a booking as in a-job-making-money, but it was my first "booked" test shoot, which I would describe as modeling's version of a screen test. The purpose of these sessions is to see how the new model photographs and discover her range of looks and strengths. The model uses the photos to build her portfolio so that when she is sent by her agent on "go-sees," the client or photographer can see how she looks on film as well as meeting her in person. It's amazing how some people are far more photogenic than others, even if they appear equally attractive in real life.

Despite the lengthy explanations I'd received at the agency, all the information in the world was not going to stop my lower lip from nervously twitching as I took in the studio located in the bowels of Manhattan. The journey there had required a commuter-train ride, two subway experiences, and a taxi I couldn't afford. I finally arrived out front in a dripping sweat brought on by nerves and a muggy Manhattan summer day.

My hair still stuck to my neck when the assistant finally walked past me and merely pointed to the dressing room. No "hellos," no "how are yous." I felt like a starving orphan looking for the bread-line; I was to find out soon enough that I'd better get used to the feeling I was experiencing because it came with the modeling ter-ritory. Photography studios quite often were brimming with con-descending, self-absorbed prima donnas, from the photographers all the way down to the assistants. Once the photographer started shooting, there was the possibility of real human contact, but not always. Modeling to me was a means to an end, a chore that would allow me to buy my horse. Other than the travel, I can't remember much of the experience that held excitement for me. Still, there were a handful of photographers like Jimmy Moore, Scavullo, and Avedon who were not only brilliant at their craft, but were also extremely bright, pleasant individuals. An exception to the often tedious job of modeling was my thirty-year stint as spokesperson for Cover Girl makeup. It was an honor to represent such a top-notch product, created by talented people, people of integrity, both on the ad-agency side and at Noxelle. We all felt like family, and my years with them were most rewarding. I still consider some of the "team" close friends. Unfortunately, once Noxelle was bought out a few years ago by a mega-corporation and the ad team changed, that good old family feeling was gone as well.

On one of my Cover Girl shoots about ten years ago, I was chatting with Scavullo, with whom I had worked since I was fifteen (lots of *Cosmopolitan* covers, etc.). The conversation came around to my first years as a model, and he told me that I was considered moody and distant. Wow! That really surprised me. I recall my paralyzing shyness caused me to keep to myself, which was obvi-ously interpreted by others as aloofness. I do know that often, when I went on a booking with a lot of other girls, I was uncomfortable with the blasé attitude most of them had about nakedness, not only in front of me but around anyone else, male or female, who happened to walk in to do hair, makeup, or styling. The European girls had even fewer inhibitions than the Americans, and I believe I was viewed as hung-up and odd because of my modesty. I must add, though, I never saw drugs, lesbianism, or overt sex on any legitimate shoot.

I quickly realized that my modesty and the way I felt about sex seemed out of sync not only with modeling circles but with the world in general, and this notion of being different grew only stronger as the 1960s progressed. My wild side, which I'd stuffed secretly away, was not so much a result of license as it was an expression of extreme emotions and neediness. I know I was not comfortable in my own skin and that was interpreted by the world in every way other than the truth. All my life, people have assumed I must possess great confidence and conviction when in fact that couldn't have been further from my reality.

Despite how I felt about myself, good news came by way of the report to Eileen from my test photographer. "She's sheer magic," he said of me. I was sure they had mixed the babies up at the hospital. I remember standing at attention watching Eileen review my test shots. My mind raced as I thought about doing anything else or being anywhere else other than where I was, because rejection was, I felt, inevitable. Maybe I could sell vacuum cleaners door-to-door, I remember thinking. At least when people slammed the door in my face, I could walk away and blame it on the quality of the vacuum cleaner. But with this modeling thing, the backside of that door meant they didn't like *me* . . . I wasn't good enough . . . or pretty enough . . . or thin enough . . . or—

"They're good." Eileen's words cut through the buzz of other voices and invaded my negative thoughts. "They . . . are?" I ventured in a small voice. I had been holding my stomach in so hard I had a cramp. Eileen gave me a big hug, and with that, suddenly I felt safe. I was always such a cheap date—give me a hug and we're family.

It turned out, miraculously to me, there was no question that

I was photogenic. Now all I had to do was to learn how to be a professional. Although modeling doesn't put any strain on one's intellectual capacity or get one's creative juices flowing, it is hard work, requiring a professional attitude, discipline, and a very thick skin. Predictably, I was going to have a hard time with the "thick skin" part.

The town of New Canaan had street dances during the summer, and that was how I met John. He was tall, blond, and looked like a "long drink of water" version of Steve McQueen. The irony was that years later I would go a round with the real Steve McQueen when I was shooting a film with James Coburn in Hollywood. Upon meeting the star, I remember thinking of him as a fond reminiscence, a more compact version of John. "Fond" was a fleeting feeling when it came to Steve McQueen, as it was to be with John. So much for that lean, blond look and appeal. Now that I think of it, I've had only two other significant relationships with blond men: the one that set me free and the one that almost killed me. But then again, my commitments to dark-haired men left me once, twice, seven times burned. Redheads and bald men didn't seem an option to me at fifteen, so you could say I was doomed as I found myself at that summer street dance in Connecticut. There I was, about to embark on my marathon search for true love, with no idea of what lay ahead. If I had had an inkling where it would lead me, I might have given the entire search up right then and there.

John and I danced. He actually chose me out of the gaggle of girls lined up for the asking. I was surprised to find myself on the sidelines, milling about as if I had nothing better to do than wait for a boy to ask me to dance. Brian—stitches, nefarious intentions, and all—was, for the moment, behind me. Fate just dropped me off at the train station when the dance activities were about to begin and I asked Dad if I could stay awhile. Dad drove off saying yes, and I said yes to the dance with John. I was immediately smitten with this college guy who possessed some smooth moves and a little experience. He seemed taken with the idea that I was a model and pursued me in a perfectly well-brought-up way for a guy in the throes of a hormonal rage. Add my "better give them what they want" conviction, which I seemed to have learned in "Insecurity 101," and *poof!* I was had, and I hadn't even turned sixteen.

As a result of many test shoots and a few bookings for real money, I finally earned bottom-line horse-buying money. As soon as I had $500 to my name (a fair amount of money in 1961, but still not much for a horse), I could buy an animal that actually had a tail. A horse . . . my very own horse! I found this sleazy horse trader, I guess you'd call him, on the back roads between New Caanan and Norwalk, who actually had horses for sale in my price range; he called them "must-be-your-lucky-day dirt-cheap give-aways."

It was a flash of red mane that first caught my attention as I was led through a maze of spit-and-glue stalls, makeshift paddocks, and piles of manure up to my hip boots. But it didn't matter, I was sure I was going to find my perfect horse. And there he was! Granted, he was a bag-of-bones chestnut who looked like DOG MEAT should be stamped on his forehead, but what could I expect for $500? I sat on him bareback with just a halter and he was quiet as a lamb, especially for a horse off the track.

I couldn't wait to get home, retrieve my money, and close the deal. Everything arranged. John's parents had a shed in their back-yard and a fenced-in field they said I could use for my horse—who was already named Sassafras by the time John dropped me off at home. I think John was relieved to see me go that day . . . I was so excited, sitting next to me was like sitting next to an explosive device.

Mom was humming a Cole Porter tune while checking on her dinner, which meant she was in a good mood. Good. Dad was refilling their cocktails in the living room looking pretty laid-back himself. Double good. I burst through the front door like an in-vading army, destroying their calm as I rattled off my plans. But there was a problem—Mom and Dad didn't have my money. Be-cause I was a minor, they received my checks from Ford and had spent my money on bills. They said they would return it to me when they could. I couldn't believe what I was hearing. I begged them, sure that Sassafras would be sold to someone else if I couldn't pay for him right off. But bottom line, there was no money and I was just going to have to wait. My parents reminded me that I was part of a family and that I needed to contribute to that family. At fifteen, it was already becoming clear that I was going to take on the role of provider more times than not, and since that was going to be my calling, I was determined to do a good job of it. That would make me valuable, right? And it would give me some control . . . some power . . . I would be needed and loved.

The slick horse trader ended up being a pretty-good-guy slick horse trader. He held Sassafras for me till I could buy him a month later. Of course I paid board, cleaned three million two hundred and eighty-six stalls, and rode a bunch of horses for his customers (which wasn't really a chore) and then Sassafras finally was mine!

It was a picture-perfect summer's day when my horse was dropped off at John's parents' place. To impress me, John helped get everything set up for Sassafras (he was, at that time, courting me fast and furiously, as we still hadn't "done it"). Sassafras found renewed strength and zeal for life at the sight of all the field grass. My lamb of a horse filled out like an inflatable doll on the summer feed and pretty soon turned into a wild lunatic. It didn't matter, though, I loved him anyway . . . And it was not so much my horse's fault, but rather the "hara-kiri" kind of riding I was doing due to lack of instruction that became so dangerous—and danger became my middle name.

John and I dated all summer, slowly becoming more intimate. I was convinced to my core that I was madly in love with him, and was already feeling the pressure of his going back to college and leaving me behind. After all, he was twenty and was used to more mature women (which is what I was trying to be). To make matters worse, John let it be known that he was getting very frustrated with my not wanting to "go all the way." (I used to wonder why he couldn't just say "making love" instead of "going all the way," "getting laid," or "doing it.") He gave me his fraternity pin before he left for school as a show of commitment, and without pulling too many punches, let me know what he expected when I went to visit him during fall break. "Everyone who has girls come up to school stays together," was the way he put it.

In hindsight, I suppose John was just doing the regular guy-thing—the problem was within me. I didn't have the self-respect and spiritual grounding to wait for the right time and the right commitment before having sex. Marriage is the right time and the right commitment, I believe. All I knew then was that I was going to lose John if I didn't comply, and I was continuing to bring my own need to be accepted into all my relationships. At fifteen, my world revolved around John and I didn't think I could stand it if he left me. It didn't matter how grown-up I could look, my immaturity decided I had to give him whatever he wanted so he would love me.

I was coming of age as the era of free love rapidly approached. It seemed the rest of the world was losing interest in that "commitment thing" right when it was becoming my only goal. I didn't value myself, yet I expected I could choose someone who would value me. Mine was not a journey of "devil may care," "wild thing" fling, mine was a frantic search . . . And what good can come of "frantic"?

n i n e

RED FLAG

*T*HAT fall I was officially back at Dalton, but rarely attended classes because of modeling, which I was doing pretty much full-time. Nonetheless, I was still able to maintain my grades—helped by my willingness to do a lot of homework—which fulfilled my parents' condition for my continuing to work . . . Work meant money and money meant horses! I brought Sassafras into Manhattan and boarded him at a stable in the nineties on the West Side. He wasn't fond of traffic and had a particular fear of yellow taxis; consequently, we were honked into some amazing runaway rides through Central Park.

I was also working hard to help Mom and Dad keep the house in Wilton so we had somewhere to go out of the city and I'd be close to John during school vacations. I was receiving some new-found respect and interest from my parents, who simply marveled at my exploding career. They seemed sincerely impressed with my maturity and ability to take care of myself, and I'd have done just about anything to hold their focus. You see, I was already a good actress, playing whatever role I thought would please everyone. But I was miscast in the role of grown woman. I was just a dressed-up little girl, an impostor who wanted only to marry John when I was a little older. After all, fall break was coming up and . . . I was going up to visit him at school . . . and . . .

I was scared when he turned the lights out and locked the door.

I was scared of what was going to happen, and afraid John wouldn't like me when it was all over. The only thing I wanted was to make him happy . . . to make him stay. And then the only thing I wanted was for it to stop hurting so much. But I never let him know. I made all the sounds and moves I thought I was supposed to make, and when finally it was over, I couldn't figure out why I felt so incredibly sad. But I never let him know this. I was happy that John seemed proud of me in front of his friends. They were impressed that I was on the cover of magazines, and the fact that I was only fifteen somehow never came up.

On my return to New York, the headmistress of Dalton called my parents and me in for a meeting. She informed us that although my grades were more than up to snuff, Dalton was not a school that would allow their students to miss so many classes. She suggested I transfer to Professional Children's School if I insisted on a full-time career. "Full-time career" . . . it was really the first time that fact really registered to me. But the truth was, I was already making $80,000 a year, a huge amount of money in 1962, so I didn't run into a big battle with my parents over changing schools.

It was not until I was writing this book at age fifty that I finally understood why my parents handled the matter so equably. I had always wondered why they were adamant about my brother attending prep school and getting a college education, a prospect Mike absolutely hated, while they let me virtually leave school to work at fifteen. And remember, *I* was the "student" of the family. I loved school. Dad actually cried recently when I asked him his reasoning on this matter, and I was surprised, yet grateful for his candid answer.

Apparently, being the daughter of Oscar D. O'Neill Jr. was different from being his son when it came to education. Dad believed, based on his upbringing, that education for a female was superfluous. After all, girls just grow up, marry, and are taken care of. That's all my mother ever wanted for her life. But for a male child, the best education was an absolute must. Now, I had the marriage part already on my agenda, but the "being taken care of" part didn't quite jibe since I was already well launched in the role of "the formally uneducated breadwinner." Another role I was to play for a lifetime.

Mom often argued with Dad about his boy vs. girl theory since she had been forced to leave school in the eighth grade because of family finances and life in World War II London. Despite her views about marriages, Mom's "lack of education" bothered her enormously (despite her intrinsic intelligence); therefore she fought for my rights. But since I began making so much money and seemed to have life by the tail, my parents saw nothing to complain about. I was already a success and my schooling was merely a time of inconvenience to be sidestepped.

In retrospect, the fact that Mom was also off working and contributing to her family at age fourteen accounts for some of her attitude. Further, my dad sent money to my mother's family in London whenever they needed it and whether he could afford to or not. My parents have always been generous beyond their means. Money is such a sticky issue; it can be a blessing, and as most of us know, it can be a curse . . . But what it really is, is "temporal." I've found one of the keys to happiness is to remember this, which is of course easier to do when you have money than when you don't.

It occurs to me now that the early teen years seemed to be a magical age for young ladies in our family, an opportunity to venture into the world like grown women and escape from a sheltered life. If asked, as I have been many times, how I felt about missing out on my youth, I can only reply that childhood was something I *wanted* to leave behind. It held little happiness and hope for me, and I was in a big hurry to feel better about every aspect of my life. If that meant growing up too fast, so be it.

Professional Children's School ended up being the toughest academy I ever attended, because the system was such that you did extra work for every class you missed, and I missed virtually all of them. I attended an initial class to meet the teachers and that was pretty much it. I told myself that I didn't really want to go to school anyway. I didn't want to meet all those kids who sat in the lunchroom squealing over a new group called the Beatles. I wanted to work and do the double homework and put all this growing-up stuff behind me as fast as I could. After all, I was on a mission to get married. During my brief times at school I felt older and more sophisticated than any of the kids around me, and they seemed to think I was invisible, especially the girls. What I took as personal rejection was often, I'm quite sure, jealousy from the female gender and shyness from the male.

Although I hadn't seen John since fall break, we spoke on the phone *constantly*. Christmas was around the corner and he would finally be home, or so I thought. When he called and said he was going skiing with some buddies instead of seeing me, I looked at the phone like it was some kind of messenger from hell. Before I could object, John promised he would come to New York so we could spend New Year's Eve together and still have the rest of Christmas break in Connecticut. I didn't understand why he had to go skiing without me, but after all, I didn't ski, and he hadn't offered to teach me. Frankly, nothing he said was making sense, probably because of the way I was brought up by Mom and Dad. I thought when two people loved each other, they wanted to spend every waking moment together, not go on vacations without each other. But I didn't want to push, so I told John to have a great time, hung up, and cried for two and a half days. I finally had to quit crying because my eyes bug out like a bullfrog's when I cry, and I couldn't work for a week after my grief. Eileen was very annoyed.

I arranged everything so John and I would have the best New Year's Eve out on the town imaginable—tickets for a totally hip club party, dinner at New York's newest hot spot. I couldn't believe how much I paid for my dress; even I thought I looked incredible in it. I was made up and ready to go a full hour before John was supposed to pick me up, something I rarely managed. My parents were sure I had John's arrival time mixed up as I sat perched on the edge of the couch, checking my makeup every five minutes. I visited with Mom and Dad during their cocktail hour and chattered incessantly as I waited for the doorbell. It never rang.

I remember feeling as if everything was starting to move in a slower motion, just a beat off normal. I called John's mother at least six times over the course of the evening until my dad said I was being rude and to stop. All John's mom knew was that he was supposed to be off for the weekend skiing. After calling his fraternity house and leaving a million messages, I was sure he must have been in an accident that had left him crippled enough to be unable to make a simple phone call! I finally gave up and went to bed at two in the morning after watching streams of colored car lights run up and down the city streets from my bedroom window till my eyes crossed. I fell into a fitful slumber, thinking, *Of course John didn't show up. I was just some easy girl that he didn't respect. Someone he had for a weekend, called a few times, and then dumped.*

John did get in touch with me a few days later and offered some feeble excuse. I told him I was worried that he had been hurt somewhere skiing or driving, but the long silence on the other end of the phone warned me not to make a big deal out of the incident (even if I thought he should have trouble breathing, his hair should fall out, and his teeth should rot for being such a crud to me). We planned to get together over the weekend in Connecticut when he returned from his alleged skiing . . .

About a year later one of John's friends told me what had really gone on that New Year's. It wasn't another girl, as I suspected, it was John's insecurities. He was intimidated about my being "some big model in New York City," and he was sure I was going to leave him, so he just didn't show up. What do you get when two immature, insecure people come together who have about as much sense as pups at play on a highway during rush hour, who don't know how to communicate, then become intimate before they are even friends? A rhetorical question. This was another experience I was going to repeat time and time again, and again, it was never discussed, understood, or healed. I just shoved it deep down inside of me along with my fury and raging insecurities.

That Saturday night John showed up at the party where I was to meet him with his best friend Deed, who had just gotten out of the Marine Corps. I had heard about this guy from John, but never met him. As they both walked through the front door, I looked at John and immediately knew I didn't want to see him anymore. My emotions just shut down; I guess he hurt me more than I had admitted to myself. I had given him absolutely everything, trusted that he would love me for it, but instead, he left me and hadn't even bothered to call. And when I looked at him, I suddenly hated him for that. It was amazing. I didn't want to care about him anymore, and thankfully, I wasn't inclined to go back for another dose of pain with him. As I write this, the word "fickle" comes to mind, but "heartbroken" was closer to the truth . . . We were children playing at being adults.

I was trying to learn the value of rising above pain before it ate me up, so I focused on the instant and intense attraction I now felt for Deed. And he was clearly feeling the same thing for me. Before the evening was over, Deed asked me what my relationship was with John, because he wanted to know if he could "see me," as he put it. I told him it was over with John and me, but I invited him to find out what John felt. And he did. As far as John was concerned, we were history. And so I told myself, "Next." However, I wasn't as free or ready as I thought. To use the cliché, I was on the rebound. And I felt I was damaged goods. As far as my heart was concerned, it was true.

Deed was six years older than I, and cocky as hell from his recent stint in the marines. After leaving school because of a not-so-stellar high school record, he was about to attend business college not far from New York. Ours was a fast and furious courtship, and I made my commitment to him early on. Only a few weeks after we started dating, Deed commented that if we had kids, they would have miniature feet, since mine were Flintstone-shaped, and his size sevens weren't much bigger. To me, that remark was as good as a ring on my wedding finger. I already knew I wanted to spend the rest of my life with this man, so I decided not much else was going to be important to me from then on. You see, if we got married, that would mean that he really loved me and would never leave me or hurt me . . . Right?

Deed also happened to do something great for me physically—
a feeling that was new for me. I was actually attracted to him as
opposed to my usual mode of trying to attract. He wore English
Leather, was a great dancer, and taught me how to drive a stick-
shift car like a man, which appealed to the old "daddy-daughter
thing" I've mentioned. Oh, and he had a fantastic tan—I have
wrinkles today from trying to keep up with him in that arena.
Obviously, I felt, we met all the requirements necessary for a serious, solid, enduring relationship. We were astoundingly naive . . .
Youth can be scary stuff, especially when it comes in adult bodies.

Although I had our entire lives planned out by our third date,
Deed was moving along at a slower pace (except for the sex part).
First times only come once, but first doesn't always mean best. I
felt different with Deed, very excited, yet it would take me years
to realize that as a woman, I had the right to enjoy sex as much
as my partner did. I had no idea at all that pleasure was designed
for both man and woman.

On the career front, things were barreling along. One day I received
a message through the agency from a man who was described as
the top entertainment attorney in the country, representing everyone from Frank Sinatra to major studios, and before I knew it, a
dinner was arranged for me and my parents to meet him at the
Copacabana in New York City. I had just turned sixteen.

I have always been grateful for my parents' training, because
posh surroundings and glitzy international company have never
intimidated me. Therefore, when this man, who was attractive, yet
easily in his fifties, swirled me around the dance floor to test my
skills, I passed with flying colors. I could tell he was impressed. As
the band music played, all of New York's high society watched
every move we made with rapt attention. There was buzz in the
air, I could feel it, and by the time he escorted me back to the table
to join my parents, he told me he was going to arrange for a major-
studio screen test in Hollywood the following week and assured
me a film contract would follow. It was a matter of only when,
not if. The rest of the evening was spent wining and dining Mom

and Dad on caviar, fancy-label vodka, and rack of lamb. It was all very impressive, and by the end of the night, I really did feel that a great adventure was looming before me as my parents and I were whisked back home in a limousine.

It was arranged that the next day the lawyer would show me some scripts at his town house so I could choose the part that felt most comfortable to me for my screen test. I told him I had never studied acting and that I really didn't know if I'd be any good at it, but he assured me that what the studios were looking for was "natural talent." Not to worry, Hollywood would fill in any blanks. The next morning the limo picked me up at ten A.M. I was surprised and impressed to see him waiting on the street by his front door with a bouquet of flowers extended in welcome.

You know, it makes absolutely no difference whether you're surrounded by priceless art or seedy furnishings when you're attacked. Such distinctions don't do anything to change the reality of fear. The front door had barely closed behind us when he pressed me hard against the wall. His mouth covered me with suffocating speed, and he told me to do things to him that I had never heard spoken before. When he finally let me go, I backed across the room; the flowers I still held fell to the floor. He looked me over inch by inch, and then he promised me that my life was about to change. He said that it was my time to grow up, and once I did, he would make sure that the world was at my feet. I remember saying that I had a boyfriend, but he just laughed and said that didn't matter to him. I could do anything I wanted on my own time, but when I was with him, I needed to please him. We didn't have to have sex, I just needed to touch him. That's all I had to do and I could have anything I wanted . . . Anything in the world.

And there it was in a nutshell. The truth is, I knew this man not only meant what he said, I also knew he could absolutely deliver everything he promised—a movie career—anything money could buy—and all I had to do was go along with his requests. What a thing to offer a young girl.

I don't know what has saved me so often in my life, what helped me make the right decision at times when my discernment was shaky at best. But I believe this is one of the many times God had His hand on my shoulder, years and years before I even knew Him. I believe His grace was covering me even if I hadn't asked for it, and although I was to be lost for so long in my search for security, God wasn't going to let me go down this road. I remember saying "I can't" as I moved cautiously toward the door. I wasn't sure if the lawyer was going to let me pass, but he did, and as I felt his breath on my back, he told me to please take his limo home. I did just that.

I never told Mom and Dad what went on that morning. But I thought, since this was the second time something like this had happened to me, *I* must be the problem. It must be my fault. In the midst of all that guilt, I was sure I would never hear another word about some movie career from that lawyer, and Mom and Dad would never have a clue about what went wrong. Imagine my surprise a week later to find myself on a plane going to Hollywood for a screen test at Paramount Studios. Everything was arranged for my shot at fame, *no strings attached*. The lawyer never approached me again and all details of the test were handled professionally through my agent. If you think this turnaround shows that Mr. Lawyer was a gentleman in the end, you couldn't be more wrong. I found out from the Paramount side that they had asked him to set up the screen test, so it was never his idea in the first place.

Once in Hollywood, I tested with James Caan, who was, at the time, shooting the movie *Red Line 7000* (1964) at the studio. I was convinced my acting was just terrible, but everyone said I was quite good. Paramount also did a "classic" screen test of me in gowns, hairdos, and different styles of makeup—one of those tests we've all seen in so many Hollywood films about the making of a star. I met the head of the studio, was invited to the commissary for lunch, and by the end of the day, I was the buzz of the studio.

After the test shoot, Jimmy and I went across the street to the studio bar to hang out with a then virtually unknown director named Francis Ford Coppola (*The Godfather*). He was a big, furry kind of guy with piercing eyes and a laugh that made you know he traveled in places most of us never imagine. Someone began playing the piano at the bar, and after a few minutes Francis joined in, performing as a human horn. Then Jimmy picked up the accompaniment by creating vocal drum sounds. I just sat there and giggled; I was absolutely fascinated with these guys, and quite starstruck. Two days later I was back in New York with a contract offer and a half-page spread in the entertainment section of *The New York Times* announcing me as Paramount's new hope as a leading lady. The article included mention of some of the broadstroke terms of my contract offer and made no bones about my huge potential for fame. I was so flattered!

Still, something in me didn't trust it all. Something in me was afraid of whatever was prowling around the big pond waiting to pounce on me . . . Something in me knew that I would get into trouble in Hollywood. I knew that the wild side that I had so carefully stored away should stay where I put it, for everyone's good. If I were married and had a family, surely I would be safe and loved. Most important of all, something in me knew I would lose Deed if I signed the contract. So I turned it down and everyone was pretty shocked . . . Even I.

Although I was really committed to my horse Sassafras, I finally made one of my first self-preservative moves by selling him to a man I met at a horse show. The horse was wildly talented but dangerous. My goal was to compete as a rider, and that required a horse that, at the very least, wouldn't sling me into the nearest tree on a whim. The man who bought Sassafras promised he'd never jump him because Sassafras had sustained injuries during his days at the racetrack. Still, one month later after class I saw my old horse limping around some backyard show after jumping class. The man had sold him as a speed horse for a quick buck. I felt like a slug—again. If I had my druthers, I would keep every animal I've known for life in a heaven of hay, carrots, and barbecue (for my dogs) as long as we all shall live. And in my dreams, I'm treated as well as I treat my pets.

A few weeks after I sold Sassafras, a girl I knew from Dalton told me she had a little dressage horse named Alezon whom she needed to sell, so I bought him for a "deal" at $500. Twice burned? I've come to the conclusion that there are no deals in life and that one gets precisely what one pays for, especially when it comes to horses. The biggest problem with Alezon was that he was not only one of the laziest horses in creation (second only to Monty), but he also absolutely loathed jumping, which was my passion. So far I had owned one glue-factory-bound survivor from the racetrack who turned out to be a warrior, and a charlatan dressed in horsehair and hooves. Nonetheless, I knew in my heart that I was destined to ride the "big sticks" some way, somehow. Unfortunately, it appeared I had matchmaking problems not only with men but also with horses, and I was painfully delusionary about their collective talents and possibilities for a future.

I remember a hot fall day when I had pushed Alezon as fast as he would go across the open field that led to the main road into town. He was actually sweating, despite his pace of a turtle racing a caterpillar. I had been boarding Alezon up in New Haven, Connecticut, because rent was cheap there and I made a deal to stay with the people who owned the barn. The long train commute didn't really bother me because I always had a ton of homework to do and I surely didn't mind some time away from work, work, and more work. Escape for me generally comes on the back of a horse.

At the end of my attempted run with Alezon, we had slowed to a crawl and were approaching a gas station where I spotted a Coke machine. Perfect; I was as dry as my horse's personality. This Coke machine was the old-fashioned kind, with the lid that lifted up. I tied Alezon to the handle so I could get some change from inside, and when I came back out, the horse was fussing with a persistent buzzing fly. Just as I was about to untie the reins from the machine, Alezon jerked his head in an attempt to foil the pesky insect. When he threw his head, the reins pulled on the Coke machine and its lid came flying up, causing Alezon to rear back. In good old slow-motion mode, I watched the entire Coke machine tip over . . . and come down square on my nose! Blood streaming from my face, I stood there dumbfounded as my horse proceeded to drag the Coke machine clear around the parking lot. Every time I *almost* calmed Alezon down, another Coke bottle would explode inside the machine and start the horse running, pawing, bucking, and rearing again. Twenty minutes later this little episode cost me a broken nose, $526.83 (thousands today) for a new Coke machine, and weeks of lost modeling work. This was the first of three broken noses scheduled for my life; the others were to result from equally ridiculous events.

"When in doubt, punt" was already a theme of mine. I taught myself to jump on the horse, but I surely needed help, and I actually did get some riding lessons after my parents and brother finally attended one of my horse shows. I was so excited that my family was actually going to be there, I entered myself in a jumping class I had absolutely no business in. Too big—too advanced—too dangerous. I ended up bringing activity at the entire show grounds to a screeching halt as Alezon and I crashed through the barrel jump at the end of the main ring. Like the little demon he was, Alezon soon recovered his balance and proceeded to run out of the ring at a dead gallop as I lay sprawled face-first in a cloud of sand. Boy, my horse was really in big trouble with me now that I saw he actually *could* move his fat body when he wanted to. Dad took off toward the out gate, yelling "I've got him, I've got him." I was now up and running toward my loose horse, arriving just in time to see Dad reach down to grab the dragging reins. As Dad began to stand, Alezon swung around to nibble some tasty-looking grass, and the next sound I heard was a *crack* as Alezon's teeth connected with the top of Dad's head. With a sickening thud, Dad reeeled in pain while Alezon curled his lip high to the sky in a gesture of righteous indignation.

You know what it feels like to carefully plant a garden in the fall and then have an unexpected spring frost not only nip all the buds but kill your plants at the root? That's what that moment felt like to me. Another *poof* in my life. Along with the bang on Dad's head went any future involvement of my parents in my horses . . . But Mike was there! Maybe he'd gotten bitten by the horse bug?

Maybe he'd like to come with me to some horse shows? . . . Maybe . . .

Mike's face turned red as he silently beat his fist against my horse's shoulder. I was so busy seeing how Mom was reacting to Dad's injury that it took me far too long to notice the dilemma my brother was in. Alezon had been grazing on a pile of green grass when I shoved the reins into Mike's hands so I could attend to Dad's rapidly swelling crown. Enthralled with his snack, my horse unwittingly stepped on my brother's foot, settling all of his twelve hundred pounds on Mike's unsuspecting appendage. Mike dealt with the onslaught in silence until I noticed what was going on and pulled the horse away. I don't think my brother's silence was about being brave so much as it was about his own cluelessness as to how to get the distracted animal off his foot . . . Once I saw Mike's black-and-blue battle wound and my dad's head, which was shooting up like a high-rise in progress, I knew I would forever be a solo act with my horse thing.

But it was during the very next show that Alezon almost put the nails in my coffin. I did have a trainer by this time, someone Dad found at the head-clunking show. His name was Wayne, and as it turned out, he was the top show trainer in the country. Apparently Wayne had commented to Dad that I showed a lot of natural talent. Dad followed up and Wayne said he'd be more than happy to work with me. I was so excited and honored!

The next thing I knew, I was making my first real move into the big pond of the horses. The problem was, I still owned a plow pony that rode like a mule. Nonetheless, in only a few short weeks I was on the show circuit. Everyone who competed was dressed to perform; shiny boots, custom jackets, grooms for their braided, fancy horses that strutted and gleamed like the BMWs and Mercedes their parents drove—and there I was, still backyard looking. I entered in the first jumping class in the morning and was first to go. Wayne had schooled me outside over a few fences and I was relieved that Alezon was at least getting all four hooves off the ground at the same time. Unfortunately, I wasn't so lucky in the show ring. We cantered around the corner to a stone wall, and to put it simply, this time the horse's hooves *never* left the ground—that is, until we hit the wall. Then we both flew. First, Alezon's refusal to jump caused me to be catapulted over the fence. I landed headfirst on the far side of the wall, my hunt cap's brim slamming into the ground like a stake. As my body completed its trajectory, my head remained anchored into the dirt. While all that was going on (in slow motion, of course) Alezon was executing his own flip high in the air over the jump and was coming down *on top of me,* all four of his legs pointing skyward. He landed on me upside down, completing my backbend under his full weight. It was a surrealistic mess . . . No, *I* was a mess.

Out of the corner of my rapidly dilating eyes, I saw Wayne run over. At first I was happy for his concern, and then it actually scared me as everyone started waving their arms, looking totally panicked. Wayne stared at me as if by doing so he could will the entire accident away. He told me to get up . . . a little movement would be good . . . He said I was scaring the parents. Before I passed out I think I said no. I was in and out of consciousness throughout the ambulance ride and the emergency-room X-ray stint. I was pretty hysterical that they had to cut my new boots off to undress me, and I refused a shot for the pain, opting to wait for some pills to work. By the way, the pain was astounding. My choice of the pills had to do with a residual phobia from my hospital stay at fourteen, when IV needles had been stuck all over me. I absolutely hate needles to this day. By the time Mom and Dad got to the hospital, I was diagnosed with a broken neck and back in three places and it was recommended that I stay in traction from six months to a year to allow all my ligaments to heal . . . "I don't think so," I remember saying to someone.

Deed sent me a get-well card from school and visited once; it was announced at the horse show that I was all right so no parents would worry. After a moment of reflection I decided I had way too much to do to stay in traction, so I left the hospital within a month and was riding again shortly thereafter. To the present, my ligaments remain permanently damaged; they could have healed properly only if I had remained in traction for the prescribed period. I decided to build up my muscles around the ligaments and spine for support instead; consequently, I continue to have a world-champion-heavyweight back that works quite well through intermittent pain. The stubbornness displayed in my thinking during this episode laid a foundation for my personal survival code: at the end of the day, Jennifer better make it happen or it won't happen at all.

It's a fact that when we're young we think we're indestructible, but every cast from broken bones I've removed too soon and every torn whatever I've suffered has come to haunt me with pain every day of my life. That accident also left me with a deep-running fear that I reexperience every time I jump a horse. I actually see that original incident replayed in my mind over and over. I would venture to say that I ride on the flat as well as anyone and I have the ribbons and winning horses to prove it. I've also won countless championships in jumping, but the jumping part still scares me to the core. By the way, I am determined to overcome that fear before I hit the retirement crowd. My need to conquer this fear is even greater than my love of horses. It is born of my desire to prevent fear from owning any part of me ever again. And that desire is born of the faith I have finally found.

ten

TOGETHER ALONE

*I*N 1963, when John Kennedy died, I was on a crosstown bus, going home from school. As I heard the news from a breathless passenger, my own breath stopped. I was so upset, but this was one time my emotions felt appropriate—everyone seemed upset and bewildered. These were unsettling times. In only a year or two the Beatles had taken over from Elvis, followed by the Rolling Stones and the Animals. Things were moving on down the road with new themes, dreams, and machines, and so was I. I bought myself a 396-425 horsepower Corvette (the first car on the East Coast with a bubble on its hood. *Hot* on fire—especially for a girl). I was going to get attention one way or another. The problem was, I couldn't figure out whether Deed was more interested in me or my car.

Eileen Ford called me at home to see if I was ready to go back to work. "Paris, the collection for *Vogue*! They want you. Can you be ready to go in two weeks?" It didn't take long for me to say yes, mostly because she sounded so excited. I assumed Deed wouldn't mind, since it wasn't a long trip. After all, this was *the* coveted job for any model, especially being booked by *Vogue*. Besides, Deed hadn't come home from school to see me in almost a month.

I had to drop another eight pounds for the magazine, so Eileen sent me off to a "fat" doctor. Whatever he gave me made dieting easy. I couldn't even look at food, let alone eat it, and I was down to the wispy weight well before I had to leave. Of course, I couldn't seem to get my lips unglued from my teeth because of the medication, but who cared, I was lean and mean and off by myself to Paris at age sixteen.

The truth was, I was more scared than excited, but since every part of me looked like an adult, I decided I'd better learn how to act like one. Eileen arranged for her "girls" to stay at a small hotel on the Left Bank. I'd always known Paris was beautiful, but I was to find out very quickly that the French are a less-than-friendly bunch. My school French helped me find my way around town, but getting lost was becoming a habit. The first observation I wrote to Mom and Dad about my trip was that I thought the French people were so crabby because they had to use cardboard for toilet paper. How's that for astute sociocultural observation!

My schedule for *Vogue* required me to work every night, since the collection clothes were shown on runways during the days, so I barely slept while in Paris. When I finally returned home in the mornings and tried to rest, workmen were just beginning their day of sandblasting the entire exterior of my hotel—there was just no getting away from the noise.

One day when I was coming back from an all-night shoot, I ran into a bunch of characteristically unfriendly models lined up in the hotel hall. I mustered up enough nerve to ask one of them what she was waiting for. She looked at me like I was stupidity's child and said, "The toilet." As the words I wished I had never uttered left my lips, I immediately knew what a fool I had made of myself. "Oh, I have a toilet in my room, don't you?" If I ever had a chance of making any friends among these girls, it vanished into thin air at that moment. I later learned that what I was referring to as a toilet was in fact a bidet. I was a laughingstock in multiple languages.

Thankfully, the work part of my trip was going very well. I was sufficiently skeletal and pretty enough to be molded into whatever image the editor and photographer imagined that day, although I was surprised on one particular shoot for footwear. I thought the editor had told the stylist to put some polish on my toes, and when I started to get ready, the editor pulled a Cruella De Vil attitude as she snickered, "Are you serious? You have the ugliest, little sawed-off feet I've ever seen." It was then that I realized I had always liked my little feet, and now even that tiny piece of pride was becoming yet another incentive for self-consciousness. But I got over the embarrassment rather quickly when I looked down and saw that the editor had size-ten feet . . . Jealousy perhaps?

A fellow I knew from New York who owned racehorses happened to be in Paris during the collections. We ran into each other at a restaurant one morning and he ended up being a good buddy to me as well as someone benign to escort me around town. I was in love with Deed and made sure this guy knew I was not available. Once that was established, he became like a big brother to me. He also let me have his rented car to cruise around town, but there was only one problem: I didn't have an international license. I can actually say I *really* learned how to drive the day I drove in French traffic around the Arc de Triomphe. It wasn't difficult to enter the circle surrounding the monument designed to change avenue direction since all cars coming from the right had the absolute right-of-way, but exiting the merry-go-round of mad drivers was a trick. The first time I tried to cross to the other side of town, I went around the Arch at least twenty times before escaping the rage of European drivers. It was nerve-racking with all the blaring horns and rude gestures, but I have to say, the experience prepared me for driving the New York City taxi territory.

Paris during the collections is like Hollywood during the Academy Awards; exciting is too limited an adjective to describe the goings-on in a town chock-full of celebrities, media beautiful people, and overflowing nightclubs. I couldn't believe I was part of that elite crowd just because *Vogue* magazine had imported me. All my life I've watched individuals hire PR firms to promote themselves, for social advancement and/or notoriety, but I just seemed to find myself in the mix without even trying. Actually, I ran from that type of attention most of the time, especially when I hit Hollywood.

I remember once Verushka, the famous model, and I were working together on the *Vogue* shoot. I had modeled with her on location many times before; she was something. This six-foot-plus blonde was never less than a surprise a minute to anyone who crossed her path. Peter Fonda and Peter Beard, the photographer, were in town for that year's festivities (it was 1964) and the four of us were having lunch at a popular bistro that afternoon. We managed to cause even the most aloof Frenchmen to focus on our table.

Peter Fonda was then a hot, up-and-coming renegade actor and Peter Beard had just been released from jail for his valiant stand for animal rights in Africa shortly after the release of one of his photography books. (Beard had courageously fended off poachers, hunters, and trappers, and this led to his arrest.) On that warm summer day, Verushka wore sandals that laced up the entire length of her long legs, and given the length of her skirt, that was like looking up a stretch of road across the desert from Los Angeles to Las Vegas with no speed limit and no sunglasses.

We were eating salad and drinking strong coffee as we discussed nothing in several languages. I didn't say much in the only language I spoke until I gasped as I watched a French tow truck hoist up my—well, my friend's—rented car. A parking violation, and I was in trouble—very big trouble. Verushka and I may not have exchanged many words prior to that moment, but she read my panicked expression and was off galloping down the busy street, displaying mountains of body language and shouting. She even went so far as to sprawl her celebrated body across the disputed vehicle, but to no avail. In her herculean attempt at saving my hide, Verushka stopped traffic but failed to rescue the car. When she finally admitted defeat, she and Peter Beard vanished into the crowd of pedestrians like a mirage.

Actor Peter smoked a joint on a street corner following our cab ride to find my car. We were in some remote section of Paris when he offered to take me back to his hotel, waving his roach at me as he spoke. I never accepted anything he offered, but I was still amazed he found me interesting enough to ask.

My stint with *Vogue* was coming to an end, and I wasn't scheduled to be home for at least a week. In fact, I planned to take a few days after the collections were over to see a little of Europe. The problem was, all I wanted to do was get home and see Deed. We had written to each other often and spoken even more on the phone, but despite all the exciting things going on in Paris, Deed was the only thing on my mind. My idea was to surprise him, so I grabbed a night flight hoping to get back to the States before he realized I had left Paris. When I landed in New York, I actually felt a moment of disappointment that no one was there to greet me . . . Of course, no one could have been there; no one knew I was coming home.

I took a cab to Manhattan, snuck into Mom and Dad's apartment on Eighty-first Street, dropped off my bags, got in my Corvette, and drove out to New Canaan to Deed's parents' house. As I entered their driveway, Deed came to the front door, having heard the massive purr of my engine—I mean, the Corvette's engine. I was so excited I thought I was going to ignite. I jumped out of the car and ran over to him, expecting, I don't know, anywhere from *Splendor in the Grass* to *Gone With the Wind,* but actually, a hug would have sufficed. Instead, Deed just looked at me and, after a very long pause, said, "What are you doing here?" He didn't do anything wrong; he just didn't seem to be excited . . . totally out of sync with my own emotions at that moment. I figured traveling halfway around the world for the last nineteen hours deserved more than a "what are you doing here?"

I've attempted similar surprises over the years and they've always been disappointing . . . My romantic beat had fallen flat. But despite that little glitch, I was sure I was in love, and as it turned out, Deed and I were married a little before my eighteenth birthday in the church I used to attend as a kid in Connecticut.

The Reverend's son was a renowned hell-raiser in the town of Wilton, so our prenuptial counseling with the Reverend seemed a bit hypocritical to Deed and me. The man spoke to us about fidelity and commitment—of course, what he preached was absolutely correct even if his son wasn't practicing it. And now I wonder why we were married in church? Was it because of tradition? Deed and I were both nonbelievers, so that's all it was, tradition. Nothing more than a white dress and rice, some ceremonial words thrown in, nothing to do with the soul, let alone the real meaning of vows. Yes, I believed this was the man I'd love for the rest of my life . . . *never* to be apart, *never* to be unfaithful, *never* to stop loving, *never* to be alone again . . . always to be protected and loved . . . forever . . . and ever . . . I was seventeen, and I was a silly little girl.

The reception was to be held at the New Canaan Country Club, so we all dressed for the wedding at the house of Deed's parents. Mom came over in the morning to assist me, but as it turned out, she needed a bit more attending to than I did. After I helped her with her hair and dress, I settled down to deal with my own nerves. I'd never thought twice about marrying Deed. I didn't have a question in my mind or heart that we would be together forever, or whether or not he was the right guy . . . But I was still nervous, which I figured was a normal bride thing.

I can't remember exactly when I first started smoking cigarettes, but it was well before my wedding day. I know because I was on my way to the church in the limo when I lit up a cigarette and burned a huge hole in my wedding veil. In slow motion, I watched it happen, helpless to stop the incendiary exchange between the lace before my face and the fire . . . Later, burned ashes framed Deed's face as I looked through my singed veil and said my vows in church. Maybe it was an omen.

But it was a happy day for me. Everything was traditional with my marriage, from the ring and silver from Tiffany's, to the wedding itself, which was simple yet elegant. Deed and I drove off for our honeymoon in my green Corvette convertible (*ours,* now that we were married). I've sometimes wondered whether Deed married me for me or for my car. I more often wondered—and still do— if he ever really loved me. I doubt it, but at least I was a catch in that Corvette and soon I became intrigued with driving fast and collecting tickets during occasional appearances of my wild side. Despite the fame I was gaining, I remained intimidated most of the time, and under Deed's spell, I became a walking paradox: a major star, minor confidence heading straight for some of her biggest nightmares.

Real financial success came, as far as I was concerned, when I was actually able to buy a top-notch show horse named Mink's Muff (she *came* with that horrible name). She was a fantastic mare that I was able to qualify for the Nationals about six months before Deed and I were married. But in keeping with my penchant for self-sabotage, I managed to break my wrist skateboarding down Deed's driveway a few weeks before the final competition. My wrist wasn't the only thing that was shattered. It was my last year to show at the Nationals as a junior and I blew it! I did, however, have the notoriety of being the only married junior rider on the circuit, which ruffled a few of the horse-show mothers' feathers. I was also a really good jock by then. "A natural," my trainer would repeat. Deed barely tolerated my "horse thing" and shortly after we were married, I sold Mink's so we could buy a house. The car went, too—fair is fair.

By the way, I did finish high school, and with excellent grades, except for one math course. This was a huge frustration for me because at Professional Children's School I was put in a second-year math class without ever taking the first year, so it was impossible for me to understand the work. I was going to retake the course but then decided to get married, so my diploma was slotted as a low priority.

Deed insisted on purchasing a house in a price range that he could afford, in terms of mortgage payments—after I took care of the down payment. It was a very good idea that, unfortunately, didn't work. To this day I regret Deed's conservatism, but there was always an imbalance in our incomes that seemed to really bother him. Some of his inability to "handle me" had to do with his inability to handle what I earned and the places my career was taking me. The irony was that during all that time I cared about nothing but Deed, not my career. But despite myself, Hollywood was going to carve out a major slice of my life for its own soon enough.

Deed was very close to his family, especially his mom, and as much as I loved the family feeling I had when I was around all of them, there was something I just couldn't identify between Deed and his mom. Any wife who has hit that mother-in-law/favorite-son brick wall knows how potentially crippling it can be to a marriage. As I was wrestling with that problem, Deed became progressively jealous and possessive about me in respect to modeling and being off on location shoots. Jealousy was not part of my package at that time because it was nothing I had any experience with. My parents had always trusted each other implicitly, so I thought it was a basic confidence you gleaned when you loved someone, especially if you were married to them.

Despite all of these early issues, my next mission was to have a baby, and my theory was that if you made love constantly, how could you miss getting pregnant? It was a fun time in Deed's and my life (this was an area in which we excelled). The problem was, Deed was working for IBM, commuting and implementing our baby plan so wholeheartedly that he lost about ten pounds and a good deal of his physical strength. After many months of candlelit dinners without success, I went to see a doctor. He explained some facts of life to me: there is only a matter of hours during every woman's monthly cycle when she can become pregnant, and usually by the time mine rolled around, Deed was so worn-out that he wasn't good for anything (or at least his sperm count wasn't). We were told to abstain for two weeks and then to try again. At first we were both thankful for the break, but after a couple of days we were chomping at the bit. Nonetheless, we managed to hold out for the higher purpose, and like magic, I became pregnant. I can't remember ever being more enthusiastic about anything in my life. Deed was also totally excited—we were having a happy chapter.

When I miscarried I was devastated. I felt like I was a total failure and worthless as a woman. The doctor assured me that I was only eighteen and it wasn't unusual to have a miscarriage at that age. I just needed to relax and try again. Deed and I waited the appropriate amount of time and started all over. Before long I was pregnant once more. I made it into my fourth month and started to show, eat lots of pizza, and glow at the prospect of becoming a mom.

I loved it when I got too big to model and could stay home and work on the house, cook dinner, and prepare for the baby. Deed and I had bought our little Victorian house in a small town in Connecticut for $22,000. It was a partial fixer upper, but since Deed was very handy and I was very creative, we did most of the work ourselves. He painted the house blue gray and I painted a yellow daisy on the back of his new Volkswagen. There was a pond across the street with soothing waters and spring found me waiting for the ducklings to hatch and my baby to arrive. I had Sally, a mutt I'd gotten from the pound the day I moved out from my parents' apartment, and her litter of puppies running rampant around the house. I even had a cat named Patches (a calico, of course). What a perfect picture.

But something insidious was lurking around the corner. It seemed to me as an eighteen-year-old pregnant newlywed that everything Deed liked, I wasn't. His taste ran toward "big boobs and blond hair," which he felt a need to remind me of on a regular basis. You see, Deed and I never were really friends. Our relationship seemed more about sexual attraction and power, not communication (Deed definitely wasn't a talker). I remember sitting with his mom one day discussing my woes and she told me that I had to learn how to get men to do what I wanted without letting them know what I was up to. "That's the name of the game," she said. I still think that's ridiculous. My mom always put everything smack-dab on the table, no beating about the bush. Then again, my mom is tough. Deed's mom played a quieter strategy, and although we became good friends, as the years went by I found she could be quite two-faced and manipulative.

I started to wonder what Deed's repeated concerns about the trouble I might get into with some guy off on location said about him? What was he doing at work and with whom? What "blonde with big boobs" might be getting his attention? As absurd as all this sounds to me now, it was very real to me at the time. Deed was never able to make me feel certain about his love for me. That may have been because I needed much more affection than the average person, but not only was Deed not forthcoming with any assurances, his own low self-esteem made him quick to tear me down to make himself feel better. We were perfect codependents in that respect because the more he minimized me, the more I needed, wanted, and had to have him love me. The more I felt unloved, the more demanding I became and dramatic in my expressions of need. My parents had never listened to me as a child and now I was an adult who insisted that someone understand and fill me up. I didn't know then that it is impossible for another person to "fill you up." The negative dynamics between Deed and me escalated. I really believed that the breadth of my love was in direct correlation to the pain I suffered, because if I didn't care, I wouldn't hurt. Based on that criterion, I was madly in love with Deed.

I couldn't have a conversation with Deed without him constantly scanning the room—I was convinced, for another woman. His eyes were always everywhere but on me. The funny thing is, most everyone else's eyes were always on me, but that made no difference to me; I only wanted Deed's attention. When I tried to talk to him about his wandering eye, my husband's favorite response was "Boys will be boys." I was so upset one day while I was pregnant that I went to the store, bought every *Playboy*-type magazine I could find, and *papered* our bedroom walls with centerfolds. My wallpapering marathon didn't go over very well with Deed. Somehow he missed my point rather than recognizing my hurt, and he remained angry and withdrawn long enough to really punish me. The wounds were growing deeper and deeper. We didn't have any of the tools to fix our problems, and not a clue about where they could be found.

Aimee was born five and a half weeks before her due date. It was a difficult experience for me, largely due to a doctor who induced my labor because he was going on vacation. Delivering a baby thirty-plus years ago was not like it is today. There was no father present for the birth and no Lamaze classes. I had absolutely zero understanding of what I was about to experience other than what my one girlfriend who already had a baby told me. Her advice was for me to go into the hospital and scream my head off so they'd give me lots of medication and I wouldn't remember a thing . . . Brilliant.

Thinking about any part of the birth procedure horrified and embarrassed me. I was very immature about those kinds of things. What a weird feeling to be so very excited and scared at the same time. Deed rushed me to the hospital even though I wasn't in labor—he said it was fun to speed without fear of getting a ticket. He visited a few times in the labor room in between the vaginal shaving, full-blown enemas, and internal exams by headnurse monsters.

I wanted a boy, Deed wanted a girl. I always thought it was right that a boy be the eldest, as we planned to have at least several kids. I'm sure now my big-brother theory was based on one of the blanks in my childhood that I was determined to fill in by means of my own children. Still, Deed wanted a girl, and I just knew I was going to have a daughter. The labor pains were beyond my imagination. You see, my baby was only half turned when induced, so there was absolutely no medication allowed during her birth. To say I was unprepared for the experience would be a great understatement.

Aimee weighed five pounds two ounces at delivery and was only four pounds eleven ounces when she came home from the hospital. It is an absolute miracle to me when I consider the total love God gives us immediately for our children. We don't even know them at birth, yet without hesitation we would lay down our lives for them. My baby girl was the best thing that ever happened to me even though I thought she looked like a chicken broiler. Half her face and little arm were all bruised from being sideways in delivery and she was very colicky from the start. But she was mine and I was filled with emotions I had never felt before. Deed wrote me a beautiful letter about how proud he was . . . times were good again.

The upstairs of our house had a master bedroom, a big bathroom, and the baby's room, which I covered with hand-painted animal murals. Deed worked hard at remodeling the attic as a small guest room for my parents, who were to stay with us for the first week of Aimee's life.

Late one afternoon, I was surrounded by the alluring aroma of Mom's dinner cooking downstairs, Deed was still at work, and I was alone nursing the baby. About the only time poor Aimee wasn't crying from her colic was when she ate, so this was a cherished time for me. The setting sun streamed in through the windows, covering the room and all it held in an ethereal light. I looked around at the pictures on the walls . . . Deed was a terrific photographer and had captured so many special moments in our new lives together. A memory stirred and I recalled the time Deed drove his Austin-Healey up from school, stopping traffic all the way: he had gone to the local grocery store and talked them into giving him a life-size poster of me advertising Coca-Cola in a red bathing suit. My five-foot-eight-inch cardboard figure was stuffed in the backseat of his little car, my feet sticking out one side of the car, my head out the other . . . Then my mind wandered to the time I visited Deed up at his school for the weekend. I had to lie to the officials about my age because Deed had me nominated for spring queen. I couldn't believe he had done that, and then I couldn't believe I won. I was crowned queen, and to me, that made up for never being a cheerleader and never going to my own senior prom. I loved that Deed thought I was pretty enough for the title. I glanced over at a picture of my aunt Elle and sadness stole the moment; Elle was sick with cancer. I felt like I was going to lose her before she'd ever get to know Aimee . . . More light suddenly filled the room as the door opened. It was Deed home from work. He stopped before entering and just looked at me and the baby on the bed with an expression that deeply touched me . . . And for that instant I felt really loved.

It was only a few days later, while Aimee was on one of her crying-for-hours sieges, that I had my first new-mom lesson. It didn't matter what I did, she wouldn't stop wailing. I had driven her around the block four times, walked her, fed her, and changed her till my fingers were almost as raw as her bottom. Her pain from the colic seemed to be taking over our lives. No one had slept in days and I was positive I was doing something wrong. I finally called the doctor for the third time that day and he asked for the third time if the baby had been fed and changed. When I told him yes, he simply said she was spoiled. I couldn't believe a six-day-old baby could be spoiled, but the doctor said to put her to bed, turn the TV up to blaring, turn on the vacuum cleaner, and let her cry. He promised if I could resist picking her up, she would eventually stop crying and go to sleep. It was the toughest twenty-eight minutes and thirty-two seconds I ever spent, but she finally went to sleep.

It was decided shortly thereafter that I should stop nursing Aimee since her colic seemed to respond better to formula. As with most everything in my life, once the decision was made, I went about the task in my usual "crash course" mode. The doctor had suggested I taper off nursing to let my milk supply dwindle slowly, but I bit the bullet and just stopped . . . Big mistake. I went from my modeling bust size of 34-B to 38-D while nursing, and when I stopped cold turkey, I was immobilized not only by the pain of engorged breasts, but by their sheer abundance. I was beached like a baby whale on my bed in ice packs for days.

But this, too, finally (and thankfully) passed. After a few months Aimee was, at last, sleeping through the night and bloomed into a picture-perfect baby. I started back modeling to make some extra money and Deed and I were actually getting along relatively well. I did have mixed feelings about returning to work, though. Part of me loved just staying at home with the baby, but then there was the other side of me that wanted to be creative and challenged. Modeling to me was strictly about making money, and soon I was determined to work at something more fulfilling. My interest began to turn toward acting. Meanwhile, some old patterns started to creep back like the little demons they are—my jealousy, Deed's jealousy, my insecurities, his insecurities, money matters, my dramas, his temper.

Nothing aroused my separation anxieties and habits of self-deprecation more than criticizing me or withholding affection. Deed was expert at both, and eventually I found myself becoming more and more depressed. And then, as if overnight, I became terrified. I finally told Deed that I needed to see someone . . . a doctor . . . anyone to help me. I felt like I wanted to die. I was feeling hopeless, and I couldn't stand the anger and distance that was destroying our marriage. I didn't know how to find any safe ground. I was afraid of the waves of destructive thoughts that flooded my mind day and night. I hated myself because it seemed that misery was all I deserved. Why else did it keep revisiting me? Why couldn't anyone hear me? It didn't matter what accolades I received from the world, I couldn't seem to get the closeness and affection I needed from my husband. My grand mission of having a family to love and love me was falling apart and I couldn't stop it. When I first met Deed, I'd told him about my suicide attempt at fourteen and I now told him that I was feeling a similar depression. The difference was, now I knew I didn't want to die; I wanted help. There was no escaping the rise of my terror. I didn't drink or take drugs; the nightmare was all mine. I was smack in the middle of a hell I didn't understand and couldn't escape.

Deed was not only confused, but overwhelmed by what he was hearing. For once he didn't respond in anger, but he did become even more withdrawn. Bottom line, I scared him. He never held me . . . He did take me to talk to a psychiatrist in New Canaan once. At the end of the session the doctor called Deed into the office with me and told him, "I've spoken to your wife, and although she seems legitimately upset, in my opinion all she needs is some TLC from you and she'll be just fine." I couldn't believe how simple that sounded . . . Then why didn't I feel better? I became angry at this doctor's casual reading of my crisis. It felt like a dismissal. "Tender loving care?" I gagged. I thought I was going to throw up. A heat suddenly rose up in me that exploded in a river of perspiration. I started to choke again and ran out of the room.

My anxiety was suffocating. That night my thoughts ran so

wild I was afraid to go to sleep. I just wanted to disappear. I couldn't stop crying and then my mind started wandering to the safety of childlike incoherence . . . my very own emotional coma. My warning voice was becoming faint, and if I didn't do something soon, I knew I would lose myself behind a mental door that would never reopen. As a last effort, I begged Mom and Dad to come and get me and I signed myself into a hospital. I knew the seriousness of everything I was feeling, even if no one else did . . . And secretly, the little girl in me hoped I could find someone to help me let them all know how much they hurt me. And make them stop. I also knew I had my own accountability to deal with.

My decision to enter a hospital was one of the hardest I have ever made, but I am more than thankful that something prompted me to go in and try to deal with my problems instead of letting them overwhelm me. But I was to learn that therapy represented only a temporary Band-Aid. It surely did not heal most of what ailed me and I was left with no real understanding of how to deal with Deed, my parents, or my brother. In addition, there was minimal interest on "the opposition side" about addressing any issues of consequence. It was much easier for everyone to call this "Jennifer's problem." Change most often comes from pain and I was in the middle of *my* pain, not theirs, so nothing changed for them.

I went home after a few weeks and then was readmitted shortly thereafter with what appeared to be a more advanced problem. I was regressing and I ended up even more isolated from my husband and everyone else because "my problems made all of them so uncomfortable." I had no place else to go, and I knew I couldn't stand where I was.

What I was told after I recovered from the shock therapy was that they had to do that procedure on me to try to bring me out of my regression. To some degree, regression was a successful recourse for me. At least I returned to a benign state or stage of my life that was somewhat tolerable. Prior to therapy, I had withdrawn to approximately age nine and I was not going to budge from there no matter what. You see, my life before nine held no memory of major pain for me, but after nine it was nothing I could bear anymore. Strapped-down, drugged, full-fledged shock therapy couldn't hold a candle to the feelings of rejection that had begun in me as a child. Always having to earn love . . . never being good enough . . . I would not come back . . . not until I wanted to . . . Where do you go when home is in your mind and love is left behind . . . and hearts need to mend but the pain just never ends . . . God, I wish I'd known You then . . . God, I wish I'd known You then . . .

eleven

NEW DANCE CARD

*T*HE meaning of right and wrong was supposed to be clear and simple. *Do* right and everything will *be* all right, but sadly, the rules kept on changing, and everything started to make less and less sense to me. The way people were, what people did. Not much seemed fair or right.

For example, my uncle Lee, Dad's brother, was so proud at the birth of his baby. He and his wife had adopted a little girl four years before, after trying unsuccessfully to have their own children. It's not unusual for a couple to conceive after adopting . . . As with most of life, things get easier when you relax. If a man could puff up and strut, that's how my uncle expressed his joy at finally having his own baby. Lee's grin was contagious and to watch him hold his child was like going to a good movie. Surely he was the happiest man alive—until the truth came out.

His wife had had an affair early in their marriage that she swore was a thing of the past. Not so. Apparently she'd kept on seeing the man, and Lee's baby, as it turned out, was not his at all. It took his wife six months to fess up. Six months of letting Lee think the baby was his. Finally she left with the children, married the other man, and Lee began his slow dance with death. He did remarry, but that relationship also ended in a bitter divorce. After that, Lee got serious about his alcoholic path to destruction.

His cause of death was listed as cancer, but we all knew what had really killed Lee.

Elle wasn't dealt a much better hand, which seemed especially unfair since she was the kindest, most loving woman on the face of the earth. Although she had stopped smoking ten years before, she had become riddled with cancer, beating her down to a weight of sixty pounds before she was finally set free. I went to see her in the hospital just before she died; she surfaced from her coma for a few minutes. Her body was nothing but a bunch of bones as she lay in a heap on the soiled bed. When she opened her eyes I could tell she was confused, as if searching to see whether she was still earthbound. Then, after a moment or two, she recognized me and she smiled . . . *How could she smile?* I remember thinking. She was in so much pain, about to die, and she smiled at me. Then, typical Elle, she asked how *I* was. She wanted to see pictures of my baby Aimee. She asked a million questions and told me how precious life was, and then she closed her eyes as she drifted back off into a deep sleep. I never saw her again. In her will, Elle left me her piano. Mom and Dad inherited her apartment on Fifty-fourth Street and were about to embark on the twenty-five happiest years of their lives, nestled in Elle's gift.

Elle's piano meant the world to me; it was a love offering, a gesture of support and encouragement. She'd always told me that I had great hidden talent, and what she liked to call "an ear to heaven," as she listened to me plunking away on the keyboard as a kid. For twenty years I moved that piano around with me until I lost most everything I had and it was sacrificed with the rest of my belongings. But the blessing of Elle's generosity, and the joy of having known this extraordinary woman, remained.

Deed and I moved to New York City to be closer to my work. Deed had become disenchanted with IBM and wanted to be involved with photography in some professional capacity, so he decided that he would try his hand at being a photographer's representative. That idea was short-lived, and even less financially rewarding, so he was soon on the lookout for new business opportunities.

It was around that time that one of the best bookers at Ford decided to open her own modeling agency and offered a position to Deed—provided I left Ford and signed with her agency. Don't tell me businesswomen aren't smart. For Deed to get the job, I felt I had no other choice than to comply, despite my loyalty and affection for Eileen . . . I tried my best to explain to Eileen why I was leaving Ford, but she seemed unable to understand, or at least she was not going to let me go gracefully. She told me that if I left her, she literally would not be able to send her kids to college. I laugh now at the guilt tactics she used to try to keep me, but at the time I was torn to pieces. I went through a stretch of diminished bookings during my transition period to the new agency, but I had a loyal enough clientele that soon I was as much in demand as ever.

Although modeling was becoming more and more of a chore to me, the financial rewards continued to speak loud and clear. The irony was that after all the trouble I went through changing agents, Deed's job at the agency was short-lived, and he quickly moved on to his next stab at career satisfaction. The day I will always rank high on my "forget list" was in 1968, in the fall of our first year in Manhattan. Starting with Aimee's sitter being late, events escalated to my missing my plane to San Juan, and after sitting in the airport for six hours, I found myself on the red-eye to Puerto Rico for my early-morning photo session. (This was a rare location shoot, as I hated to leave Aimee and Deed was still uneasy in my absence.) My only hope that night for a little rest presented itself when the seat next to mine on the plane came up empty. If I could only remove the armrest, I could lie down and take a real snooze. I pulled, I yanked, I wiggled, I smacked the divider, but to no avail. Determined to make one last-ditch effort, I got on my knees in my seat and yanked with all my might . . . The armrest suddenly came loose and smashed into my face with the force of a heavyweight boxer's punch. I was slammed back into my seat by the sheer velocity of the impact. Within a split second my newly rebroken nose was gushing blood, and within another few minutes my lip looked like I'd been stung by a nestful of wasps.

Let me put it this way, dinner could have been served on the swollen parts of my face with room to spare.

When I arrived in Puerto Rico, there was no one to meet me at the airport since I had missed my earlier plane. I finally found a taxi and toured most of the island on a wild-goose chase charge-the-stupid-American-as-much-as-we-can taxi ride. When at last I reached my destination, I found a note at the hotel desk telling me what room to go to and that my makeup call was in thirty minutes. I made it to my room but found myself locked out by the sleeping model inside. She had a later call than I and "didn't want to be disturbed by my late arrival." Mega-rude sometimes comes in pretty packages.

I waited in the hall until the photographer and stylist came by to get me. They were paralyzed at the vision of my ravaged face. Thankfully it was a bathing-suit shoot instead of a lipstick ad, the focus being on the bod not the schnoz. My face was photographed either turned away or looking to the sky in all the shots, and we somehow managed to make our quota.

My return flight was totally packed and within an hour of departure I started to feel sick. My body was turning beet red and swelling before my eyes: a wicked case of sun poisoning, I soon learned. Although I had spent the entire day in the pool shooting pictures, I hadn't paid any attention to the possibility of getting burned as we were under an overcast sky. The word "dumb" pops into my mind as I think about what happened, but at that moment I had more immediate concerns. Nausea was now claiming my attention just about the same time as the plane hit a major patch of turbulence. As we began to gyrate earthquake style, I barely made it to the bathroom before falling to my knees to vomit. Suddenly I felt a hand on my back pulling me out of the bathroom. The stewardess informed me that I had to put my seat belt on and pushed me down next to some poor, unsuspecting man who tried his best not to stare at the bruised, red-faced, wrenching, swelling lunatic in the seat next to him . . . I never thought of a simple modeling location as on-the-job combat.

*   *   *

There is a theory that says that when one plays hard to get, it makes one all the more sought after. Although I never put that theory to practice with men, I surely did with the film industry. Paramount was hot to sign me, even more so since I had turned them down a few years before. Thankfully, I had the presence of mind at that point to tell the studio I wanted to study acting before beginning any kind of acting career.

At the time Bob Evans was head honcho of Paramount, and he'd call me in for a meeting whenever he was in New York. Those meetings always followed the same story line: Bob would have me come up to his impressive office, piled high with scripts, and walk around the stacks of opportunities like he was showing off a herd of prized cattle. He always exuded an air of sexual promise with me, but in the end he remained respectful of my marital status. This didn't stop him, however, from insinuating that nothing should deter me from pursuing what promised to be an incredible film career. What put him off was that I refused to do nude scenes (the "in" thing to do in the late sixties). I also refused to swear on screen and I wouldn't move out to live in Hollywood . . . Bob said I was making his job "very difficult." Then he would take me out to dinner at a "spot to be seen" restaurant, and the next time he was in town the whole dance of finding me a project would repeat itself. I never did do a movie for him. *Love Story* was one film opportunity that came close, but the studio said I couldn't play a Jewish girl . . . so they gave the part to Ali MacGraw. MacGraw . . . O'Neill . . . Jewish? (Bob ended up marrying Ali.)

Deed would invariably throw a fit when I'd get home from a "Bob meeting" and we'd fall into all the old arguments and pain. My husband was never very supportive of my impending film career, so I didn't pursue it with much gusto. If he'd only recognized all of the legitimate opportunities I turned down along with the illegitimate ones I skirted, he would have been proud of me instead of defensive. Aimee was growing, but as a couple, Deed and I weren't. Still, I was hoping for another baby. One night, during our regular conciliatory moments of lovemaking, Deed felt a lump in my breast. "What's that?" he said, withdrawing his hand like he had burned himself. "I don't know," I lied.

The doctor told me the lump must be removed immediately . . . exclamation point! I had ignored its presence for months, hoping, like a wishful five-year-old, that it would just go away. Back then breast cancer was not part of everyday conversation, and little effort had been made to educate women about its danger and their own role in diagnosing the disease. There was little focus on self-examination or early detection, let alone less intrusive analysis. A lump to me meant either I had cancer or I didn't, and if I did, then I would die like Elle, but I would not let them cut me up! What a fool. My fears had extended from needles to doctors in general. After my stint in the hospital where I underwent shock therapy, the medical world was a place I did not want to revisit.

Due to my delaying tactics, the operation I finally underwent was more extensive than it should have been. The doctor informed me prior to surgery in his best lack-of-bedside manner that he was going to cut out my lump, ascertain whether it was cancerous or not while I was still on the table, and if it wasn't cancer, he would sew me back up . . . But if it was cancer, he would "finish the job." I refused to give him permission to "finish the job." He didn't like that a lick. Matter of fact, we didn't get along after that. It's not a good idea to go under the knife of someone who doesn't like you; they definitely have the advantage.

The growth in my left breast was the size of an egg. Luckily for me it was benign. A few years following my surgery, I decided to become the chairperson for the American Cancer Society in order to use the celebrity I had gained after *Rio Lobo* and *Summer of '42* to inform others of what my own experience had taught me. The society and I shot one of the first instructional films for women about breast cancer and its prevention, detection, and cure. I had been a frightened little girl about the entire subject and could very well have died from my fears and ignorance.

Once I was on my feet after surgery, I began to attend acting school, which turned out to be better than I ever imagined. Paramount was paying for my classes and I was learning fast and furiously. I found that the process of discovering how to act naturally supports you as an individual whether you end up working professionally as an actor or not. This is especially true if you find a good teacher, and I was blessed with a fantastic one. Robert Modica was schooled in Sandy Meisner's Actors Studio method, and to this day I think Bob ranks tops in his field. His relentless insistence on finding one's truth within a moment, his compassion for the difficulties of learning the art, his eye for detail, his kind presence and humor, and his genius of discovery place him heads above the rest.

And under his tutelage, I was unfolding like a frostbitten flower given a sunny second chance—my outer layers fell dead to the floor, exposing tender fresh life just under the surface. Bob told me early on in my study that I should do films rather than stage because I possessed a vulnerability and a mode of delivery that was more internal than broad . . . one the camera could capture more readily. He also often gave me deliberately disgusting and loathsome characters to play. I fell into tears in the middle of class one night, embarrassed by the roles he kept insisting I portray. Now that I think of it, they were always manipulative, promiscuous, or sultry creatures who lived in a place I wanted to move away from rather than investigate through any kind of character study. In fact, I usually felt they had *no* character to study at all and I preferred to be enveloped by more morally and intellectually expansive persons to portray. "Crap," he'd bellow, matching emotions to mine as he overwhelmed me with his point of view. He told me that as he had observed me over the last six months, he had come to realize that I believed people were going to identify me with whatever character I was playing, and that I needed to get over that misconception. I needed to stop worrying so much about what everyone thought of me and start acting. I was not the character I was portraying, and I couldn't portray any "character" until I took myself out of the equation. Once I accepted his wisdom, I began to find acting extremely liberating.

Other changes were going on as well. Something had happened

to me since I'd become a mother: my fascination with speed had waned. I had already survived a head-on collision between my parents' Corvair and a stone wall when I was sixteen. I was playing racecar driver and overshot the turn. I could actually see the face of the driver in the car coming around the bend in the opposite direction; we locked eyes in a slow-motion panic and simultaneously swerved to avoid each other. The weight of the rear-mounted engine caused my car to swing into the wall. The other car drove on without incident. I wondered why the driver didn't stop, at least to see if I was dead or injured. The crash brought to my previously broken neck and back a rebirth of constant crippling pain that ravaged me for months, and my right arm and hand were already functioning at reduced capacity from being severed and broken. Before I was out of my teens, my body was a walking battle zone.

At the prompting of my acting teacher, I finally got a theatrical agent, who immediately set me up for some auditions. On my second try I landed a part in a low-budget film called *Glass Houses* to be shot in Los Angeles. The producers and I battled over their insistence of a nude scene for me as I was playing some older character's mistress—but I stood my ground and they finally gave me the part anyway. However, the nude-scene issue did cost me many a role in the future. I've marveled at times about my staunch conviction on this matter at such an impressionable age and at such a financial cost (another one of those "God's hand on my shoulder" issues). There was also Deed to consider—although he clearly enjoyed looking at nude women, he didn't want his wife on public display. I interpreted Deed's position as being protective of me, although the truth probably was based on jealousy . . . Typically I chose the more romantic notion.

Glass Houses was shot for under $500,000 over four weeks. I stayed with the producer's family for budgeting purposes, and as a first film experience, everything went quite well. All the cast and crew were pleasant and professional, even if the story line of the film was trite. A year later *Glass Houses* finally achieved general release based on the success of *Summer of '42*. My first film had a short, forgettable run.

While I was in L.A. I was able to see my brother Mike. He was on a trip across country after graduating from college and looked me up. Having just come off a stay at a commune, Mike was full of ideas about hippie communal living and free everything. At the time my own mind was on a tour through Eastern philosophy, so Mike and I had some "deep" discussions to share . . . You know, early-twenties know-it-all stuff. We talked and talked, and I momentarily felt reconnected with Mike, safe under my older brother's care.

Since he'd gone off to school, Mike had been virtually out of my life and as my career blossomed and my family grew, we seemed to have less and less in common—but not that night. Mike came to see the rushes of my film and have dinner with me at the producer's house. It was to be an evening I'd never forget. When we got out of the car to go inside, he handed me a miniature pill and said to take it. He had the oddest expression on his face, as he was obviously already under the influence of whatever the drug was. He finally confessed it was mescaline not acid and he promised it would be "cool." I had never tried any drugs, and frankly, I was scared to death of them; Mike swore to me that it was no big deal. Then he broke the tiny pill in half.

I had all but forgotten about the drug as the evening proceeded along with no disturbances . . . But when dessert was served, I knew something was wrong when the apple pie *walked across the table* all by itself. Panicked, I looked at Mike, who appeared to have no skin on his face. I excused myself and went into the bathroom. That was a *big* mistake, because the bathroom had a mirror, and when I looked in that mirror, I had no skin on *my* face. I freaked. Mike and I left the dinner and wandered around for a few nightmarish hours till the stupid little pill that was "cool" let go of my mind, which was floating around in pieces somewhere in my head. I know now that without question, hallucinogenic drugs open one up to demonic forces, powerful forces that can manipulate you for the rest of your life. That night with Mike absolutely terrified me. As far as I'm concerned, drugs are not even slightly cool. They are as bad as it gets and really can cost you your life and/or your sanity. As usual, it was going to take stubborn me a few rounds of punishment in my life to figure out that simple fact.

As my marriage was becoming more troubled, my career was moving ahead full force. Although I was intent on becoming a good actress, it was never the center of my focus. The drama of my failing marriage permeated every part of me, and I kept worrying that I was falling short as a mother. But Hollywood kept pushing me, and my next stop on the movie trail was signing with the top theatrical agency, CMA. My agent, Jerry Steiner, was a real go-getter and determined to release all my potential (I was never again to have such a good agent). One of his first appointments for me was with Howard Hawks for the lead in the next John Wayne movie, *Rio Lobo*.

Mr. Hawks had made many a brilliant movie—*Bringing Up Baby, Red River,* and *Rio Bravo,* to name a few—but when I met him, he was in his seventies and deteriorating fast mentally. My appointment was at his studio office. When I entered, he was sitting behind an enormous desk, sun streaming in through the windows, creating a heavenly aura about his head. Our conversation was brief, and within a few minutes he cast me in the lead female role. Once that was settled, he told me to approach him. As I stepped tentatively forward, he kept motioning me to come closer. I thought a million horrible thoughts. What was this old man going to do to me? What did he want me to do to him? I was expecting the worst because I had experienced the worst . . . I finally made it to his side when, out of nowhere, he lifted his arm and punched me hard in the stomach. I gagged, staggering to the front of the desk for protection and distance. "That's where I want you to speak from," he boomed. "From your diaphragm, not your throat. You are special! Know it, not only in the way you look, but how you sound." I was still trying to recover from the blow as he continued. "You will be a Hawks girl! I've made them all, including Lauren Bacall, and I will make you a star . . ."

Mr. Hawks told me to go home and scream at a tree for fifteen minutes six times a day until the film shoot started, and that doing this would lower my voice. He was wrong. When I arrived on the set on the first day, my voice wasn't lower, it was nonexistent . . . I was hoarse. My register remained pitifully high for the duration of that movie, which embarrasses me to this day whenever the film is rerun (which it is constantly). It took years of smoking (stupid, stupid) and lots of voice lessons before my tone progressively dropped to one of the lower decibels in the business.

John Wayne was a total delight to work with. In a few months I had gone from a half-million-dollar movie to a ten-million-dollar film (remember this was the early seventies), costarring with one of the world's best-known heroes. I never considered "The Duke" a great actor; he was more a larger-than-life personality. Nonetheless, it was during the filming of *Rio Lobo* that John Wayne won his Academy Award for *True Grit*—truly a wonderful moment for him. He always told me that the most important thing about acting is to *really* listen. That advice came in handy years later when I worked on a film in Europe where everyone was speaking different languages. Talk about listening for your cue!

I was in a mischievous mood one day on the *Rio Lobo* set, so I decided to glue a huge handlebar mustache over my lip for a joke. The shot I was doing required me to come into the frame, sneak around the sheriff's office, and leave the frame. Hawks was sitting in his director's chair when he yelled "action." I did my bit with the mustache on, and the crew went into hysterics, but things really got crazy when Hawks yelled, "Cut, print." Obviously, Mr. Hawks was not only a bit senile, his eyesight wasn't much to speak of either.

The Duke did *Rio Lobo* out of respect for Hawks, as they had made many classic films together in the past, but it was rather sad to see this once-renowned director losing his touch. A constant stream of well-wishers, supportive friends, and fans of Hawks passed through the set during the entire filming schedule including the legendary director John Ford and actor Robert Mitchum. A book about Hawks was being written while we shot: the set was hopping, accolades were flying, and I felt honored to be present at what seemed like a giant wrap party for an era gone by.

I only saw the Duke lose his patience once. It was after a gun battle in the saloon where I shot the bad guy and then fainted into the Duke's arms. He was to carry me up the long flight of stairs to exit frame. Remember, John Wayne had had one of his lungs removed due to cancer, so this scene was no easy task for him to perform. I shot the gun, fainted, was caught, and tried to will myself to be as light as possible while still playing unconscious. As we ascended the stairs, the Duke's breathing became heavier and heavier . . . I really wasn't sure if he would make it to the top. But he did, and Hawks yelled "cut" . . . only to have the cameraman announce that they didn't film the shot because Hawks forgot to tell him to follow us up the stairs with the camera. With that, the Duke dropped me hard on the floor and stormed off the set swearing that he wouldn't do the scene again . . . But of course he did. He was a real pro. There were, however, a few things you didn't do with the Duke; you never talked about religion or politics, and you never played cards with him if you expected to win. In my opinion, John Wayne more than deserved his hero status.

Hawks wanted to sign me to a multipicture deal with a loan-out clause. The clause meant that he could sell my option to anyone he wanted to without my approval. When I declined his offer, he became livid and told me he would "blackball" me from the industry so I would never work again. He really didn't have the power to do all that he threatened, but I didn't know this. He scared me, I admit. At the end of the day, what he did do was spell my name wrong in the film credits and poster to get back at me for refusing his offer.

Deed and I rented a house in L.A. while I was shooting *Rio Lobo* so I could be with Aimee and him, but the resurrection of our marriage wasn't working. Location shoots are as tough on relationships as long business trips away from home. I believe lengthy separations should be avoided if at all possible in a marriage—I have found that any separation is potentially injurious.

With that in mind, I went back to New York right after the film wrapped, to stay "home," even though my agent said I should remain in L.A. for the sake of my career. In a last-ditch effort to save my marriage, I bought a house in Bronxville not far from New York City for an easy commute with a country feel. Aimee was a toddler now and I felt she needed a safe atmosphere to roam about and play. Still, after all Deed and I had done to make things better, tensions continued to grow. Deed bought a dune buggy and any spare time he had was spent in the garage tinkering on the sand machine. I started riding again to try to fill my missing-husband gap. It was during that period that Aunt May (my mother's sister) came to live with us to look after Aimee when Deed and I were at work . . . And so we chugged along. Our fun times were spent dancing at the clubs in New York City, but basically we argued a lot and I fought off recurring threats of depression as I continued to feel inadequate in my relationship.

By now Deed had become incredibly cold and I told him so one night when we had some friends over. Without a word, he ushered me down the hall, pushed me around the door, and twisted my arm back to the breaking point. While he was doing all this, he kept talking to our friends in the living room, saying, "You know how Jennifer gets . . . Maybe she needs to go back to the mental hospital until she feels better." It was a low point for me . . . for us. Although I became hysterical, Deed wouldn't let go of my arm. Finally the tension grew unbearable and the other couple went home. After they left, Deed took me to the emergency room to see if my arm was broken. I decided right then that I wouldn't be spending any more time with him—or in a mental hospital, for that matter. I was going to take charge of my life whether I liked it or not. My knight in shining armor existed only in my mind; if my future needed to be rescued, I'd have to do it myself.

Deed and I were legally separated shortly thereafter, although our attraction for each other pulled us back together for a few more rounds. Deed had taken an apartment in New York City when we seemed to be heading rapidly for a divorce, but after a few steamy reconciliatory nights together, he moved back in. Not long after, I was offered a part in a small film called the *Summer of '42* to be shot in Northern California. Deed and I considered the project and decided that a break from each other might even be a good thing for our marriage. It's interesting how easily a "break" from each other can turn into a permanent separation.

twelve

LEAPS AND REBOUNDS

THE *Summer of '42* offer was another coup for my agent, who knocked himself out to get me the role. At first, Robert Mulligan, the director, refused to see anyone under thirty years old for the role of the "older woman" Dorothy. I was twenty-two and considered too young. But after Jerry beat the doors down, Mulligan agreed to see me. My agent recognized that this magical little script could launch me as a household name and a major international star. He was right, but first I had to get the part.

And there was a hitch . . . When I read the script about this boy's bittersweet first love with the character Dorothy, I was concerned once again about the lovemaking scene. My agent was furious when I told him I couldn't test for the role if there were nude scenes. He begged me to test anyway, and if I got the role we could address that issue later. He kept reminding me that we were dealing with Robert Mulligan, a director with impeccable taste and talent! But I didn't want to waste the director's time with a test if I wasn't going to do something he required, so I made Jerry call Mulligan to explain my position. The word we finally got back was, "If Jennifer is that right for the role, we'll work around the nudity." Over the years I have had producers and others swear that I was nude in the bed scene of *Summer of '42;* what a perfect example of leaving a little to the imagination. We *do not* have to show graphically what we all know happens in the bedroom to get a point across.

There was something else about the project that concerned me. Although Herman Rauchen had written a tender and humorous account based on his own coming-of-age story, the fact remained that Dorothy was an older woman who loses her husband in the war and takes a young boy to bed. How could I play Dorothy so that the audience would fall in love with her instead of hate her? I have to admit, the balance of sympathy and judgment was not an easy one to maintain. After reading the script many times over, I decided if Hermie, the boy, hadn't arrived at Dorothy's house at the beach exactly when he did, their relationship would have remained as before, an innocent friendship between an awakening young man and an older war bride. But Dorothy had just received news of the death of her husband, was lost in memories and grief when Hermie arrived, and, in a moment of need, leaned on him for human contact, for comfort. They were both vulnerable. A caring moment amid devastating news. An interlude that held no future, but was, nonetheless, a brief, bittersweet exchange of love born of loss. And that is how I played the role. I could relate to Dorothy's deep despair, her need to be held . . . to feel loved and alive when her world was dying around her. She was flawed, she was human, she was lost. I understood her.

The actual filming of *Summer of '42* was a delightful professional experience. Every aspect from director to crew was top-notch, but on a personal level I was suffering. I was still so shy in those days that it would never have occurred to me to go to get something to eat in a restaurant by myself. Since Mulligan had put me in a motel away from the rest of the cast, I spent most of my off time in my room eating peanut-butter sandwiches and playing with two stray cats I had rescued. I named Reneé and Oscar after my parents (those felines were madly in love).

I understood the choice on the director's part to keep me out of everyday contact with the three young male leads in an effort to assist the boys in reacting to me on camera with awe and awkwardness. They were fifteen years old, I was twenty-two and the mother of a three-year-old, so that still made me "the older woman." Had we shared lunches or dinners or all become friends, it would have required more acting on the boys' part to respond in a starstruck manner to "Dorothy."

I giggle about being best known out of my thirty-plus movies for my portrayal of Dorothy, "the older woman," when I was but twenty-two when I made the film. Where does one go from there, and how does one age gracefully almost thirty years after the film's debut? At fifty I am now just beginning to feel a little like an older woman on a bad day. On a good day, watch out.

Deed visited this location as he had the others, but as usual, our time became a painful succession of nasty flashbacks. Just recently I recognized that during most of my major jobs, whether it be a Cover Girl shoot (which I had been doing since I was sixteen) or a role in a new movie, stress was always raging around me, making a good performance on my part very difficult. Although my participation in that pattern made me a *full* partner in the debacle, it's also clear that no man ever served as a support system for me, either personally or careerwise. Was it all about control? Competition? A replay of my relationship with my brother? There I was again, shooting *Summer of '42,* and all I could think about was my personal unhappiness. Deed and I again agreed on a "trial separation." I believe for most marriages that's a hard choice to recover from, especially if you make no gains in mutual understanding and healing. Without that, confidence and trust in your partner go straight out the window. Deed's visit was brief. Adding to the tension, his dad had been very sick and Deed was understandably under a lot of strain when he went back east.

About halfway through the '42 shooting schedule, my mom broke her back—according to the phone message at my motel from Dad. They were coming back from Deed's father's funeral when a truck hit their car head-on. I knew I needed to get home, even though my mom was in stable condition. Thanks to the producer, Richard Roth, and Mulligan's understanding, I was allowed to make a quick trip home to see her. It was another one of those impossible all-night flying gigs that landed me in Bronxville, New York, some thirty-six hours later.

The biggest problem I had was getting into the house quietly past my two dogs, who were beside themselves with joy and howls at my sudden appearance. After I practically suffocated them in a bid for silence, then rolled on the floor with them long enough to be completely covered with fur, they allowed me to sneak up to the bedroom to surprise Deed. I undressed in record time, slipped into our bed, and ever so slowly moved my naked body meaningfully against his . . . After a little coaxing, Deed finally awoke, looked me right in the eye, and said his old line. "What are you doing here?" Oh well, another surprise bites the dust. I've always seen life as a series of memorable moments, either good or bad, but so many potentially good surprises end up on the "cutting-room floor." This one certainly did.

Later that morning I went off to see Mom in the hospital and was pleased that she knew that I loved her more than a lot. Showing up is usually all it takes to let someone know how much you care . . . I struck gold on this part of the surprise.

The rest of my short stay confirmed all of my worst fears about my chances for sustaining any relationship with Deed. We were both lost without a clue about how to heal and fix ourselves. It was finally over. Marriage was forever as far as I was concerned. So if forever didn't exist, what did that leave . . . never?

When Mulligan invited the entire cast and crew to watch the last rushes of *Summer of '42* after eight weeks of filming, everyone showed up. What does it mean when you're shooting the dance at the end of the film and the entire crew have been crying like babies for days because they were overwhelmed by the scene? What does it mean when a prop master who has been in the business for forty years hands your character a bag of groceries for a shot and his eyes are spilling tears? It means that you have a hit movie on your hands, one that touches everyone to the core. My character, Dorothy, was on screen in *Summer of '42* for a mere eleven minutes . . . That's it. What does that mean? Maybe the best times can be short times as long as they count.

I'm such a product of my training as an actor that I have never used any kind of aid such as glycerine to bring on or show emotions. "If it's not real, don't shoot it," I say. But when I shot '42, I also didn't know how to "save it" for the close-up. After crying for days, I literally had to wait for my tear ducts to refill before we could continue the scene. It was particularly frustrating since there wasn't a dry eye on the set.

Getting a performance right in a movie is a phenomenal feeling that ranks up there with executing a perfect jump on a horse or hitting a solid, unencumbered note in singing. When you're on and completely "in character" and "in the moment," you have absolutely no awareness of anything around you, including the camera and crew. It's when a line is never searched for and everything flows freely, no matter where your emotions take you; you may be startled by your own voice—a yell or a laugh comes without warning or inhibitions. Being real within imaginary circumstances requires trust, and although I had very little of that for people (or myself), I was able to make up for it when I was acting. The thought of "performing" made me very nervous, but at least conquering that problem was in my control, and as I became better as an actress, I began to enjoy a freedom of spirit that lived through the characters I played on screen. It would take me years, however, to get in touch with my real *spiritual* freedom, and until I did, I seemed personally doomed to ride an emotional roller coaster. But for the time being, there were many of those soaring acting moments in the *Summer of '42,* and I am forever grateful for that opportunity.

It was 1974. Although fame and fortune had knocked on my door, I still hadn't plugged into the Hollywood way of career advancement. After the rave reviews and record-breaking attendance for *Summer of '42,* I was contacted by the biggest PR firm in the film industry. They wanted to represent me and basically guaranteed me an Academy Award nomination for Best Supporting Actress if I signed on. Just a nomination would have assured me major salary increases and prestige for the rest of my career, but I never looked at acting as a business. Naively, I felt that if the Academy wanted to nominate me, they would do so based on the merit of my performance, not because of publicity.

That attitude may have been my major career-strategy blunder of a lifetime. I continued to let film opportunities pass me by as I wrestled with my sadness over my failed marriage. I was asked to work in Europe as well as on various other projects around the States, but opted to return to New York to see if there was any life left in my relationship with Deed—I refused to accept the fact that we were through. But even with my continued choice to bypass roles, I eventually managed to amass a substantial body of film work.

Years after '42 had been released and its success and stature established, I had lunch with Richard Roth, the film's producer, at the Beverly Hills Hotel pool. The sun was beating down on Hollywood at its best. Well-toned bodies were draped across lounge chairs that surrounded the tent-striped bungalows created for privacy and provocative mingling. Waiters bustled about tending to the guests' every whim, as the parade of flesh and the growl of high finance moved through the manicured set. Richard and I dined on shrimp and wine at one of the umbrella tables. We chatted about how many international film festivals we had both attended during *Summer of '42*'s release. I had won countless Best Actress awards abroad as well as in the States and had heard the film dubbed in multiple languages. (As you can imagine, hearing myself speak in foreign languages was sometimes extremely funny.) The film was such a huge success in Japan that they actually ran a national Jennifer O'Neill look-alike contest . . . for Japanese women?

Amid all the types at poolside, I was telling Richard about the time I'd found myself in Yugoslavia for yet another film festival at which '42 was shown. After having passed without incident through the machine-gun-protected barricade in the airport, I attended an international press conference held for me and the notorious director Sam Peckinpah, who wanted to know why I hadn't been cast in his films *Straw Dogs* with Dustin Hoffman or *The Getaway* with Steve McQueen. He was drunk at nine in the morning. I told him I hadn't appeared in these films because he never asked for me . . . He said, "Good point." And then belched.

Richard waited till I finished my story by the pool, then said what was on his mind. He was excited about *Summer of '42* for so many reasons, not the least of their being that its financial success meant, as he put it, "I'll never have to work again in my life." He was amazed, and said, "Can you believe it? Never again in my life!" I told him I was happy for him. This seemed to bring him back to reality. He realized suddenly that his great good fortune was not mine as well, since I'd worked on the film for scale wages and had no ownership in the film. I told him that just being a part of the film was more than enough for me. He repeated how guilty he felt nonetheless, so I suggested that if he wanted to give me some points in the movie, I would be honored to accept in order to ease his conscience. He laughed and the subject never came up again.

Although I didn't receive a nomination for Best Supporting Actress, I was asked to be a presenter at the Academy Awards. Obviously I had not hired the PR firm, but I did end up handing Michel LeGrand his Oscar for writing the theme song of *Summer of '42*. What a thrill that was! LeGrand's sublime score lifted the film to another dimension. It was then that I truly understood the power and beauty of the right image melding with the right music. Together, their effect is greater than either's individual possibilities. And from then on, music became more a part of my inspiration, representing magical experiences as satisfying as my best moments in film. Although professional pursuits were still lower on my list than personal ones, I was about to embark on a whirlwind of artistic expression: acting, writing, music, painting, singing, directing, and producing.

It was also at that time that I bought a fantastic four-year-old Thoroughbred mare . . . the best horse I had ever ridden. Her show name was Spur of the Moment, but Aimee wanted to call her "Mabel." My three-year-old daughter was so excited about naming my new horse that I allowed Mabel to stick (although it always made me feel like I was calling Audrey Hepburn "Hey you"). I showed Mabel three times, she won all her classes, and then she went lame. I was so frustrated! I was still recovering from the experience of buying a horse in Canada that, once we brought him down to New York, turned out to have arthritis in his back (apparently he was drugged when I tried him). The people I bought him from just laughed at me when I told them I wanted my money back. "Sue us," they said, "but you'll have to do it here in Canada and it will cost you more than you paid for the horse." I had no recourse, so I sent the horse out to be retired and never sued those slimy people. No matter how many times I have been taken to the cleaners (and I have been ridden hard and put up wet by some of the most dishonorable con artists in the world), I'm always surprised and hurt by the world's lack of ethics. It's been proven to me over and over that I'm wrong to assume people will do the right thing, but I still keep hoping they will.

I sent Mabel up to my trainer's farm to try to heal her lameness, but all our efforts just brought me thousands of dollars of vet bills and no horse to ride. I had also been trying to breed her while she was recuperating, but also to no avail. Finally, there was nothing to do for my horse but to make her comfortable. She could never be ridden again. When I was loading Mabel to be shipped to Virginia to have her hind legs operated on, I asked my vet if she was barren on top of being lame. The vet looked rather embarrassed as he admitted, "I realize I've had Mabel on hormones to help her joints, so in essence you've been trying to breed your horse while she's been on birth control." I considered punching the man, but it was just a fleeting thought. By the way, Mabel is still alive and well in Malibu, California, enjoying over thirty years on Jennifer's meal ticket. I have had so many horses die young or become lame, yet Miss Mabel is still trudging along. She did finally give me three beautiful babies over the years.

Newly divorced, I moved Aimee and me into New York City's West Side, to a fabulous funky apartment that used to be an artist's studio. It had a two-story living room, slate floors in the kitchen and dining room, and a balcony surrounding two bedrooms. Above the fireplace loomed an enormous etching of a knight in armor, which shook when my mega–music system was turned up full blast. The Stones, Carly Simon, and Dory Previn echoed at all hours. I was not about to give up on "cool" or romanticism.

Although men were courting me right and left in New York, I was still deeply despondent about my divorce. In my heart, I felt I had failed in my most important mission. I was convinced it was all my fault and that there was definitely something wrong with me . . . Surely I was unlovable. But then there were those times when I would wake up early in the morning and look at the sun spilling over the Manhattan skyline and feel such excitement for life. There were those times when just being young was enough, even if I felt used up. My life had become this odd mixture of ups and downs, of extremes, and there was never a middle ground in which to find peace and solace.

For my next film project I chose to work with Otto Preminger because his movie was to be shot in New York City and I didn't want to move Aimee around on locations so soon after the divorce. Dyan Cannon was the lead in *Such Good Friends,* and although Preminger had done some remarkably good films in the past, this would not turn out to be one of them. It was a bad career choice for me and my agents pulled no punches in telling me so. Then, in the midst of the big career-move debate, my main agent Jerry killed himself. *Boom*—just like that. When the head of CMA called me with the horrible news, he had no explanation for the tragedy. No one seemed to know what sent Jerry over the edge. If they didn't know what went wrong with him, I surely didn't, since my relationship with Jerry was only about work. Following his death, the job of representing me was scattered among the rest of the agency; I no longer had a central person who cared much about me. The people there seemed more interested in their doodle pads and their next hit and I didn't fall into the "hot" category because I wouldn't comply with the unspoken rules of Hollywood. I admit I did tie my agents' hands many times over the years because my priorities were different from theirs. The sixteen-year-old model who turned down Paramount had become a twenty-four-year-old movie star who took a similarly cavalier attitude toward new film roles.

It was hard to believe Jerry was dead. One day I was talking to him, the next day he was gone . . . Someone must have known he was upset. Everyone including me missed noticing his pain. I wanted to tell Jerry that I knew how he felt, that life is not ours to take. What a thief despair is . . . What a powerful enemy waits for us in ambush.

So many people I met early on in my acting career now run Hollywood in one capacity or another, but when I knew them they were wide-eyed with dreams on their lips and determination in their stride. Two such interns on *Such Good Friends* were Steve Tish, who went on to produce *Forrest Gump* and *Risky Business,* and Don Phillips, who also produces and has discovered in casting many up-and-coming stars (Nicolas Cage and Anthony Edwards, for example). Don and Steve were my buddies on the set and off, helping me move into my apartment and just hanging out together. They were also there the day I almost passed out on Mr. Preminger's set . . .

For the most part, Otto was a rather nasty individual with a lethal temper and a tongue that could dismantle even the thickest-skinned customer. Everyone was terrified of provoking his wrath and my turn was about to come.

I had a scene to shoot in *Such Good Friends* in which I visit my lover in the hospital, and upon seeing that he is dying, I faint. I'm taken to a room to lie down and recover. As I come to with the aid of smelling salts, I have a dialog with a nurse. We were all set to roll so I lay back on the gurney where I was supposed to be unconscious. Otto yelled "action," the nurse popped the fake "popper" (amyl nitrate, a drug meant to dilate capillaries in people with heart disease). The only problem was, the popper was *real* and I inhaled it with such a vengeance that my heart started racing, my face turned puce, and the rush from the drug put my mind on a track that I couldn't follow. I was so scared that Otto would scream at me for stopping the scene that I tried to go on with my lines despite my disoriented state. I couldn't even think, let alone speak, and Otto gave me an unforgettable tongue-lashing for forgetting my lines. It's never fun to be chastised and I've occasionally wondered what any of that day had to do with acting.

Shortly after wrapping *Such Good Friends* romance again entered my life. It came in the form of a blind date that turned into a two-year-plus relationship. Creg was extremely wealthy and powerful yet conservative—so much so that he would cut the gold buckles off his Gucci shoes because he thought they looked too flashy, too nouveau riche. He didn't like me to wear makeup and he didn't want me to work. It was refreshing however to be with someone who thought I was very bright and talented—that I was more than a dim-bulb movie star. He encouraged me in my oil painting, music writing, and reading—under his tutelage I added several newspapers a day to my usual fare, and for all of the above I am grateful. Creg treated me like a princess. Traveling extensively, we moved through the world like it was his personal garden party. He was an early riser, a hardworker, and following him required my rearranging most of my interests. My horses completely fell by the wayside. Tennis was his sport and it became mine. I played pro-celeb at Forest Hills center court . . . My life was changing.

His time was spent promoting causes, negotiating mergers, and pulling off business ventures of staggering proportions. At first the private planes, designer jewelry, and the high life were exhilarating, but in the end they left me cold, since they were offered without deep commitment or real intimacy.

Creg was in the midst of a complicated divorce and had several young children to attend to. The circumstances were less than perfect, yet I found him to be an exceptional father, and as time went by, I fell very much in love with him. Experiencing love again was a miracle to me, since I thought I would never feel that way about anyone after Deed. However, hobnobbing with the power elite led only to more disillusionment for me as I discovered some truths behind the guarded doors of politics and big business that are per-haps better left hidden. My interest in politics is only recently re-surfacing, based on what I believe to be not only our right, but an obligation we all have to get involved with the running of our country.

It became increasingly evident then that I needed either to get on with my career or to give it up and focus on my life with this dynamic man. The problem was his impending divorce, which be-gan to seem like an endless obstacle, and although he seemed very much taken with me, he really hadn't shown much interest in en-tering a new marriage. This was the seventies, mind you, and it felt like I was the last person on earth who wanted to choose marriage over the much-talked-about "freedom." And then suddenly the nitty-gritty problem reared its ugly head: he did not want any more children, ever. Not with me or anyone else.

In my early twenties with a four-year-old child, I found myself considering the prospect of never having a larger family. No, just one more child; that's all I wanted. One that was ours . . . together. I pleaded. But once again I'd hit a brick wall. It was another hint of what was to come, but again I chose to ignore the early-warning signs. Instead, I searched for answers in intensive therapy and the study of philosophy. I was already in love with Creg and I knew my feelings weren't going to change for a long time, if ever. I needed to know if I was being unreasonable or if he was just not available for what really mattered to me. The more rejected I felt, the more "difficult" I became, and I began to feel myself at the mercy of waves of sadness that overwhelmed me with memories of past disappointments. I would lash out again and again, I cried out to be heard. I was scary and I was obnoxious; he was distant, and over time the distance increased.

I told Creg I had to go back to work because I was running out of money. I needed to earn my own keep. Of course, he always tried to take care of me financially, but in the end I wouldn't let him. We weren't married so I couldn't allow him to support me. The last thing I was looking for was a handout.

During some of our time together, I had kept my own apartment and Aimee and I would commute between his apartment and our own while she attended private preschool. I had a feeling Creg didn't think I was a very good mother, or at least he never recognized me as such. I felt unacceptable again. We never really talked about our true feelings—there was a lack of real closeness between us. "It" was happening again . . . I was losing my sense of self to another man's agenda and unavailability.

I decided to take the movie *Lady Ice* with Donald Sutherland and Robert Duvall, which was to be shot in Miami. This represented a first move away from my current relationship. *Lady Ice* turned out to be a difficult shoot; the film was already in the throes of serious problems when I was called in to replace Susan George. It's always uncomfortable to arrive on a set after filming has begun, because everyone has already formed their cliques and behavior patterns. In addition to personality conflicts and script problems, the location was suffocatingly hot and humid in Miami. The real trick was to get a scene shot before our makeup was washed away in a flood of perspiration. Donald was a demanding costar who would delight in indulging such pranks as mooning the cast and crew whenever the spirit moved him. Duvall, on the other hand, fascinated me as an actor. While I was working on a scene with him, I found all his responses virtually undetectable, but later, when I watched that same scene at rushes, his effect on the screen was intense and meaningful. His artistry had this uncanny quality to it.

It wasn't long before my then-estranged boyfriend decided to fly in from New York and finally ask me to marry him. I was swept off my feet and back in love—a love I had never really lost.

Once the film wrapped, I flew back to New York with renewed hope that my dreams were finally going to work out. This marriage proposal gave me a sense of being respected and an emotional security that freed me from the dark mistrust that always haunted me with men. Even though the marriage had to be put off until his divorce was finalized, I was content just knowing his intentions meant "forever." I had told Creg when we became involved that due to recurrent health problems and the removal of a breast tumor a few years earlier, I couldn't take any kind of birth control (every method had side effects or dangers for me). He knew deep down that I wanted more children and it was up to him to handle contraception. And so it had been.

Following his proposal, our time together was better than ever, and when we made love, Creg took no precautions. I talked to my therapist about his new behavior and he suggested that sometimes when people want something but don't want to admit it, their behavior may actively bring about the very desire they refuse to acknowledge consciously. If this was the case, my fiancé really wanted everything with me—marriage *and children*. This filled me with hope, and when I found out I was pregnant not long after, I was ecstatic. I confirmed my condition with my doctor and even made him write a note that I was pregnant on his office stationery so I could surprise my fiancé with the good news.

I didn't recognize the person I was standing in front of as he read the letter saying we were expecting a child. This couldn't be the man I loved . . . the man who had asked me to marry him. His words were precise and unequivocal: "I don't want it," Creg said. Over the next month my life became a dark spiral that sucked me down. At first I told him that I refused to get an abortion as he suggested, I was prepared to have the baby on my own. He shed layers of his personality, like a human onion, leaving less and less compassion as he searched for the right method to coerce me into doing what he wished. But after all his approaches had fallen on deaf ears, he pulled out the big guns.

His eyes never flickered, his voice was precise and even in phrasing and tone. His body language was frightening enough, but his words sealed his threat with a promise I knew he could keep. "I am going to do everything in my power to have you get rid of this pregnancy," he said. "But if you insist on having my baby, I promise you, the moment it is born, I will take it away from you and you will never have anything to do with it . . . Ever. I give you my word that I will prove you unfit, emotionally unstable, and I will bury you. Do you understand me?"

I knew that his promises to love me forever now belonged to

another life and another time. I also knew that this new promise was one he would keep. He wouldn't let me have the baby on my own. He would stop at nothing to convince me to have an abortion, but if I found a way to have my baby, he would take it away from me forever.

I was inconsolable as I lay waiting on the table for the doctor to begin the "procedure." My doctor knew that I wanted this baby more than anything in the world, so he offered to speak to Creg on my behalf. He couldn't see why things couldn't be worked out . . . When the doctor returned to the examination room, his expression was grim—it took him a few minutes to find words. He told me that he was sorry . . . that he had never met anyone so absolute and unswayable in their decision. The abortion was to go forward.

I was told in the seventies that a pregnancy was just a blob of tissue in my uterus up until three months gestation. I was told that an abortion was not unlike passing a heavy period—it's not a real baby or individual, it's just a mistake—an inconvenience. There are too many people in the world as it is. We have no moral responsibility to a blob of tissue—that microscopic entity without a name or a face is no one.

I was told by everyone including my doctor that abortion of the "tissue" prior to three-month maturity was all right. Ignorance on my part is a weak excuse, but an accurate one. I now feel that despite all the overwhelming outside pressure, I was pitiful in my inability to stand up against someone else's reasoning, no matter how powerful. I buckled under fear. I didn't know then where to find real strength, to find real truth. Deep down I knew I was wrong when everyone was saying it was all right. Nothing in the world could ever make me opt for that choice again. I hated myself, no question about it.

thirteen

MERRY-GO-ROUND

$\mathcal{I}$ HAD become great friends with a man with whom I had been studying Eastern philosophy. His name was Joseph and he was the most sensitive, supportive individual I had ever known. Aware of the torture I was going through with the impending abortion, he offered to marry me and raise the baby as ours because he truly loved me. His gesture was beyond gallant, yet I knew the position the real father had taken made it impossible for me to accept. But I could marry this kind man . . . and I did.

Joseph, my second husband, had gone from a carousing ad-agency executive with an exceptionally rapid and eclectic mind to a gentle philosopher and thinker. He had tamed his temper and turned his intense energies from temporal to spiritual matters through his study of Eastern philosophy, gurus, and mysticism. He was a compelling example of the kind of transformation for which I was searching.

New Age thinking and Eastern philosophies are certainly appealing, especially for people who question the meaning of life, the role of consciousness, and desire spiritual growth. Their hook is seductive because, in simple terms, they appear to offer an avenue through developing consciousness that takes one to God's doorstep and beyond. In a nutshell, God is everywhere, everything, and all-powerful. God is consciousness, and through meditation and study one can evolve to higher and higher levels in order to become one with God. Therefore, the philosophy purports *you can become God*. Egos love that concept, and this is what I believed in my twenties. I wanted mystic readings to guide my life and teach me to know the future. I wanted to be filled with higher energies and experience total enlightenment. I wanted to travel the astral planes and cultivate psychic powers, read auras, commune with the universe . . . you name it.

The only problem is, *it's not the truth*. What I achieved in my travels through the seven levels of consciousness and out-of-body experiences was only to open myself up spiritually to all kinds of negative forces and influences posing as enlightenment . . . In fact they were more demonic than divine. But I didn't know any of that in my twenties and through most of my thirties. I thought *Jonathan Livingston Seagull* was more than a sweet story, it was a spiritual breakthrough in the form of a bird. The profound observations (and there are many) of Eastern philosophers titillated my mind. Astrology promised to chart our course through life—we could even speak to the dead and come back incarnation after incarnation till we "got it right" and then graduate to a higher level. The truth is, we can never get it right because we are human and we all fall short of the glory of God. The truth is, we need grace and forgiveness . . . The truth is, *we are not God* and never will be.

Like my study of Eastern mysticism, my years in therapy never brought me any real peace. Therapy explained things about my subconscious mind, but it never connected the information to my heart; the pain was never healed and the patterns never changed. I am thankful for my years of philosophical study and my encounters with various psychological approaches because they broadened the base of my understanding and strengthened my conceptual thinking, but in the end both were damaging to me because they promised something they couldn't deliver. They promised the *whole* truth, and all they delivered was a lot of what I wanted to hear so I would "feel" better and temporarily "feel" more in control.

Just after Joseph and I married, I bought my favorite house of all time, in Bedford, New York. Thirty acres one hour outside of the city, this awesome stone home had courtyards, paneling created in France, hand-painted walls, a barn, and pastures for my growing herd of eight horses.

My husband contributed his wonderful antique furniture to the farm and negotiated its purchase price with as much expertise as I have ever seen. However, his wheeling and dealing made me nervous; at every bid I was afraid we were going to lose my dream house. Bargaining for something I desperately want is not one of my talents, which is probably why I've paid top dollar so much of the time for my objects of desire. What I am good at is envisioning glorious end results and bearing fruit from dilapidated beginnings. My Long Meadow Farm was a good example. Although originally a splendid home, it had been deserted for so long and was in a state of such disrepair that the property hadn't sparked interest from anyone in years. I experienced some of my greatest joys turning that home into a showplace.

Just as my depressions were becoming a memory and I had a new home and marriage, the next wave of unpleasant surprises began to swell. From the very beginning of our marriage my husband and I were extremely close. We shared our interest in spiritual development, and even better, Joseph had a son who lived with us who was just a few years older than Aimee. I encouraged my husband to take time off and become a writer, an area in which he showed so much promise. Besides, I was making enough money to support us until he could contribute. And for the first time in my life I was with a man who cared about making *me* happy sexually. Up to then, I had always been focused on making *him* happy so *he* would want more of me. I honestly had no idea what a woman was capable of experiencing physically until this relationship. He was tender and patient with me . . . He let me know everything was all right and I was safe.

But not long after we moved to the farm, Joseph changed. He started meditating five to six hours a day, searching for enlightenment. After this he would shut himself in the office and write for the rest of the time to the exclusion of me and the children. When he finally came up for air, it was to cook brown rice in special copper pots or to have discussions with friends I considered radicals about such topics as the value of drinking one's own urine, which was touted as the ultimate body-cleaning process. The love-making stopped as the outside world grew more unappealing to him. I'm not sure whether his sexual interest waned for me or in general, but again, I was sure it was all my fault. I felt completely rejected.

The taxicab came early that evening; his suitcases were at the front door. The theme from the movie version of *Jonathan Living-ston Seagull* filled the air . . . I didn't hear the door close when he left. We had been married a year when I told him I missed him and that I was unhappy. He didn't argue, he didn't yell, he just left with his son. I never saw him again . . . The divorce was swift.

So Aimee and I lived on our twenty-two-room horse farm alone. The big question was whether we should move back into New York City like all good little divorcées do to regroup and remarry, or stay out in the country . . . I chose the country. After Aimee had grown up, she told me she had hated living in the country during our eleven years at Long Meadow Farm because she was the only kid in her class with divorced parents. Here I thought I was doing the best for her. The fact was, we were just at the beginning of a tumultuous mother-daughter relationship that has only really begun to heal in the last few years. At the time, the distance between us seemed insurmountable.

I was never very physically demonstrative with her. I'm not sure why, because when my other two children finally came along, I was much more affectionate and tactile. Perhaps some of the difference had to do with becoming a mom for the first time when I was so young; it was as if Aimee and I were growing up together as siblings instead of mother and daughter. My sorrows when Aimee was a child often paralyzed me emotionally, and sadly, my daughter paid for my unhappy times. During all the relational upheavals, I was withdrawn and unavailable to everyone, including her. I was doing to my daughter the same thing my parents had done to me! Most children reap the ravaged harvest of their parents' hurts and inherit some of their negative patterns along the way. It's a sad fact that we don't have one lifetime of behavioral soap operas, we have generations of them. Another option to try to right the wrongs of our own upbringing is to take matters in completely the opposite direction when we become parents. And most often all we succeed in doing, according to our children, is create another set of wrongs. And so it goes . . . I've learned that this merry-go-round does not have to continue, but you need the right tools to break the cycle, something I know now but didn't have a clue about when I was younger. If you ever want to find compassion for your parents, become a parent.

After my second divorce, I had a string of engagements that thankfully got nipped in the bud before blooming into yet more disappointments. But despite my flickerings of discernment, I was still barreling the wrong way down a one-way street with something new to contend with: drinking was becoming more of a pattern for me. If I was sad, I would drink so I wouldn't have to think for a short while, but then I would become increasingly sad on the other side of that release . . . Surprise: drinking is a depressant, that is a clinical fact. And just because it comes in the pretty package of "relaxing," or "celebrating," or "forgetting," or "sleeping," doesn't mean that it isn't ALWAYS destructive one way or another *in excess*. I don't believe there is anything wrong with moderate drinking. I know there is everything wrong with drunkenness, which only leads to debauchery.

I was very fortunate to have a wonderful housekeeper named Claudette, who lived with me for over ten years. For some reason Claudette adored me and took care of me, my house, my animals, and oversaw Aimee as well. And of course, I took care of Claudette. We had a marvelous relationship. She was reliable, honest, and caring, and I considered her an absolute angel sent to me as a surrogate mom while I was winding my way through my mid-twenties to early thirties.

As I was working extremely hard in films and making a lot of money (*Reincarnation of Peter Proud, Carey Treatment*, etc.) I gave myself professional challenges to fill me up and keep me busy. My mind never stopped, my body never rested. I still believed deep down inside that the void I felt so intensely could be filled only by love in the form of a good man, a good marriage, and more children. The problem was, I couldn't seem to find the right guy and it would take me eight more miscarriages to finally end up with two more children. The only thing I could count on was that I wasn't about to give up trying on any front.

Aimee was always very close to her dad and his family, especially his mother. I was very happy about that since my family was basically nonexistent in the grandparent/uncle area. If I couldn't create a real family from my side, I was relieved to see that Aimee was getting that important feeling from her paternal relatives.

My brother Mike did marry briefly following college, but quickly divorced, and so far has remained spouseless and childless. His early desire was to carve out a career for himself as a drummer and comedian, but despite his talent, he couldn't quite make that dream come true. Nonetheless, he's always been a big thinker and shamelessly persistent about proving his point of view. Always wanting a closer relationship with Mike, I invited him to stay at my farm for a while in the mid-seventies because he needed a place to live and play his drums. As it turned out, I was away most of that time shooting a film and Claudette almost lost her mind during his residence. Apparently, the house exploded with tension; Mike was an extremely messy bachelor and boarder.

My world at Long Meadow Farm included some fantastic moments intermingled with the tougher ones. I gave grand sit-down dinner parties. Quiet moments were spent enjoying my horses, dogs, cats, and country life. At one point I had eighteen dogs and seven cats that I had rescued from the animal pound. But despite all those animals, Aimee wanted another: a yellow Labrador. She was determined, so I finally bought her a pup she named Sunshine. I also bought her a pony named Training Wheels, which she rode a little bit, and, as she grew older, a horse named Minor Detail.

But Aimee never seemed all that interested in horses. In fact, none of my kids cared much for them even though horses were and continue to be a core passion of mine. Reality was, Aimee wanted rats, snakes, and birds for pets. Although that was difficult for me to relate to, I got her some that she kept in her bedroom. The part I really couldn't understand was how she could actually kill mice to feed her snake. I guess I'm a wimp when it comes to things like that.

Aimee took piano lessons for a while, but when I started to play and write music, she quit and took up the drums. There was an early, deep-running competition between my daughter and me. I also felt a great burden of criticism from Deed and his family. I had thought his mother and I were friends, and as I said, I loved her for being a wonderful grandmother to my daughter. Several times I had her stay with Aimee and me at Long Meadow to visit or to watch over Aimee when I had to work. However, although I received praise from her to my face, I was to find out later that she criticized me severely behind my back. Our tongues can be the smallest, most lethal weapons in our arsenal.

As I made more movies, I always tried to schedule them so that Aimee could join me on location. But there would be a time when she asked if I could please leave her at home . . . She didn't want to travel with me and attend new schools. I certainly could understand that since I had had such a hard time with new schools myself.

When Aimee was eight, she said she wanted to live with her dad. Deed remarried and had one son and another child on the way. It seemed his new wife was to Aimee what my aunt had been to me when I was Aimee's age. My aunt had animals and a garden and we did fun things together that my mom and I didn't share. Aimee's stepmom was more the hippie earth-mother type who baked, sewed, and stayed at home. I now understood how my interest in my aunt must have hurt my mother, because Aimee seemed to share a closeness with her stepmom that she and I didn't have . . . and that hurt. When Aimee expressed her desire to live with them, I was crushed. Because my parenting skills were based solely on what I had experienced as a child with my parents, I simply did not have the tools then to be the kind of mom I wanted to be or Aimee deserved.

I agreed to let her go to her dad's because she seemed so set on it—I truly wanted her to be happy. Unfortunately, when she called Deed, all excited about her plans, her father said he wouldn't take her. It broke Aimee's heart. It appeared now that she'd have to make do with me.

Around this time I was in rehearsal in Los Angeles for a picture with Elliot Gould called *Whiffs* when I was slotted to do Johnny Carson's show. As always, the producers wanted to do a preshow interview to go over what I would discuss with Johnny. I was in one of my "let's push Jennifer to the limit" moods and told my agency (then William Morris) that I would sing on the show. The agency said, "We didn't know you could sing." "Sure I do," I said, hoping I could speak it into being with confidence. The agency called up *The Tonight Show* and the response was "Great, we didn't know she sings. Have her come in tomorrow for rehearsal with Doc Severinsen."

Although I was in the middle of rehearsing for my film, I had to find a song to prepare by the next day. Doing *The Tonight Show* was second only to appearing on the Academy Awards as far as numbers of viewers and massive exposure. It was always nerve-racking because of the clout the show carried. The first time I did *The Tonight Show* was when it still was being shot in New York City. My mom met me at my dressing room to help me get ready. I had called her in a panic because I was going to wear a clingy pink Halston dress and was sure I would perspire right through it from nerves. I asked Mom to bring some antiperspirant deodorant. She brought four different kinds and I put them all on, layer after layer, until my armpits were literally stuck to my sides.

Everything seemed to be under control as Mom and I were ushered to the green room to watch the beginning of the show. Just as I was settling down, we were offered a glass of wine. Mom took hers and inadvertently spilled it all down the front of my outfit. So there I was, standing in the wings about to go on with Johnny Carson and Ed McMahon for the first time, with the wardrobe lady madly trying to dry my dress with a hair dryer.

All I heard was "Please welcome Miss Jennifer O'Neill!" and

someone shoved me out onstage. I made it through the kissing-greeting part and settled into my seat. During all the many times I did that show, both Johnny and Ed were as delightful with me as they were that first night. I was chatting about I can't remember what when it happened . . . I felt an explosion of perspiration flowing down my arms. The tension was just too much, even though my armpits were glued together. Horrified, I looked down midstory to find dark pools gathering on my arms. I didn't have the experience at that stage to point out my dilemma and make light of it on the show, so I suffered in silence, bumbling my story beyond recognition.

And now—oh, boy—the song. I had called Mom up for her thoughts only a day before the show. "You're going to do what?" She was surprised. "I'm going to sing on the Carson show tomorrow night." "Oh, Jen . . . I didn't know you sang." Mom was already suffering with me. We decided on the song "The Look of Love" because Mom said not to sing anything famous like a Streisand tune, so the audience wouldn't compare voices; her message to me was loud and clear.

I couldn't find the sheet music of the song anywhere and Mom and I couldn't remember all the lyrics, but finally a friend came up with a ratty old copy, so at least I could read all of the words. I was still learning them as I arrived at the studio that day. At the entrance was an enormous monitor airing the rehearsal in progress, and as the door swung open, I saw Johnny Mathis on the screen holding a note for eternity as he was finishing his number . . . I was not only going to be singing on the Johnny Carson show, but I was going to be singing on the Johnny Carson show with Johnny Mathis singing on the Johnny Carson show! Bad idea.

As I gingerly entered the stage area, Johnny Mathis bellowed across the floor, "Jennifer, I didn't know you could sing. Mind if I stay for rehearsal and listen?" I didn't even know this man and he was being supportive. I was dying. Just then I turned to see not one but a fleet of agents from William Morris moving toward me, their arms outstretched in Hollywood's greeting . . . And yes, they were all saying that they didn't know I could sing.

Mathis's players were leaving the house band with their piles of arrangement sheets when I handed Doc Severinsen my ratty piece of paper. "I hear you're going to sing with me tonight," Doc said, nodding his head in encouragement. "I didn't know you were a singer!" I felt like I was going to faint . . . "What key?" he asked. *"Low,"* I replied.

I had never held a mike for a live performance before and my lips were already starting to gyrate from nerves. And suddenly there I was standing in the middle of the stage, trying to strike a Sinatra pose while singing "The Look of Love" in front of half my agency and Johnny Mathis. Well, singing actually isn't exactly the right word; I was making various unrelated noises totally off-key. This was my first public experience with my "goat voice." Doc stopped the band. "Sorry, Jennifer, my fault. I'll drop the key lower." He smiled again, but this time not so enthusiastically.

"Lower" didn't help a bit as I limped through the song. I had already decided that I couldn't bear to make such a spectacle of myself on national TV when I saw the show's producer moving rapidly in my direction with my league of agents and their furrowed brows close behind. Before I had a chance to tell the producer I wasn't going to sing, he attempted a pleasant expression as he said, "Jennifer, let's save it." I said, "Sure thing."

I just did my talk bit on the show that night, but after my debacle as a chanteuse, I was on a mission to get this singing thing organized. I hate when something intimidates me and I wanted to conquer my vocal fears. I loved music far too much to be afraid of it. I had danced and sung two duets with Tom Jones on a TV show (*The London Bridge Special*) in which we co-starred and I later had a recording deal with Famous Music for about a minute and a half . . . The company folded after I cut my first songs for them and I have always joked that I was single-handedly responsible for its demise. Except for a rare few such as Streisand, Kristofferson, and Liza, performers don't usually succeed both as singers and actors. It's hard enough to build one career, let alone two.

After the Carson fiasco, I called William Morris and told them

I wanted to do a nightclub act and to please find me a director and book me somewhere. They reluctantly complied, and before I knew it, I had choreographed myself into another one of my famous corners. The agency set me to open at a hotel in Puerto Rico in three and a half weeks! Thankfully they found a director with an impressive reputation to work with me. His name was Nick and he was an absolute slave driver. He was also about to become my next husband.

fourteen
FOREIGN TERRITORIES

WE arrived at the hotel in Puerto Rico like a long-lost caravan of wandering gnomes. This excursion of mine to do a nightclub act intrigued my daughter, particularly as she considered the sun, fun, and swimming that came along with it . . . *And,* our own condo overlooking the ocean—Aimee was raring to join me on this one. I brought my dogs Sally and Samantha with us to round out the homey feeling.

Nick told me I was in for the workout of my life and he was not exaggerating. To write, mount, and rehearse a two-hour, one-woman song-and-dance show within a few weeks' time is an awesome feat for a pro, let alone a first-timer. Relying on his expertise, I welcomed Nick not only as the director but the choreographer as well . . . Sort of a road-show Bob Fosse.

We argued, we screamed, we laughed, we cried our way through the days leading up to the looming deadline. I don't think I've ever been so tired and sore. I was either going to make it or break it, he said, and "break" wasn't in my vocabulary. Nick had me singing everything from some of my original songs to "La Bamba," but when he said he wanted me to sing "Tea for Two," I flipped. It just seemed too corny and old-fashioned. But as it turned out, he was right. It was probably my best number in the entire show because of the way he staged it—very *very* slow, low, and sexy, sitting on a stool wooing the audience. The dance numbers ran from broad and energetic to undulating. I had never worked with anyone who had the kind of precision, energy, and vision Nick had. Frankly, I had never met anyone like Nick, period . . . And he seemed quite fascinated with me as well.

Nick was the first person I'd ever known who was totally excited and supportive of me as a performer. Not only did he want me to succeed, he expected me to be nothing less than brilliant. He instilled in me unequaled confidence and a sense of rare beauty: I felt very appreciated. Nick was also used to running the show, literally, so he was extremely dominant and stubborn. I liked the dominant part. Still, there were times I could have killed him at the end of our marathon eighteen-hour rehearsal days and nights. I know he respected me for never giving up, and he was determined to harness what he called my "raw talent." As my opening date neared, I actually felt ready and able to do a professional show.

Nick's musical arranger flew down to Puerto Rico once we'd chosen all of the material. Since our booking was in a new hotel, the stage literally was being built around us as we rehearsed the show. What that meant was little rehearsal time with my band and none at all with lights and sound before opening night. Nick would scream at me that I was not making a movie—that no matter what, the show must go on. In other words, I couldn't stop and ask for another take if things didn't feel right. My biggest worry was my infamous goat voice, which reared its ugly head whenever I became very nervous. Would it attack me during the show? I told Nick that if it started, there was no controlling it except by stopping. Nick exploded: "No stopping! . . . Ever!" In his wisdom, he decided to have me open the show with a huge song-and-dance number so if my voice started to wobble, it wouldn't be noticeable as I whirled, leaped, and spun around the stage. Thanks to all my performances at Mom and Dad's parties, the leaping part was easy for me. I was a very good dancer with a leg extension for kicks that wowed even Nick—and that was saying something.

Opening night was packed. I stood backstage literally shaking in my black high-heeled boots as I pondered my predicament. Aimee, Sally, and Samantha were lined up next to me as a support team, but no breathing pattern or meditation technique I tried would quiet my nerves. Then I wondered why I did these kinds of torturous things to myself. There was no place to run, no place to hide . . . *Boom.* Applause . . . "Please welcome Miss Jennifer O'Neill!" . . . Music . . . Cue . . . And suddenly I was on the fly, dancing across the stage in a whirl of movement amid a cacophony of sound. The song accompanying me was "Bird of Beauty" by Stevie Wonder, and the choreography made this the toughest number of the evening. Blinded by the lights I had never rehearsed with, I groped for the stage boundaries yet somehow managed to keep dancing. Although my goat voice was there, I was too busy flying through the air for anyone to notice my failing vocals.

The opening number ended in waves of applause. Wow, what a feeling! A live audience was actually interacting with every move I made—and I liked it. Next, Nick planned for me a short "rap" while the guests settled into the evening, and I settled into me. My following number was "Tea for Two," and after I talked and the audience laughed, I pulled the stool up for my ballad. *Please . . . please . . . please, voice, just don't start goating around,* I silently chanted to myself. I heard my first notes and relaxed. I sounded great! On key! Solid! . . . So—*why was everyone laughing?* A snicker started in the audience and traveled through the room like wildfire across a drought-ridden range. All I could think of was Nick saying, "No matter what happens, don't stop. I don't care if your bra breaks, your costume falls off, you sprain your ankle, or you hate me, *don't stop!*" And as the sound of laughter grew stronger, *all* I wanted to do was stop.

I didn't understand until I finally saw, out of the corner of my eye, my dog Samantha wagging her way across the stage as I sang the guts out in this torch song. I wanted to tell the band to hold up, but I remembered Nick's command: "Don't stop." I had no options; the more I sang, the more my dog begged me for at least a pat. And then came the *next* distraction: my daughter stood on the side of the stage, clapping her hands frantically, pleading with Samantha to come to her. This went on through the entire "Tea for Two" number—which was a smash hit! The audience thought the dog was a brilliant setup. I received a standing ovation for my trouble, and in the end the show was a huge success.

Everything Nick and I did happened in a whirlwind of intensity. The brief but constant period of rehearsals for the show threw us into a high pitch of emotion. In general, putting on an act requires pulling out all the stops, including those between artist and director. In our case, the experience left Nick and me emotionally raw and involved with each other on a personal level. We married within a few months.

I was as sure as the sun rises that I was in love again with Nick, even when he confessed to me just before we were married that he was gay. I assumed if we were getting married, that meant he "used to be" gay. I appreciated his candor, and for me our plans had been made and I didn't feel I could change them. But one thing was clear, *used to be* gay was a must. If Nick and I were going to be married, obviously he couldn't continue to be so and he assured me his gay life was a thing of his past.

Our marriage was a short and at times wonderful interlude before reality, as always, came crashing in. Nick was a control freak who had met another control freak—me. My first European film opportunity came up virtually moments after we were married and we were off to Sicily before the remains of our wedding cake could be sliced up and put in the freezer.

Nick's parents were much older than mine. Nick had arrived late in their lives, and "Mama" absolutely adored and spoiled her last son. Mama and Dad were of Italian descent, born in the old country, and absolutely the sweetest people I'd ever met. Mama doted on Nick and had sewn the costumes for all the shows he had directed and danced in since he was a kid. Yet again, there seemed to be maternal attachments that distanced me from my husband, as well as his "past preferences" that bothered me in a place I couldn't identify. I was in foreign territory.

The shooting of my first film in Europe, *Gentle People*, directed by the renowned Zampa, starring Franco Nero and James Mason, was very difficult. Nick accompanied me to serve as a support system, but in short order found that he hated being relegated to the sidelines. It was his calling to direct, and this complex, creative guy couldn't easily take a secondary role. He was very emotional about expressing his displeasure and anger at finding himself in such a position.

James Mason was another one of those legendary actors whom I felt very grateful to work with. He was a gentleman both on and off the set, portraying his character with precision and elegance. Franco, on the other hand, seemed to have his nose out of joint because, although he had enormous European name value, I was the lead in the film and he was hired for a supporting role. For whatever reason, Franco felt an almost daily need to tell me how much money the producers were paying him—much more than I was being paid—for his relatively small role in the film.

And then there was our love scene. The shooting of any love scene is always awkward—at least for me. "Acting" intimate in a roomful of people with a fellow actor you're not in love with, starting and stopping at the words "action" and "cut," is difficult enough, but if your partner in the scene needs to brush his teeth or take a bath, the experience can be particularly unpleasant. In that regard, Franco was a Sicilian with shower habits that left everything to be desired. It was a pungent day on the set no matter how handsome he was or how much he was paid.

By the end of the movie, Nick decided he needed to pursue his own career in the States as I was pursuing mine in Italy. It was right that his career was a priority, but again, separation rarely helps a marriage. In addition, he found Long Meadow Farm and Aimee overwhelming, and as hard as he tried to fit in . . . well, it was a bit of round-peg-in-square-hole situation. Nick's mother accompanied me to Europe in Nick's absence for my next film, which was to be directed by Luchino Visconti. God bless her, at seventy-plus years, to be doing that for her son—although I believe she was also thrilled for the chance to revisit her homeland. She came to help me watch over Aimee, who was put in the American School in Rome during the five-month shoot.

To be chosen for a role in *L'Innocente* was an honor beyond my wildest dreams, because in my mind, Visconti was *the* master filmmaker of the era. With only ten movies to his credit, his main work had been creating extraordinary operas on the stage. Visconti's ten films included many masterworks, from *Death in Venice* to *The Damned* to *The Leopard*. *L'Innocente* was this great auteur's last film before his death, and even at age twenty-six, I appreciated being in the presence of so great a genius. He had already suffered a stroke when we shot the film and performed his directorial wizardry, half-paralyzed, from a wheelchair. I'll always remember his amazing eyes—transparent, deep blue caverns, full of knowledge and wisdom. And when I met him at his villa to discuss my role, I knew if I were cast, the change in my life would be major. More than a new part, working with Visconti meant a transcendence of one's old sensibilities.

It was 1974 when my agent, a European William Morris rep, accompanied me on the two-hour motor ride outside of Rome to meet with the master on his new film, starring Giancarlo Giannini (of *Swept Away* fame). The story of *L'Innocente* was based on a seventeenth-century novel dealing with infidelity, in which the breakdown of a marriage brings death to the "innocent." Working in Europe at that time heightened my awareness of the arts and enhanced my feeling for and knowledge of history. It meant more than stretching my imagination beyond the language and politics, it opened me up as an artist and a woman in a manner I had never experienced before.

While I sat with Visconti in his villa discussing my role as the mistress in a three-character story, I waited for my agent to speak about the potential nude scenes. Although this subject was of ongoing concern to me in American-made movies, European films held even fewer restrictions on nudity. My agent refused to address the issue with the director, as he was afraid I would lose the coveted role, so I was forced to question Visconti. After my bumbling discourse, the great director seemed almost amused at my plight and merely said, "Don't be preoccupied, the other one will do it." His eyes twinkled and the subject was closed. "The other one" meant Laura Antonelli, who was playing the role of the wife, would do the naked scenes. This was all very interesting because

Laura had started her career in porno pictures and had only recently been considered lead-actress material. (By the way, I thought she did a wonderful acting job in her role.) When the film was finished, it was shown in the main theater at the Cannes Film Festival after Visconti's death and the reviews were superlative. Most critics noted how brilliant it was of Visconti to have the mistress (me) covered up to her neck in lace while the wife's bed scenes with Giannini were extremely erotic . . . I laughed . . . I really laughed.

Every moment of work on Signor Visconti's film was a gift. I studied editing with him and we became friends. He loved horses and I drew a portrait of him, which he seemed quite taken with when I presented it as a gift at the end of the shoot. But there were also some difficult times intermingled with the excitement. To begin with, I spoke absolutely no Italian when I arrived on the set. Giannini, with whom I had all my scenes, spoke absolutely no English. The dialogue was lengthy and complex, and we each had to deliver it to an actor who didn't understand what the other was saying. But Visconti didn't seem the least bit concerned over the language barrier, as most films shot in Europe are dubbed into various languages in the end. My director told me that I had a week before I began to shoot to learn my lines in English set amid Italian cues and that he would have a dialogue coach assist me with that task.

I worked like a dog learning that script and following my coach's lead, I believed I had a handle on the technique. But a problem arose on my very first day of shooting. Visconti never rehearsed scenes, which was difficult for me to deal with as an actress. The point was, I hadn't worked at all with Giannini prior to the day we began filming. I didn't know him in the slightest, and we were playing lovers with a long history. Visconti apologized for the fact that I was being forced to shoot the death scene on my first day on the set, a necessary recourse because of location scheduling. Again, the twinkle in his eye preceded his word of sympathy. *"Poverito,"* he said. "Poor baby."

Five hours of makeup and hair styling were required every day to ready me for the period-costume look, with corsets that literally took my breath away. So there I was on the set of a Visconti epic, about to do the final death scene, surrounded by a non-English-speaking crew and an actor I couldn't even say good morning to. "Action" was called and I rushed into the sumptuous room to settle on my mark for the scene, a chaise longue by the fire. I remember feeling thankful for all my dance classes, as I was sure I wouldn't have been able to handle the voluminous period dress with any grace without that training.

Visconti was so obsessed with period authenticity that he and the costumer actually discussed the fact that I shaved under my arms and seventeenth-century women did not. Despite their request, I refused to grow armpit hair for the role—that meant I could not raise my arms during my descent onto the lounge—and that made my movements even more difficult. I was struggling when Giannini (in character) entered the scene, handing me a glass of wine before our dialogue started. I drank from the glass, expecting the normal grape juice that is used in Hollywood, but I was filming in Europe where they serve wine at lunch and dinner even when working. The point is, it wasn't grape juice, it was real wine and I gagged on my first swallow, all the while trying to look cool and elegant.

In the midst of attempting to keep my armpits hidden and recover from my wine surprise, the second major glitch hit me the moment Giannini started his dialogue. He spoke his lines so fast in Italian, I didn't have the foggiest idea what he was saying, let alone "where" he was in the scene. When I'd worked with the dialogue coach, he spoke the Italian lines very slowly so I could find my cue, but Giannini's speech at his normal pace sounded like Daffy Duck on speed.

I just sat there with my mouth hanging open, holding my glass of wine, totally lost, staring stupidly at Visconti. But what was really amazing was that after the first few days of shooting with Giannini and listening (as the Duke had told me to), there was absolutely no language barrier between us whatsoever. In fact, I believe I did some of my best work in that film, never totally understanding my costar's lines but just reacting to him.

Nick's mother returned to the States about halfway through the shoot. Things had disintegrated between Nick and me to the point of separation and she wanted to go home to him; our divorce was just a formality at that point. How did I feel? . . . Numb. It's a fact of life that one can become accustomed to almost anything, and failed relationships didn't surprise me anymore.

As everything was falling apart, I was glad I had brought my dog Samantha and my cat Oscar to Rome with us for company. At the end of the day, I would come back from work to find Oscar hanging like a bat off of the grass-cloth-covered ceilings and walls. (He was furious I'd left his mate, Renée, home, and let me know his feelings by tearing the walls to shreds.)

Now that Nick's mom had left Rome, my routine was to take Aimee to school at 7:30 A.M. (accompanied by Samantha), then grab a cab over to a riding stable on the outskirts of Rome where the soccer matches in the Olympic Stadium were played, ride "Roberto," a jumper I had leased, go home, bathe, and arrive at the set by eleven to prepare to shoot until seven P.M. Fortunately for me, this was not the normal twelve-to-sixteen-hour movie-shoot day—the extremely gentle schedule was due to Visconti's failing health. I hired a nanny to fetch Aimee from school and give her dinner before I returned to our residence next to the zoo in Rome's main park for her bedtime. And so it went for the next few months.

Europeans have an entirely different view of animals than Americans do. For example, in Europe, dogs may accompany their owners into the best restaurants, while their treatment of pets can be frightening compared with U.S. standards. This may be because Europeans have seen the ravages of war at their back door and have struggled so often for life and food that animals are not such a priority to them. Nonetheless, some of the conditions I saw animals suffer seemed less than humane.

So when I lost Samantha while working on *L'Innocente*, I just about lost my mind. My dog accompanied me to the set in my private car every day; she was my best friend and I adored her. She stayed in my dressing room when she wasn't playing with the drivers and crew outside or overseeing my purse by my cast chair. A mixed shepherd collie, Samantha was as smart as a whip and a total charmer from the day she hit the ground. She was entirely dedicated to me, unlike her mama dog, Sally, who would suck up to anyone who had a bone or a pat to offer. Sally was cute but unreliable; still I loved her to pieces. (I had her for eighteen years.) As my life was unraveling, it seemed I found far more consistency with my pets than with any of the human relationships I had.

According to my driver, Franco, for no apparent reason, Samantha ran out of my dressing room that afternoon, through the building, and down into the heavy Friday-afternoon traffic in the middle of Rome. To this day, I believe someone must have frightened or threatened her, because she *never* left my side or my dressing room if I was on set. I was working amid one-hundred-plus extras in a huge dance scene when my driver told me about Samantha running away—I was gone without a word to anyone. In costume, I ran through the streets of Rome looking for her. I was hysterical, my tiara was askew, and my makeup and dress had wilted by the time I returned fifteen minutes later to see if she had somehow returned to the set . . . But Samantha had simply vanished.

Shooting couldn't continue without me and every minute wasted cost the production a fortune. Back in my dressing room, I was inconsolable; my makeup was smeared from crying, my eyes were swelling fast and furiously when I was told that the director had called me back to the set.

This was one of the longest walks of my life; in my mind I can still see the extras, in full costume, parting to allow me to pass. Visconti happened to be sitting in his wheelchair under an arc light, which shed an almost celestial illumination about him as he watched me advance. Once I reached him, I burst into tears, the story of my lost dog spilling out in wails and moans. This was a "could hear a pin drop" moment as the entourage of producers, agents, crew, and extras waited for the director's response. In the past, Visconti had been famous not only for his immense talent but also for his explosive temper. But for whatever reason, he showed mercy on me and told me to take his personal driver to look for my dog. Then he dismissed a hundred extras and called the day a wrap . . . He was so kind.

I never found Samantha, although I searched for her for three months and offered major rewards on Italian television, radio, and press for her return. It was as if some force plucked her off the face of the earth. I believe I saw every stray dog within a fifty-mile radius of Rome, but Samantha was gone as if she had never existed. There was an actor in *L'Innocente* who lived in my residence and took on the task of searching for my dog with me. His name was Marc and he played the part of the author in *L'Innocente*. He was French but spoke perfect Italian and English—with no accent to boot—and was a totally handsome scamp.

He was engaged when I met him, but then his fiancée left him and my life changed again in a way that surprised even me. I'm always amazed by the experiences that bring people together— emergencies are on the top of the list for throwing people into each other's arms. But perhaps because we are so needy during such times of crisis, the relationships they inspire often have the shortest runs.

In any case, Marc was charming, funny, and mischievous to the bone . . . a wiry, sexy Olympic boxer who had been born in Sweden, a European James Dean who was an expert in film history, music, and ways to make a girl wonder. He drove me around Rome after filming together every day, looking for my dog, taking me into the various quarters in town. He knew nearly everyone he ran into at restaurants, all the "underworld" denizens and the gypsies who ran the streets. It was a whole different world for me; I was always a bit off balance with Marc because he spoke languages I didn't. Clearly, we met on his turf, and he liked it that way.

Marc moved me in what I thought were all the important ways. He was without question the most romantic man I had ever met. But there was more, the down side. My family used to say I was moody, but I was a piece of cake compared to the obnoxious side of Marc. The word "brat" springs to mind—guess it takes one to know one. Knowing Marc inspired me to "get over myself" in the moody department. And then there was that old syndrome of mine that always got me into so much trouble; Marc gave me a hard time and that fascinated me.

He asked me to marry him on our fourth outing in search of Samantha. I didn't respond at the time except for filing his request under my "wow, that's so romantic!" category. My dad had asked my mom to marry him on their second date, so I figured this could be a good omen, no? No. By the time we were cast as costars in our second picture together, Marc had visited my farm several times in the States. Aimee and I had visited him in Paris and met his mom and his little girl, who was Aimee's age. There was a hitch, however, in our courting ritual—my parents absolutely hated him. "This actor," they called him, "was a creep." And what my parents thought always carried a lot of weight with me.

They were right. Marc turned out to be the most irresponsible lightweight I was ever going to run into, but I was caught up by his charm and manipulated by his touch. This was a very sexy man. He would post "the banns" of our intended marriage on the doors of European churches, which always melted me. He wanted babies, which double-melted me, and he pursued me hard to have a child with him. Marriage had to come first for me, but with all Marc's intense courting, before we could arrange our wedding, I became pregnant. He was elated. A few weeks later I miscarried and he became totally furious at what he called "my womanly failure." Marc was someone who had jabbed at my conservatism with a hot poker and challenged me to give up some of my sexual hang-ups. The problem was, this guy was a boy, not a man. He was also a weaver of illusions that somehow kept me wanting more of what was to end in nothing.

He led me a merry chase for several years before we separated, and then he died of an overdose of heroin. At least that's what I was told by his mother, almost a year after I'd last spoken with him. In those days heroin, especially in France, was an inner sanctum death run of the "cool." When I met Marc, he told me he had a past in drugs, but he was "finished with all that." He lied with most every breath he took and in the end I knew that if I were to stay with him, I would die as well. He was doomed. Nothing scared me more than heroin and I was committed *never* to get near that nightmare. I never did.

I remember when Marc and I were to be married in Rome, I called my parents to ask for their blessing—Mom took an amazing stand on the phone. "If you marry that twerp, I swear to God I will never speak to you again . . . *never*! Now, you get on the next plane home and talk to your father and me." And I did just that, because, of course, even as an adult, nothing frightened me more than losing the approval of my parents.

I flew home, and called off the marriage. It was hard even for me to ignore Marc's outrageous behavior when I had the miscarriage, and when I was out of his presence I realized how much he actually scared me. To this day I'm grateful to Mom for bashing some sense into me. She always saw through Marc even if I couldn't. I believe my mom was truly worried for me, and it was one time when her threats of withdrawing her love worked in a positive fashion.

fifteen
WHIRLWINDS

A YEAR to the day after losing Samantha, I landed in the Rome airport for another of my Italian trips and found myself at a kennel by the airport. I had seen an advertisement along the road for German shepherds and was drawn to investigate.

The moment I saw Bête ("beast" in French), I knew she was going to be mine. Although she was supposed to be a trained protection dog, all she knew how to do was cower or bite. She was a small shepherd, bred in Germany out of working stock, but when I found her, she was being used as a brood bitch. Her face was a clone of Samantha's. It was almost eerie. This kennel's idea of training was to intimidate the animal into attacking with no obedience or control to back up the behavior. It was very sad. I had my hands full with this dog, but Bête and I bonded immediately.

It was after being put in school in Rome again for my second film shot in Siena that Aimee begged me to let her stay home from then on. She remained with me until we finished that movie and then headed home to Long Meadow Farm. I knew that Claudette was not up for caring for Aimee full-time (the two had never been really close), so I decided to hire a nanny. I wanted someone young and fun. Someone to be a loving, responsible pal for Aimee while I was gone as well as when I was home. I wanted to fill in the gaps for my daughter.

I know now that Aimee had had a hard time with Marc because

he and I were always in some sort of emotional hurricane and that worried her. What a hard thing for a little girl to go through at age nine . . . At the time I didn't think Aimee cared a lick about me. She seemed not to want to have much to do with me, and apparently she thought I felt the same way about her. We were both wrong. We just didn't know how to reach each other, and of course, I was the adult, so I take full responsibility for our failure to do so before many more complex issues pulled us even further apart—before they finally brought us together.

I hired a girl named Pam. She was in her early twenties, with long black hair and an absolutely delightful personality. There was a separate apartment in the back wing of the house that would accommodate her and her boyfriend. I thought twice about the "boyfriend" part, as John and Pam were not married, but they said they were engaged and planned to marry soon. (With my own track record, who was I to judge them?) What I was far more concerned about was that John was scheduled to serve a one-year jail term for a felony shortly after Pam intended to start working for me. When I think about it now, I cannot fathom how on earth I let this man into my house. What possessed me to allow someone who was about to do hard time step even a *toe* into my life? But then, John never looked or acted like a felon. In fact, as a package, Pam and John looked to be the most wholesome couple you could imagine. During Pam's interview, John brought up his impending jail sentence and promised that he would never come near my property if I was concerned about him or if by doing so, it would cost Pam her job. "She's been through so much," he said in a deep, emotional voice. He explained that he had been running a farm for several years after he'd gotten out of Vietnam—that's when he had leased one of his barns to a buddy. I had never met anyone who was in Vietnam, and John had his handy basket of heart-wrenching stories that could melt anyone on the one hand, or shock their pants off on the other: it all depended on the effect he was going for.

He continued his tale of woe by saying he had no idea the cars being stored in his barn were stolen, and when the police showed up, he ended up taking the fall instead of turning in his friend. By the time he finished, I actually felt John had been done a disservice and that, by watching out for his friend, he was the only one involved in the mess who was honorable. What can I say? John could sell ice to an Eskimo. He certainly sold himself to Pam and her entire family, who supported him one hundred percent. And now I was just as snowed by him as they were.

John came from a good family who lived in the same town where Deed grew up in Connecticut. His dad had a very successful career in advertising. According to John, he had chosen farming and dog training over numerous other careers only because he loved animals and the outdoors so much. Pam's mom ended up becoming my secretary, and suddenly I felt like there was one big blossoming family at Long Meadow Farm—my dream come true. I didn't have to marry anyone to create a family, I could borrow from everyone else's life. Aimee absolutely adored Pam and we created a support team for her as she bided her time without John. (He started his jail term immediately after I first met him.)

Pam's year alone exposed some sides of her that were disturbing to me, but then everything that was to unfold during this period of my life was unpredictable. The most consistent and reliable of all the newcomers was Pam's mom, Helen, who truly was a dear, hardworking woman. I was writing scripts and music and had a captive audience in Helen and Pam . . . My first screenplay, *Fanny and the White Knight,* had an MTV approach, which at the time was very innovative. I decided to write the music and lyrics to the film's score and never considered that I couldn't—even though I only plunked on the piano, didn't read music, and had never studied. Despite all my obstacles, CBS Records demoed the project and I was off on a creative twirl of marathon recordings and script and song rewrites. It was an exciting time. There was also a real camaraderie in this house full of menless women—everything was going along swimmingly until the end of John's jail stint.

When John came to the farm to live with Pam, our happy arrangement began to falter. There was strife between John and Pam from the moment he walked through the door. It was revealed that

Pam had had an affair with a woman in John's absence. Not only did that shock me, but John accepted it, which shocked me even more. I came to realize that Pam always had her eye on me sexually, an attraction she tended to verbally express when she was drinking too much. She did control herself under normal circumstances, however, knowing that a sexual relationship with me was never going to happen. And since she was always perfectly well behaved around Aimee, and my daughter absolutely adored her, I fell into the thinking that what Pam did on her own time was none of my business, as long as it didn't hurt anyone.

And then there were the extenuating circumstances. Pam had an extremely serious medical problem that involved allergies; she would go into anaphylactic shock that could literally kill her at any given moment. The fact that Pam seemed to be living on borrowed time made her sometimes erratic behavior more excusable, or at least understandable. Watching the ambulance take her off into the night had become an all-too-regular occurrence. It was just so frightening and hard on her. As for me, I was trying to repair myself from all my broken relationships by holding up in my room during creative binges . . . I was driven to try to produce something of substance and value—I just had to express myself in some meaningful way. My pace was frantic and I couldn't seem to slow down my restless nature. The emotional hole in me wasn't healing; if anything, it was getting bigger . . . But as with all untamed addictions, my need for love would again lead me by the nose soon enough.

At the prompting of everyone in the household, I became partners with John in a dog-training business and built a kennel on the farm. This seemed like a great idea—I loved the dogs, John promised big financial returns, and Pam was happy to have him working at home so he could be near her. (She had given up her relationship with the other woman.) Aimee couldn't wait to spend time with John, who took on the role of a stand-in dad since he was the only man on the farm. He also unofficially oversaw the farm duties and supervised Long Meadow at large. John was a natural and was comfortable handling the horses even though he didn't ride. He was also an excellent dog trainer and always gave me the sense that he was taking care of things in my absence as if they were his own. I later learned that ownership was his plan all along. I always responded positively to the sense of being protected because I've never really felt that way, so whenever a man came along and offered that service, I was like a kid on Christmas morning.

James Michener's *Caravans* was one of the bigger films being cast in Hollywood in 1978. My agent called and said the director wanted to meet me at my farm to talk about the project. It was to be a five-month shoot in the desert in Iran. The bottom line was, they were interested in my doing the film because they knew I was an athlete and the location promised to be a test of fortitude. The filmmakers felt I would be tough enough to stand the rigors of the climate and culture, which I took as a huge compliment. My co-stars would be Anthony Quinn and Michael Sarrazin, with whom I had worked on *The Reincarnation of Peter Proud*. The studio wanted to pair us up again since *Reincarnation* had been a big box-office hit. I was told I would need to wear a blond wig in the film to be true to the novel's character . . . I accepted. Besides, I'd always wanted to be a blonde. Also, the money was great and the location sounded interesting. Of course, no one had a clue that in a matter of months the Shah of Iran would be deposed by the Ayatollah Khomeini.

Everyone at home assured me that if I took the film, Long Meadow Farm would be taken care of from house to stable, and Aimee would be well watched over. (She *really* didn't want to go on this location!) Everyone said I should go and take the film, they insisted, giving me their united word of honor. Deed and his new family got along fabulously with Pam and everything seemed to point to my being able to depart without a worry. John had re-trained Bête into an incredible personal protection dog. I was so proud of her and felt safe in her presence.

I took Bête and Heinz with me to Iran. Heinz was a hundred-plus-pound German shepherd straight off the police force. Bête had already proven her talents by warding off a mugger one night in the park in Rome. Some guy ran up from behind me to grab my purse while Bête was off in the bushes. She appeared on her own out of nowhere and valiantly attacked the assailant. We all fell in a heap on the ground. In a panic, I got all my German Shutzen commands backward: *fosse* mean "off," *füse* means "attack." Despite my blubbering, Bête nailed the guy by the arm and pinned him to the ground. Her tendency was to attack more like a Doberman, which goes for the throat, than a shepherd. As we all floundered on the ground, I could see she was about to lunge at my assailant's throat. All the fancy German words and training left me and the only thing that escaped my mouth was *no!* Bête let go of the man, who ran off terrified; I doubted he'd be grabbing for any more purses in the near future. It was then that I realized my nifty little shepherd was really a lethal weapon in a fur coat. For herself, Bête was meek and mild, but as my protector, she was an irresistible force. She would be ever by my side for the next fifteen years. As far as Heinz went, he was a full-fledged walking shield, and between the two dogs, John said I would be well protected on my trip to the Middle East.

I had traveled a lot in my life and I perceived this trip would be just another adventure. After all, how different could one place be from another? As things turned out, it was like going to the moon. I hadn't realized before I traveled there that Iran was saturated in drugs. Anyone over sixty could legally get morphine-based drugs . . . Grandparents were very welcome in their children's homes in Iran. Most everyone was hooked and there was a general absence of honor and morals that made my stay one of the most frightening experiences I have ever endured. Five days after I left the country, the overthrow took place. Getting out of a falling building always provides a good time to reassess one's life.

The *Caravans* shoot promised to be difficult, but it was even worse than I imagined. We had an amazing crew from all around Europe (mostly England). Everyone was as strong as an ox, yet most of us became very ill. My normal weight was about one hundred and twenty pounds. When I got back from Iran, I weighed a fraction over a hundred and was sick as a dog. And speaking of dogs, mine weren't in much better shape. We were all in a stress state that is difficult to describe. It wasn't just the bad water and unfamiliar food, it was the tension and stress of being in the middle of a live minefield: Iran was going to erupt any moment and you could taste it.

The film was co-produced by the Iranian government, so all involved with the production were dealing with politics as well as filmmaking. I was able to sidestep some invitations to the palace, using my dogs as an excuse, but I recall one dinner invitation I couldn't decline. When asked to attend by not only the royalty but by the producers of the film, I tried to say I couldn't leave my dogs in the hotel. It didn't fly this time because the princess informed me that her family would be sending a private car for my dogs and me so I would be sure to appear at their festivities. And thus my dogs attended a black-tie sit-down dinner at the palace, even though Iranians hate dogs . . . While I was in their country, I saw dogs spinning and vomiting in the streets, having been poisoned by animal-control officers. It was disgusting. (Cats, on the other hand, are revered in Iran and run rampant about town.) I did realize the animal atrocities were the least of the problems going on in that country.

Michener's novel focused on a happy caravan, which became the backdrop for a political love story. While shooting the film, the Buluchi and Kashki tribes were hired to portray the carefree little caravan. The only problem with using these tribes as extras was that they had been arch enemies for centuries. An average day on the set consisted of people madly running to the Porta Potties with crippling diarrhea from the food, and stone and fist fights between the two tribes. An ambulance was called to the set on a regular basis helmed by the set doctor, who wore a long black cloak; this incompetent character misdiagnosed everyone and everything. One of his bigger flubs was insisting that my wardrobe lady wasn't sick, but rather that she was suffering the effects of pregnancy. He offered this diagnosis *after* she told him she had had a hysterectomy.

We had prepared for months to choreograph and shoot the film's epic flood scene. A dam had been built, all sixteen cameras were set, and the caravan was gathered to cross the roaring waters. I was to do my own stunt, which consisted of carrying a twelve-year-old child on horseback halfway across the river, then making the horse rear, falling into the water, and then dragging the child to the safety of the riverbank. While all this was happening, the rest of the caravan would be attempting to cross the perilous rapids. This entire sequence was a one-shot, one-time deal.

I started into the waters with my horse dodging goats, mules, and people being swept down the river. As I made my horse rear, I became aware that two very important things had not been accounted for—one: the child who was with me didn't know how to swim, so when she hit the water, she was terrified and pulled me under in her panic, and two: when the seven skirts of my costume got wet, their weight felt like I was wearing a cement suit. Both the girl and I almost drowned before we were fished out of the water downstream.

What was equally ridiculous was that right in the middle of the flood shot, Princess Ashraph, the Shah's sister, arrived with her entourage to watch the filming. As her limo pulled up, the tribespeople recognized her, and wherever they were—on camel back, floundering around midrapids, pulling others out of the waters, etc.—they all stopped and started bowing to their royal princess. As a result, many animals were lost and most of the flood sequence could not be used.

On the costar front, I soon found out that Anthony Quinn was a real piece of work wrapped up in a star ego. I certainly respected him as a wonderful actor and great survivor of the film business, but I saw little to respect in his methods of achievement in either arena. As an actor, I found him to be self-serving and stingy with his fellow performers. Quinn, of course, was playing the head of the caravan, a character who dies at the end of Michener's novel. However, Quinn decided he didn't want to die in the movie because he had just died in *The Greek Tycoon*. But what was more outrageous was how he went about getting his way.

In my typical fashion, I went to see all of the rushes after work every day. There were multiple problems with the shoot and everyone had legitimate gripes to voice in the up-and-coming production meeting we all were set to attend. Quinn had arrived one month later on set than anyone else, so we all looked to him for some fresh ideas and guidance. He had me fill him in on all the past and present details and assured me, after many a meeting, that he would take care of every one of my concerns. We had reached a point in filming when it would be financially disastrous to fire Quinn, and he knew this. Thus, he chose that meeting to deliver his power speech and not address any of the relevant issues. Rather, he informed everyone that he had decided his character was not to die, and with that in mind, the biggest problem facing everyone on the set was coming up with rewrites in order to accommodate his desires. With that, he simply walked out of the room. I didn't know whether to cry or applaud. It was, after all, a brilliant performance.

Once the power play had time to register with the producer, the next question was who to kill instead of Quinn. I immediately piped up, "Me. I'm not having more fun as a blonde." They took me at my word and blew me up at the end of the movie.

I had been divorced from Nick for about three years when I met Jeff. My thirtieth birthday was celebrated on the set of *Cloud Dancer,* a film I was shooting with David Carradine in Arizona. On my way back home through L.A., a mutual friend set up a meeting between Jeff and me, thinking we might like each other. I would say that Jeff is one of the most sensitive individuals ever to walk the planet, a romantic to the core. His craft was songwriting and he had embraced incredible success for his efforts at the keyboard—he was respected by his peers and friends alike. When I met him, he was also on the rebound from a long relationship with a very well-known actress. Jeff and I related to each other instantly because I, too, was on the rebound from Marc, so we commiserated with each other. What a perfect setup for bad judgment and big fantasies for two such as we.

Jeff actually earned a paycheck, owned his own house in Bel Air, and led a reasonable and meaningful life. His two children were delightful and happened to be about Aimee's age. Add all the perfect pieces that fit into the puzzle, including our shared propensity for hasty marriages—he, too, had several "priors" under his belt—and we were headed down the aisle.

It turned out that being friends, having kids of similar ages, and sharing interests in both film and music does not a marriage make. Add bicoastal living with long absences that began only days after we were married and . . . you guessed it . . . trouble in paradise. Again.

Not long ago I had the opportunity to run into Jeff in Nashville. We found each other to be happily remarried after twenty years had passed . . . I was so pleased that I had the chance to apologize to this nice man for my part in the breakup of our short marriage. Once I realized that we had made a mistake by trying to turn our brief friendship into a lifelong commitment, I became depressed and unmanageable. Jeff told me that I overwhelmed him when we were married. He felt unworthy of everything—my farm, my career, my celebrity, my intense personality. He explained that he had been totally intimidated by me, to the point of not functioning, and the less he functioned, the more abandoned and angry I felt. I beame impossible. Jeff and I cried and laughed and forgave each other in that chance meeting and I am so very grateful that we had that moment. I hold it as an honor in my heart to have known Jeff, even if the time we spent together was miscast.

Not long before we divorced, I went down to Kentucky to shoot a film with Lee Majors called *Steel* and became extremely ill. I had a serious uterine infection that left me with a lot of scar tissue and a dim prognosis for having any more children. I felt robbed. Deep down, I thought that I was being punished for having had the abortion years before as my life was slipping away between poor choices and poor health related to childbearing. I have enormous sympathy for couples who cannot bear children, and though I already had my daughter, I knew that there was much more to motherhood than I was experiencing. And I wanted it so badly.

We all grow up trying to figure out who we are and what we're supposed to do with our lives. We search ourselves for the meaning of life, but why are we asking *ourselves,* when we're the ones who are confused? No matter how much I studied, searched, insisted, or yearned, until I became aligned in right relationship with God, I was running in circles. I was insatiable. The truth is, there was not ever going to be anyone who could fill me up. I expected when the right man came along, he would make me whole. Now I know that no one can do that for someone else . . . *No one.* I have a dog that's particularly unhappy at being left at home, and when I close her inside, she'll scratch and eat right through the door in a total panic. My other dogs just wait for my return, sure I'll be back to love them and feed them. I was like the dog who tears down doors. It's very tough to deal with such frenzied behavior and there's no lack of destruction for anyone involved with such a person.

I thank God that He gave me a veritable iron machine for a body and a steel trap for a mind that didn't wear out from my boot-camp pace until I found a place to rest and a direction that had been perfectly planned out just for me. Unfortunately, I wasn't going to have a clue about that right relationship for the next eight years, which were to bear witness to some of the most dangerous episodes in my life, both emotionally and physically.

Meanwhile, "back at the farm," John's and my kennel business was not delivering the level of success he'd promised, and although Claudette made sure the household ran smoothly and Helen diligently watched over her secretarial duties, the sense of harmony we had known had slowly turned into discord. Aimee was yet again trying to digest her mother's most recently failed marriage. She moved closer to Pam and her father . . . and who could blame her?

I had a gift in a dear friend and accountant named Aaron, who watched over my finances. I felt secure in my ability to work and safe that my money was in honest hands. As things were later to fall apart in that realm, I realized how lucky I was to be acquainted with Aaron and able to rely on his expertise. My acting career was solid and my ongoing relationship with Cover Girl cosmetics filled in the financial cracks so I wouldn't have to take film work I didn't want to. Since the early seventies I had been under an annual contract with Cover Girl that provided me with a handsome fee for my participation in one commercial-and-print-ad campaign a year. My first work for the company was in a Noxema commercial shot at a train station when I was fifteen, and the rest was history. I believe I am as well known for my affiliation with that product as for any film work I have done. What a blessing for me for so many years.

I was home to spend a few months when I realized that Pam and John were having some very serious relationship problems. They never did get married and it appeared that they were never going to. Aimee was already suffering at the thought of John leaving. They had become such good friends and Pam was clearly still in love with John. Things were a mess, a veritable soap opera.

At this juncture another big movie deal, a space-travel film this time, came along from a major studio; it was to be a six-month shoot in L.A. that would require I commit to being in California for at least five out of the six months. My agents pressed hard for this job, as they felt it would be the studio's next huge box-office success. John agreed to stay at the farm and try to work things out with Pam while I was gone, and it was decided Claudette would accompany me to the coast. Again, Aimee begged to stay home with John and Pam and Helen, who would be there to oversee the day-to-day running of the household and her.

This major studio lot was the first one that ever required Bête to stay in my trailer; she was not allowed to accompany me on the set. Another less-than-favorable omen came when I arrived at hair and makeup the first day to be greeted by a roomful of surprised faces. It appeared that everyone thought I had blond hair. This was confusing. At that point I had made at least ten movies in my natural hair color and only *Caravans* in a blond wig, but apparently it was *Caravans* that had registered with the producers. I guess there's something to the old saying about being only as good or as bad—or as blond!—as your last film.

The thought of wearing a wig again for the next six months appealed to me about as much as thumbscrews, so I said they could cut my hair a little and dye it blond. After four separate trips to the salon for color that repeatedly was not light enough for them

(I started to think they really wanted Sandra Dee) my hair started to break off and turn green. This was going to be a big problem.

Aaron had come into L.A. to see one of his other clients, Chita Rivera, perform at a club and invited me and my agent to join him. It was always great to see Aaron, even if he didn't recognize me in my now blond-green short-cropped 'do. After a terrific evening, I was on my way home in my car with Bête when another car going in the opposite direction on Sunset Boulevard crossed over into my lane. I swerved to avoid hitting it and careened out of control, smashing into a parked car head-on.

I did have a sense of what was happening as the police and medics tried to pry me out of my car, but it all seemed so far away. I remember willing Bête to be still because she was protecting me and wouldn't let anyone in. I heard the policeman say he might have to shoot the dog if they couldn't get in the car—and then miraculously, Bête withdrew and they pulled me out, locking my dog into the soon-to-be-towed-away car.

My sense of detached observation continued throughout the ambulance ride as well as in the hospital. I could hear what everyone was saying and at times I could see them, but I didn't seem to be able to get my own body to respond to my commands. It was scary when I stopped breathing and all hell broke loose in the emergency room. They ripped my hospital gown open and started twisting my nipples to try to get me to respond. Very strange, I thought. They pounded hard on my chest . . . *very* hard. A breathing tube of some sort was being shoved down my throat with great difficulty. A nurse told the doctor/intern person handling the tube that it was meant for a man's much larger throat, but his response was, "What the hell." When I saw the electronic paddle prods headed my way—flashbacks of shock therapy—something woke up in me and my breathing returned, at which point I screamed for them to leave me alone. But it wasn't until I repeated to the doctors and nurses exactly what they all had said in detail while I was on the machine, unconscious and not breathing, that I got their attention.

Given my meditative out-of-body studies, I told myself the experience didn't surprise me, but today, I'll admit, I'm not sure what really happened. After I regained consciousness, the injuries I sustained amounted only to superficial bruising and a very sore chest from being pounded on. Unfortunately, the studio producers took the car accident as an excuse to fire me from the movie before the next day was over. Some get-well card. My agents were livid, as I had medical permission to return to work in only a few days. But really, it wasn't about my bruised arm; it was about my *green hair* and my *dog*. I was an inconvenience that they felt they had an opportunity to dump and they went for it. I had never been fired from anything in my career. It was very humiliating. It was only later in my life that I would learn to translate difficult events as humbling instead of humiliating, and so very long before I knew that God turns all things to good in His name. But for now I just felt miserable and embarrassed, and it was getting the best of me.

Once I had come to in the hospital, I sent my agent to get Bête from the wreckers, and as soon as I knew she was okay, I just wanted to close the entire chapter. My agent pushed for me to sue for damages, but I decided to take another movie instead, short hair and all—*A Force of One*, with Chuck Norris. By working, I destroyed my chances to recover any money for my losses, but I was determined to move on.

John picked me up from the hospital two days later. I was so surprised to see him there. Claudette and John were always very close and she had phoned him in a panic when she heard about my accident. John never told anyone at home I was hurt until he called Pam and Helen from the airport, already on his way out to L.A. The fact that he singularly made this decision to come to L.A. was unknown to me. He led me to believe it was a mutual decision.

So there he was, and in no time flat he was "protecting" me full-time—everything from speaking to agents and lawyers to picking up groceries. I was amazed at John's ability to move through various worlds with such ease. He took over everything and told me just to rest and heal. Claudette was pleased with his visit, happy to see someone treat me with care. And of course, John had worked her so well. John also told me that although it was over between Pam and him, he wanted to make sure I was all right and Aimee was settled before he moved on. But in truth, he never moved on; he simply moved *in*.

Pam left the farm before I returned home and Helen bridged the gap with Aimee at the house. It continued to astound me how fast things changed in life, at least in mine. Two years before, John came into my world as the boyfriend of my daughter's nanny, and within what felt like a blink of an eye, that "boyfriend" became my husband. John was a con artist to the bone—clear to the marrow—but I wasn't to know that for many years. If the energy he put into deceiving and manipulating people had been rerouted into positive endeavors, the sky would have been the limit for him. He had an uncanny knack for intuiting what someone needed and then supplying it before they even thought of asking. It's very difficult to get your arms around reality when your partner lies more easily and plausibly than he tells the truth.

But for the time being, Aimee and I seemed to have a real shot at becoming a family with John at the helm. My daughter and John were already very good friends, and that was an amazing joy to me. They would spend afternoons at the kennel, go errand shopping, or train her pets together—all the things she and I didn't do with each other—all the things a family should share.

John had also taken over managing my career and, as it turned out, my finances as well. Not long after we were married, Aaron asked me to come in to the city to meet him for lunch without John. Aaron had been working with John and me for about six months and had decided he'd better bow out of my life as an accountant so as to preserve our friendship. I was shocked; how could Cinderella lose her slipper? Aaron wouldn't go into much more detail about his reasons for ending our business relationship, since he was trying to be respectful of my marriage. I was to find out years later that his concerns were well founded, and that my error in judgment was going to have serious, in fact ruinous, consequences.

But in the meantime, everything seemed to be rolling along

smoothly. John promised me a baby, no two ways about it. He looked at me not long after our return from California and said that we were going to have a son, he was going to marry me, and I was finally going to be taken care of, protected, and happy. When I became pregnant shortly after we married, John already had his hooks buried deep into my soul. But the son didn't arrive right off. In fact, I ended up having to consult several fertility experts after my first three pregnancies with John ended in miscarriage. I was advised to have my tubes surgically "blown out," because of all the scar tissue. At that time I was also having crippling pain in my feet, a result of neuromas (tumors) on the nerves. Although painful, I was told this condition was also reparable by surgery. The procedure was to cut the nerves in my feet at the sites of the tumors, thereby avoiding any sensations of pain. "If it hurts, cut it off," I announced, trying to present a brave attitude. I was concerned about being out of commission for so long that my ability to work would suffer, so I opted to have the surgery performed on both feet in conjunction with the tubal laparoscopy.

Surgery on two feet rather than one put me in a wheelchair instead of crutches, but undergoing the ovarian surgery in tandem was even a bigger mistake. When the surgeons pumped dye into my ovarian tubes by incision through my navel, they distended my stomach with gas to allow observation and entry into the area. All the air that entered my body to allow the laparoscopy left masses of gas that now gathered in my stomach and required postop walking to disperse. The problem was, I couldn't walk after my foot surgery. Talk about being caught between a rock and a hard place. Since I couldn't stand, I couldn't pass the trapped air. I was doomed to agony.

The doctors prescribed for me the painkiller Percoset. As it turned out, Percoset was also the drug John had decided was the only cure for the post-Vietnam stress he apparently suffered from. And so it started . . . I healed, but I still had pills for my pain, which I gave to John for relief of his alleged headaches.

Just a few months after the operations, my agents called to offer me a movie of the week entitled *Love's Savage Fury,* Aaron Spelling's epic TV version of *Gone With the Wind.* I had never done TV, nor was I interested in doing it. In those days you were either a film actress or a TV actress, and never the twain should or would meet as far as I was concerned. But my agents insisted, pointing out the excellence of TV programming currently in production (the miniseries *Roots,* etc.) which they insisted was changing the complexion of TV. I finally accepted the role, hoping my ever-inventive agents weren't misguiding me in the name of a big paycheck.

The shoot was a period-costume piece filmed in Mississippi in incredibly humid heat. Again I was wearing a wig, because my hair was still recovering from the spiked-frog look it acquired from the studio dye job. I was also accustomed to a film schedule, which is leisurely compared with TV shows. But none of the above was important to me as long as the performance was there.

The director and I worked very closely on the project, reviewing rushes every night and rewriting as we went along to improve the script. I was pleased with the results, but when I was called in to dub and was shown a cut of the film in its entirety, I was shattered. The editors had butchered the film, transforming and debasing what had been a moving story about a spoiled Southern belle, who matures as she survives the ravages of war—what I viewed was a sappy love story. I dubbed the film and went home to lick my wounds. I have always been a perfectionist about my work as an actress, and after this edit, I felt like I had been artistically raped.

Aaron Spelling called me at the Beverly Hills Hotel just before I was to catch my plane for New York. He knew I was upset and wanted to make things right with me. He said he was doing "a little show called *Charlie's Angels*" and wanted to know if I was interested in becoming an Angel. At that moment I lost it. I demanded to know what he had done to my film, and frankly, I was surprised when he apologized profusely, promising he would change anything I didn't like. I then apologized for being so upset and began to suggest some edit changes as he had requested I do. After a few minutes something occurred to me. "Mr. Spelling," I asked, "have you already scored the picture?" "Yes," he replied in his cheeriest voice, "we're on the air in nine days." That did it; I blew up again. "Do you think I just fell off a cabbage truck? You can't re-edit a picture once you've scored it!" A long silence greeted my words, then Spelling tried to reassure me that the film was wonderful and asked that I trust him. I wanted to know if I could re-edit the footage for European release; I knew we had shot a great film, even if this wasn't apparent in his cut. He told me he couldn't let me have the footage because the network owned the negative. I was so frustrated.

Ten days later Spelling called me again. He sounded triumphant and quickly offered me accolades and congratulations. *Love's Savage Fury* had, it seems, received a forty share, making it the highest-rated TV movie of the year. So much for what I knew. Maybe that's why I worked for Aaron Spelling instead of Mr. Spelling working for me. He and I have shared a laugh or two over the years about that story.

John was learning the film business by the seat of his pants as he accompanied me on location and took on more managerial roles . . . whatever they were. There is nothing worse than an actress's husband managing her. Although this was a joke of the industry, I was determined to make our working relationship succeed because I knew that the future of our marriage hinged on it.

Soon another film offer cropped up. David Cronenberg asked me to do his next picture, *Scanners* (1979), to be shot in Canada. I liked this soft-spoken, sincere, and immensely talented writer/director, but I was concerned about the subject matter of his film. I've never much cared for science-fiction movies and I really wasn't sure I wanted to be involved in one. But what was interesting about *Scanners* was that it didn't have monsters or creatures from outer space; rather, it dealt intelligently with the theme of ill-used human mental powers. I found the idea fascinating.

I accepted the lead in the film in good faith, having heard only a description of the story without benefit of a finished script. But when I arrived on location in Canada and read the screenplay, I was disappointed. I felt it had little to do with what David and I had discussed. This mild-mannered director had written a gory, heads-exploding, eyes-popping-out story, with special effects that made me queasy just to think about.

I'll never forget the producers, John, Cronenberg, and me sitting around the huge dinner table that night, writing up a contract expressing our passionate negotiations about how many eyeballs could splatter out of their sockets or heads explode if I were to be in the film. As it turned out, *Scanners* became a cult classic despite my concerns and I consider it to be a very good film. And since then, I've watched the growing body of Cronenberg's film work with great respect. He's become one of my favorite directors.

The making of any film takes on a life of its own and carves out a piece of one's history in the process. I've come to chronicle my life by a collection of film shoots and chunks of time surrounding locations, rather than by specific years. The sequence of my marriages forms a second string of continuity. And as I lived my life, my world seemed to reinvent itself with every new character I played and every new relationship I was in . . . an endless stream of setting up temporary house on locations and starting over again and again with new dreams, a new husband, a new family dynamic, and new painful surprises. I guess I've been lucky as an actress, for I was never at a loss for emotional depths from which to draw. My personal life was a compilation of new story lines that always seemed to have the same sad ending . . . If only I could have hired a new writer?

sixteen

LOST AND FOUND OUT

$\mathscr{I}$T was an extremely hot August at the end of my pregnancy. An unappealing season to be so heavy with child, but such an exciting time nonetheless. Every precaution was taken with this baby in my womb. Weekly hormone shots to ensure my ability to carry him to term. Diet, exercise, medical examinations. John seemed triumphant at the news of the pregnancy, and yet he became increasingly distant as the baby neared. Or was it me? Was I perceiving correctly or was I only projecting and inventing again?

Aimee and John were also spending more time together as my pregnancy progressed. My daughter was now a young teenager, bursting at the seams both physically and emotionally. I was concerned about some of her behavior, which I felt was flirtatious and precociously sexual, especially in front of her stepfather. But I suppressed these feelings when John told me that I was being ridiculous and emotional because I was pregnant. I acquiesced, convinced I was overreacting.

Even though it was two weeks before my due date, I was dilating and ready to deliver, so my doctor broke my water August 25, 1980, in the Greenwich, Connecticut, hospital. It had been thirteen and a half years since I had given birth to Aimee and I was determined this time to experience the miracle of childbirth in a positive way. John and I wanted to have the baby naturally, so as I lay in bed waiting for the contractions to begin, I thought back to our classes, reviewing the breathing methods and all the information we had been given.

I was the only woman in my Lamaze class, including the instructor, who had already had a baby, so when we all watched a film about actual delivery and the birthing mothers were smiling angelically while overseeing their babies being born, I felt compelled to tell these ladies-in-waiting that sometimes it's not as easy as it looks. I didn't want any of us to feel like some sort of failure if we weren't all smiles through the entire delivery. I thought I was being practical, John thought I was complaining.

I was swimming in waves of excitement. Boy, what an amazing thing it is to have a baby. I can't think of a greater joy, a more important mission, and then *ooooh,* more pain. After twelve hours of labor, I had managed to sucessfully use my learned breathing method, but at the very last push, the final moment, I screamed once . . . and my baby boy was born! Seven pounds, two ounces. He was extraordinary. He had all the standard parts and was already handsome as far as I was concerned. John was wonderful throughout the delivery and seemed very taken with his new son. I was a happy woman who was very thankful for this second-chance child.

They took my baby Reis (a family name on his father's side) away to be cleaned up and to let me rest for about forty-five minutes before I went to my room. As the two nurses were wheeling me down the hall on a gurney, I remember noticing that all the doors to the hospital rooms were open. About halfway down the hall, I heard myself scream. I sat up and looked around. I wasn't aware of having made a sound . . . but even *I* heard it. The nurses asked me what was wrong and then I heard myself scream again! The nurses didn't seem to notice anything unusual, so I told them I was fine and lay back down. When I finally got to my room, Aimee was there watching television. "Look, Mom, you're on TV!" she cried, bouncing on the bed as she greeted me . . . And there I was in the middle of my rape scene in *Love's Savage Fury,* yelling my head off. Apparently everyone in the entire row of the hospital rooms was watching my movie. Rape in stereo. That's when I knew

I was really a good actress—my scream on screen was the same as my scream when I was delivering Reis.

It was that night, four hours after Reis was born, that the pediatrician woke me out of the best sleep I had had in months. I remember I was in the middle of such a sweet dream. "Your baby is very sick and we have to take him by ambulance to New York Hospital right away where the experts can give him better care." His voice was dry and unemotional. "Your husband is on his way to the hospital to go along with your son," he continued. "What's wrong with my baby?" I was still trying to get my bearings. "Pneumonia." Apparently Reis had swallowed some amniotic fluid during the birth and had caused the pneumonia. His prognosis was bleak.

John was fantastic during this emergency, spending his time between New York Hospital and the hospital in Greenwich. His mom and stepdad were a great comfort to me and I convinced myself that my baby would be fine even though he was so very sick. My mom and dad were on vacation in California and did not come back to be with me . . . They said they couldn't do any good for the baby by cutting their vacation short. Still, we spoke on the phone a lot.

All the new moms in the hospital got their babies at feeding time. I got the breast pump and stared at the Polaroids of little Reis that John brought me daily from New York. It was decided that I should stay in Greenwich Hospital once it appeared that Reis was not going to die. That way, when he got out of critical condition, we could have a few days together under hospital supervision. What a nightmare my poor baby had been through by the time I finally held his frail, little body in my arms one week later. I considered it a miracle that Reis was alive. You think you can never love anything more than your child, until your next child comes along. It was then I really understood that love is something we never run out of.

Reis improved by leaps and bounds, and by the time he was three months old, you would never have known he'd been sick.

But as well as my baby was doing, Aimee was the reverse. Of course I had heard about the difficult teen years and how impossible parent-child communication becomes, but my problem with Aimee wasn't that we couldn't talk—my problem was that I didn't even know where to find her. It was like she had traveled to another planet and I didn't have the spaceship I needed to visit her. I hired a nanny for the baby, a lady named Rhoda. She fell absolutely in love with baby Reis and was to become part of our family for the next seven years.

Things were settling down a bit and I was confident about Reis's health when John and I decided to take everyone on vacation to Florida before I started back to work. I was feeling more and more excluded from the interaction between John and Aimee, which John kept telling me was jealousy on my part. That thought terrified me—I had been through that jealousy thing with Deed and I knew what torture it was. What on earth was wrong with me that I seemed jealous of the time my daughter spent with her stepfather? It's what I had wanted all my life . . . a close family. The only problem was, I didn't seem to be part of the equation. I felt that old addictive need to be loved rising up in me. I felt abandoned and criticized again and I didn't know why. I felt depressed, led by feelings out of my control.

John repeatedly convinced me that I was just overreacting; after all, he'd ask me, didn't I want him to have a good relationship with my daughter? Weren't we a family? "Yes," I'd say. "Of course," I'd say. "I'm sorry," I'd say. John would tell me that my hormones were still probably out of whack from the pregnancy. He'd tell me I just needed to relax. He'd run me a tub and bring me a glass of wine.

But things didn't get any better on our vacation. Actually, things felt worse as I kept fighting with my emotions. I would constantly talk to Rhoda about it, but she didn't see anything wrong with the time Aimee and John were spending together—I began to think I was losing my mind. My daughter seemed to flaunt her relationship with John. She was closer to him than I was. She actually seemed to be flirting with him at times, parading around on the beach in her bathing suit. Something was radically wrong, but I couldn't quite put my finger on it . . . The way she stood in front of him. The way she'd smile at him. *Stop it, Jennifer,* I'd command myself. *This is crazy!* I was so upset and I didn't understand why.

Memories began to torment me. I thought back on the day before we had all left on vacation. I was in bed feeding the baby, John was lying next to me, reading, when Aimee came in to the room. She had had a bath and was wearing a robe, which was open, exposing her legs as she climbed onto the bed with us. I could see she had nothing on underneath, and this disturbed me, but what was more disturbing was that she made no effort to cover herself in front of John. I reached over and pushed her robe closed and told her to be more careful. Her response was a flash of annoyance as she flounced out of the room.

This was only one of several such incidents. One afternoon at the pool in Florida, Aimee, John, and I were out sunning. Aimee decided to show John her tan line by pulling her bathing suit up, exposing her rear. When I told her not to do this, she made no bones about letting her resentment be known. But it was when Aimee asked John to take her deep-sea fishing the next day that I reached my limit. They both knew I couldn't stand fishing and so of course that meant they could scurry off on another excursion by themselves. They left before dawn and, by nightfall, still hadn't called or returned. I was getting more upset with every passing hour and every glass of wine. By the time they returned, I was livid. As is always the case with too much alcohol, everything becomes more explosive and dramatic, and I ended up leaving the condo where we were vacationing in fury. John and Aimee later came out looking for me in the car. I told them flatly that I was leaving in the morning.

We all left Florida the next day, and for whatever reason, things began to change, or at least it seemed that way from my perspective. John became more attentive to me and we both immersed ourselves in my next work project, which was to be the launching of my own clothing line. With John, things always seemed to move just to this side of irrevocable—and then suddenly they would be rectified. But then the process would begin all over again in a new way.

The clothing-line venture involved a big contract, one that looked like it just might be my annuity for life. Warren Hersh was the project's mastermind (having put together the Gloria Vanderbilt clothing line, he had a wonderful track record in his field.) As soon as he contacted me, we began a whirlwind business relationship. I remember that my legal fees alone for the agreement were close to $40,000 to negotiate trademarks, percentages, and a million-dollar-plus guarantee a year. This contract arrived just in time, since I hadn't worked during my pregnancy and my film offers were dwindling . . . according to John. But with this new business deal, things were solid again. John seemed to have reinvested his energies in our marriage and it looked like we were on a major roll.

Determined to stretch my creative side, I put together an ad campaign and pitched it to Hersh at the same time several other top New York advertising agencies were vying for the job. I won the account fair and square. I was especially excited because I had written the song for the campaign, sang it, conceived the commercial, and directed it. So many of my areas of interest were fusing in this one deal . . . I was on cloud nine.

Direct from his run at Radio City Music Hall, Peter Allen was hired to perform at the clothing-line launch. In addition, we put together a top-notch fashion show to present the collection, which was called "Jennifer O'Neill Separates." The evening came off beautifully, and won rave reviews and a lot of press. Peter had everyone in hysterics at the end of the show when he offered a little comedic wordplay on the name of my collection, calling it "Jennifer O'Neill . . . Separates Again." With orders from Macy's and Bloomingdale's, it looked like my clothing line was an instant winner.

But dark clouds seemed always to hover nearby. At the same time John and I were improving, things were falling apart with Aimee. I became aware of a tension between Aimee and John that

I hadn't noticed before, but I wrote it off as just another round of adolescent mood swings on Aimee's part. Before she turned fifteen, Aimee cut her hair and permed it; she also started having a bit of a weight problem and acne. One day she informed me that she wanted to leave the farm to attend boarding school as most of her friends were doing . . . and so it was agreed.

John and I ran off to Europe for ten days while Aimee stayed with some friends and at home, and visited with her dad on the weekend. We were celebrating the clothing-line coup and baby Reis's health and made the trip a honeymoon of sorts, since we never had taken one when we married. It was a fantastic trip— except that I miscarried again in the middle of our stay in Rome. I had experienced this loss so many times that I had become almost numb to the disappointment. It would probably be more correct to say that I became very fatalistic about such losses. "What will be will be" became my motto as far as miscarried children were concerned.

When I was on my feet again, we went on to Venice, where we bought cratesful of art that we had shipped to the States. By the time we got home, we had spent money we didn't have to purchase things we shouldn't even have considered. And when my clothing-line company was "cross-collateralized" with some of Hersh's other floundering endeavors and taken down with his sinking ship, it looked like my farm was going to be sucked right under in the wake. John assured me we would be fine financially if I could find a way to get an infusion of funds to tide us over until I was able to land another movie role.

I had a friend in New York who was extremely successful and didn't blink at personally loaning me $250,000. I had always owned my farm outright because I never wanted to lose my home for any reason; it was, after all, the only ongoing stable factor in my life. But now it was being held as collateral against the loan, and before I knew it, my farm was up for sale to pay off that loan. Carl Icahn bought my place for far less than it was worth, but I was in a corner. It is impossible to negotiate meaningfully from a weak position and Icahn knew I needed to sell. He made a low bid. When I countered higher, his next bid was even lower than his original . . . The kill was swift, and bloody.

All I can say is that it smashed my heart to sell Long Meadow Farm. It was without a doubt the most incredible, magical home I will ever own. At the time I told myself something better would come along, but how many "perfect 10s" did I expect to have in a lifetime? I bought another stone home not far from Long Meadow; it was on nine acres and required a massive renovation job. It was another one of those places no one wanted, and I was determined to make this shambles with grand potential into my next showstopper. The biggest problem was that it didn't have a barn, so my horses had to be boarded out until I could manage to create an area for them. I had recently lost a colt when he broke his back in the field so I sent Miss Mabel to a nearby barn, hoping for another foal within the year. To this day, I always yearn for my horses if I can't see them on a regular basis. It feels like a part of me is missing. But the new house did, however, have a separate building for offices and another to house a caretaker family, which John hired in short order.

Because of the Long Meadow's sale, we were able to buy this less expensive house and still have some money left over, but it was not enough to pay back the loan. And there seemed to be so many other pressing expenses. John insisted we put up a ten-foot fence around the entire new property for area-protection dogs. Suddenly my home felt like a prison, with floodlit security systems and alarms suitable for presidential protection. Once John released the night dogs to patrol, no one was able to set foot outside the house. The biggest hassle, though, was having to make sure all the cats were brought inside every evening so they didn't wind up being late-night snacks for the dogs.

John also had guns around the house, which terrified me. If you think I find fishing distasteful, hunting makes me nuts and guns completely paralyze me, especially when children are anywhere in the vicinity. John and I had many an argument about that issue since Reis was then a toddler and we finally agreed that John would have only one shotgun, stored high up on a closet shelf, *unloaded*.

By the time John finished explaining to me how important it was that he be able to protect his family, I couldn't help but retort, "Protect us from *what*?" I never received an answer to that question. I concluded that his attitude might be related to the trauma of having fought in Vietnam, and that this experience still caused him to view the world in life-and-death terms. John's theme was to tell me not to worry, he'd take care of everything—all I needed to do was to concentrate on my work and on making money. As it turned out, *money* was all that mattered. When John looked at me he saw dollar signs. The truth is, it was his only real interest in me.

Although the atmosphere was less volatile now that Aimee was away at school, the house felt empty without her. I missed her, and that was not a new feeling for me. I felt like I had missed her all her life: I had.

When the call came from a woman who said she was a psychologist and that she needed to speak to me immediately about my daughter, I was scared. I was to bring my husband with me to her office some forty minutes away. I didn't know how to interpret the call—I couldn't imagine what was wrong. The voice on the phone refused to explain the emergency, and when I insisted on speaking with my daughter, she allowed me a few words merely to confirm that Aimee was in her office and down from boarding school . . . But that was it. Something was wrong with my girl and I had to go, no matter how odd the voice sounded.

During the ride to the psychologist's office, I kept asking John what he thought was going on, but he seemed as confused as I was. There had been an urgency in the woman's tone that made chills run down my spine. When we entered the psychologist's, I saw Deed waiting outside the office as Aimee clung to her stepmother on the far side of the room. Surprisingly, the psychologist asked to speak with John first, alone, and before I could make any sense of what was happening, my husband disappeared behind a closed door. Aimee came over to me, but she refused point-blank to tell me what was wrong. This was torture; my daughter was in trouble and she wouldn't tell me why. Her father wouldn't talk to me either and his wife was, as always, punishing in her aloofness. We all sat in a kind of mute standoff for about half an hour. The tension reminded me of an impending execution. Finally I had had enough. I banged on the psychologist's door and then just walked in. I insisted that she tell me what was wrong with my daughter. Why was she talking to John and not me?

I looked at John, whose complexion had taken on the tone of the bottom side of a dead fish's belly. Once again everything started to go in slow motion as I caught a distortion of the psychologist's words. "Your daughter says . . . she has been having sexual contact . . . with your husband . . . since she was eleven years old." My eyes found John's and locked on them like a death ray. "She's lying," he responded without looking away. Before I could assimilate this information, the psychologist called Aimee into the room.

I know I was crying when I held Aimee in my arms, because I saw my tears stain her shirt amidst her tangled hair. I was numb. "How could you do this to my little girl?" I heard myself say to the room in general and then to John directly. Events resumed normal speed, but sounds echoed oddly in my ears. I felt like I was in the twilight zone.

Seventeen years ago, sexual abuse was not a subject for dinner-table conversation or TV talk shows. The recent onslaught of information about sexual-abuse cases has caused people to drop their old sweep-it-under-the-carpet attitude and join their voices in an aggressive war cry against these crimes. This is, of course, as it should be. But seventeen years ago I had never heard about sexual abuse, nor could I imagine how such a monstrous thing could possibly happen between my daughter and my husband.

I kept telling John in that unventilated, harmonious-colored cell of an office that everything would be all right if he would just admit to his responsibility. There was help for him, for all of us, I said, if he would just tell the truth . . . But John looked everyone in the eye, one by one, including Aimee, and stated over and over in no uncertain terms that absolutely nothing inappropriate had happened between Aimee and him. *Ever!* I always figured you could see a lie coming if you looked hard enough, because lying makes most people uncomfortable, and other people can detect this. Not so for John . . . He was unswayable.

It was obvious that the psychologist had questioned him prior to my invasion of the office. Her theme was that he needed to "own" to his behavior and he would be given help with his problem, but if he continued to deny any sexual exchange with Aimee, the state would criminally prosecute him. There was nothing in the world John responded to more viscerally than the thought of ever going back to jail. It seemed implausible that he would risk going to jail over anything he could handle with something as benign as "therapy."

There was no more to be said in that office. Aimee tearfully and repeatedly confronted John with her version of things—sex four or five times a week . . . alcohol . . . drugs . . . nights together in and out of the house . . . He categorically denied any wrongdoing, stating that Aimee had always had a crush on him, had mistaken their friendship for personal interest, and that Aimee had enormous problems and competition issues with her mother. It was all those mother/daughter problems, he concluded, that were at the core of her ridiculous allegations. He said he felt sorry that Aimee was so upset, but the fact was, both Aimee's father, Deed, and John's ex-girlfriend, Pam (who Aimee was still in touch with) had their own reasons to seek vengeance against Aimee's mother and all they were doing was exacerbating a young girl's craving for attention.

Sides parted . . . Aimee went home with her dad for the time being and I went home with John to further investigate this . . . *thing* that had just happened . . . this thing that was beyond reason to me . . . this thing that was pulling Aimee and me even further apart. There had been four adults who lived full-time in the main house at Long Meadow in addition to John, Pam (part of the time), me, and of course Aimee. With regard to the alleged four-plus years of sexual, alcohol, and drug abuse four to five times a week, all four of these people agreed that they never saw or heard anything of that nature going on between Aimee and John. "Impossible" was the general answer to these charges from outside friends and people who had not only known John, but had had Aimee over to their home for the night or weekends. There was concern for Aimee's promiscuous tendencies, but recognition as well of the difficult times she had spent in the backwash of all my marriages and angry behavior. Clearly, help was needed all around.

The year that followed Aimee's accusations was a full four seasons in hell for everyone involved. I discovered that among all the people whose opinions on the subject really mattered, every single one supported John. Suddenly I felt like a fool for not believing my husband at the psychologist's office. And then there was John himself, always finding time, day in and day out, to reaffirm his innocence. As always, he was brilliantly convincing.

My experience in family court lasted the entire year, and with it came staggering legal fees to represent my husband. John's lie detector test results supported his testimony, all potential eyewitnesses believed John's position. The only explanation was that Aimee had been exaggerating events or that she was simply fabricating. It appeared her motivation was her desire to hurt me, because she herself had been hurt. It was hard to believe her statement that she had gone up to boarding school, read an article in a magazine about incest, and suddenly realized what she had allegedly been doing with John for four years was wrong. How could she not have known something like that was wrong to begin with? I couldn't believe that for almost four years, four years of alleged sex four or five times a week, plus drugs and alcohol, no one in the household ever saw anything out of line occur with John and Aimee—ever caught them drinking together—ever saw Aimee under the influence of drugs—ever caught them red-handed. None of it made any sense to me. Aimee was almost fifteen years old when she made these allegations. When I was fifteen, I was out on my own working in an adult world. It seemed incomprehensible that she didn't know what she was doing. I couldn't believe what she said had been going on, and she couldn't believe I didn't believe her.

And then there was Pam and Deed and all their hatred and anger for me. Who was telling the truth? Who could I trust? It was a no-win situation. Someone was lying, and it was either my husband or my daughter. This was crazy . . . My household was breaking down into enemy camps.

John kept chopping away at the credibility of Aimee's tale. He was brilliantly convincing at expressing compassion for Aimee even though he was the one she accused of wrongdoing. He talked incessantly about the competition my daughter felt toward me and her need for attention. He reminded me that when I was her exact age, I had tried to kill myself because I needed my parents to hear my pain. Aimee was simply doing the same thing in her own way that her mother had done at that age. She needed me to know how much I had hurt her and how angry she was at me for not being there for her, and this was how she was expressing it. He went on about how Pam and Deed jumped on the wagon as soon as they thought it gave them a way to get revenge on me—how all of them, especially Pam, wanted to see our marriage fail. He said Aimee had always wanted all of his attention, and after our return from Florida, when he realized how wrong he was to have hurt me by spending so much time with Aimee, she got angry with him. She was jealous because he began focusing more on me, which, he said, is what he should have been doing in the first place. He concluded that this explained all the sudden tension that sprang up between Aimee and him, when before, they had always been such good friends. Aimee was flat-out jealous of me. John brought me documented court cases of teenagers who invented false charges against parents, teachers, and stepparents—people who actually went to jail because these kids lied and later confessed to their lies . . . We spoke to two psychologists who supported John's position. Bottom line, Aimee was just trying to hurt me. She would have been more effective if she had talked about one or two isolated incidents, but trysts four or five times a week? . . . Impossible. Everyone agreed, it was impossible.

The only problem was, *Aimee was telling the truth*! This man had manipulated her since she was eleven. Being a willing participant was not the issue. Aimee was a child abused by a pedophile in a most insidious manner. She was taught to lie and manipulate.

Although no intercourse ever occurred, just about every other sexual activity did. And my blowup in Florida had brought things to the surface. Yes, they did go out to find me in the car, but only after they had oral sex, and, as Aimee now explains, during this session she suddenly felt disgusted for the first time. She withdrew at that point and John never pressed the sexual issue with her again, knowing intuitively that he didn't have a willing victim in her anymore.

seventeen

SILVER THREAD

*I*T was years before I realized my daughter had actually been sexually abused. After one year in family court, the judge stated that in his opinion, Aimee had been molested, but no criminal charges were brought because there was absolutely no corroborating evidence. John never admitted the abuse until it suited his purpose. And it wasn't until he repeated the crime with his next stepdaughter, Melissa, while his wife, Cindy, was pregnant as I had been, he was finally criminally charged, pleaded guilty, and spent time in jail. Unbelievably, through all of that he repeated his old refrain, denying any wrongdoing, yet again. John didn't do jail time as a pedophile until 1996, but if we believe the statistics, we can expect that he will repeat his crime until he seeks serious psychological help—which may or may not do any good. A condition of his plea-bargain agreement requires John to register as a sex offender for the rest of his life and the judge ordered him to have no contact with children under the age of eighteen.

When Aimee saw the exact same dynamic happen with Melissa and Cindy, and knew the mother had absolutely no idea her daughter was being molested, she finally believed that I was unaware of what was happening to her during her abuse by John. Aimee hadn't believed me any more than I had believed her. It became clear to both of us how it is possible, at the hands of one such as John, for these atrocities to go on for long periods of time completely undetected and unconfessed. It is only now that Aimee and I are really beginning to heal some of the deepest of wounds, and believe me, this is no overnight process. But she and I are determined to tell this story in the hope of providing some support to others experiencing the same nightmare. We believe it can make a difference if warning signs are recognized and support systems offered. I respect and applaud Aimee for surviving her abuse with such understanding, and for her determination during her recovery. I love her for her intelligence, courage, and deep dedication to stopping further abuse, as she did so brilliantly with Melissa. But above all, I wish I hadn't been blind to the truth she had tried to tell me.

Thinking of all this takes me back to the day in 1982 when I came home from yet another lunch with John's lawyer during the family-court case. John couldn't make the meeting, so I heard a review of the work the lawyer had done to warrant his fee of more than $100,000—the time spent with "expert witnesses," etc. No finding had been handed down by the court as yet, so the only thing that didn't feel like it was in limbo was my debt.

I was worn out. I just wanted to go upstairs, close the world out, and sleep, when Rhoda told me three-year-old Reis had an earache and wouldn't stop crying. I called the doctor and took the baby over to his office, knowing how much pain he was in. (I used to suffer from earaches as a kid and they really stink.) An exam, antibiotics, and an ear flush later, Reis finally lay down for a nap when we got home while Rhoda made him some dinner.

I had gone up with Bête to my bedroom to rest when I noticed that the safe in the closet was wide open. John was the only one who knew the combination. On closer inspection, I saw there was a gun, lying in a bowl of bullets, in perfect reach of Reis, had he toddled in. Instantly livid, I began imagining what could have happened if the baby had found the lethal package. I picked up the gun in the bowl and headed for the phone next to the bed. I was going to call John and let him have it: his guns were to be removed from the house, *immediately*! The bed was an English four-poster that stood easily three to four feet off the ground. I jumped sideways as I always did to mount the bed, holding the bowl against my lap . . . And it was at the moment when I landed on top of the bed that the thirty-eight caliber gun went off . . .

The noise of the firing weapon overrode my thoughts. The bullet entered my lower right side, exploded through my hipbone, and exited my back within a fraction of a second. Muscle, tissues, nerves, and ligaments recoiled, snapping like rubber bands. It was a pain unlike any I had ever felt. Breaking my neck and back at age fifteen or giving birth to my children paled by comparison— perhaps because this pain was unannounced, this pain was so invasive, this pain was so dangerous.

The gun now rested on the bed next to me. Everything was moving in another slow-motion dance. I was viewing my surroundings through shutter frames, and in the corner of one of those frames, were . . . my pink suede shoes, fastened to my feet, which were attached to my legs, which, unfortunately, were attached to the rest of me. As I looked down at my body, I seemed to be detaching from myself. I remember thinking, *Those can't be my pink suede shoes. I'm thirty-four years old. I had those shoes when I was nine.* A small laugh escaped my heaving chest . . . I told myself, this is the part where your life flashes before you. Unfortunately I found no consolation in that explanation. *What the hell are those stupid shoes doing in my death scene?* I wondered, then refocused on the bullet that had just split through me.

Reaching the phone next to me seemed an insurmountable task, but I managed, then struggled to remember the caretaker's number. I was sure that at any moment someone, anyone, would come running to my rescue. The phone rang . . . once . . . twice—a distant sound compared with my labored breathing. The waiting was interminable, and the notion that it would be easier just to close my eyes and slip away crossed my blurred thoughts.

I'm not sure how many times the phone rang before it occurred to me that no one was going to answer. By instinct, my mind sought escape from my body's pain. I tried to ponder the bigger picture like the good little New Ager I was in those days. I realized I had blasted my way through life in a whirlwind of extreme behavior, foolish relationships, and horrifying, if not predictable consequences. I had given God no real authority so far because I was convinced that I was in the driver's seat. But now I hoped, and somehow believed, He would grant me a reprieve.

Mostly I realized how terribly I'd spun out of control. My life was a maelstrom. While this latest and most horrific instance of chaos and destruction had not been caused by my hand, all the choices that led up to this moment were mine. I had filled my dance card with some pretty twisted characters and now the day of reckoning was upon me.

I dialed and again the phone rang over and over. My mind drifted once more, my eyes scanning the room for something familiar, something to attach myself to in an effort to stay earthbound. I tried to focus on the pictures of my children on the walls. I remembered every detail of the time I had spent antiquing the paneling, I heard every argument that had taken place in that room. Then, suddenly, something closer to me shot into focus— my own hand. I counted my fingers like I was counting the extremities of one of my newborn children to make sure all were present and accounted for. Anything to keep my mind from getting weaker. I put the receiver down, as close to hopelessness as I had ever felt. Everything started to fuzz out like a late night TV after the day's programming is over. And then a voice within me beckoned: *"Try again, pick up the phone . . .* Call the operator. One digit, dial."

Focus, Jennifer. Focus.

Being such an obedient type, I summoned my last bit of strength and dialed the operator as the voice had told me. There, the phone was ringing again—then, finally, a voice! "Operator. Can I help you?" All I could muster in response was some labored breathing into the receiver. I knew the operator was going to hang up on me. "Wait, please!" I begged through wisps of breath. I managed to tell her that I had been shot. She responded mechanically, "You must dial 911 for emergencies."

I honestly don't recall the words I used. I don't know how I managed to awaken this operator's heart, but she finally must have taken me seriously, because, just as I was losing my battle to hang on to consciousness, the police showed up. Then more chaos and panic as John burst into the room screaming to the police and medical attendants, "It's all my fault—I don't know what happened—I love her—it's my gun—is she dead?" I focused on odd, disembodied details: the vein bulging in John's forehead, his nose, which seemed to grow longer and longer with every lie he told. At best, everyone seemed to be running around doing nothing. At worst, I had only imagined that help had arrived.

I remember very little of the next several hours—the ambulance ride, the X rays, the IVs, the operation.

Apparently I had refused to sign the surgery consent form, all the while arguing with anyone who would listen that I was just fine. Shock makes a wild film director: under its influence, I no longer edited thoughts; I expressed everything that popped into my head. One actual voice, that of the attending doctor, managed to filter through; he told me that because there was no blood coming from my wounds, I was obviously hemorrhaging internally. That got my attention. "If we don't operate immediately, you'll be dead in five minutes." That did it—I managed to sign the release.

John hovered around like a concerned husband—the panic in his eyes was real, only the source of his concern remained a mystery . . . Clearly I was incapable of getting a true reading on this man. The previous year of my life had pressed every alarm button I knew I had, and some I couldn't have imagined. A raging debate erupted between my heart, mind, and soul as to whether I just wanted to let it all go. Staying alive had become increasingly less attractive with every new disappointment. I struck a wary bargain with myself; I vaguely remember deciding at least to enjoy my time under anesthesia, to exist in limbo between life and death. At least I'd have a short break from the stress and sadness that had been sapping my energy for years. That seemed marginally preferable to my old strategy: "when in doubt, regress." Somehow it even seemed funny. An inspired headline surfaced in my mind: JENNIFER O'NEILL SURVIVES GUNSHOT WOUND UNSCATHED. OTHER THAN SUCKING HER THUMB ON A REGULAR BASIS, SHE'S BACK TO NORMAL.

Just as this stream of mental drivel peaked, a serene silence washed over me, and I saw the anesthesiologist appear before me. He first wore the illuminated garb of a merciful angel, then suddenly, horribly, he was covered in the maggot-riddled hide of a half man/half buzzard. I don't remember a thing about my travels while under the knife, as the team of doctors searched for the source of my internal hemorrhaging. (By the way, there was none. In fact, it would turn out that most of the healing time I needed was a result of the exploratory surgery rather than the bullet wound.) Then—however long afterward—I found myself thinking consciously: *I'm coming to . . . here I go again.* I came reeling back to earth at breakneck speed . . . back to the hospital . . . the pain . . . *the TV?*

The anchorperson's voice was the first outside stimulus to penetrate my drugged sleep. A blaring TV in front of me announced the late-night world news report. More jolting than my return to reality was the realization that I was watching myself on TV and that I was the headline story. The anchor's voice hummed, "She became a household name with her starring role in the internationally acclaimed film *Summer of '42.* Cover girl/actress Jennifer O'Neill has suffered a gunshot wound and remains in critical condition at the local hospital near her home in Mt. Kisco, New York."

I foraged through layers of sheets to my abdomen, hoping I was in one piece, hoping all I was seeing, hearing, and feeling was just a bad dream. My hands rested on a mound of tubes protruding from my stomach like a random pile of straws. I felt nauseous. My arms were invaded with IVs, my body was yelling "uncle" to the recurring physical pain that showed me no mercy. This was no dream. Fragmented memories of the last hours bounced into my mind—every one of them terrified me.

I wondered why anyone would have left the TV on in my room, knowing I would wake up to the news of my own lurid story. *Don't get paranoid,* I thought. *There's no conspiracy going on here . . . Yes, there is!*

The door to my room burst open, and the intruder entered unannounced. I felt like my surroundings were being sucked away into a giant vacuum, leaving my breath hanging in the air. I was so disoriented I couldn't even speak when the nurse told me that my daughter was waiting downstairs for a visit. She studied my eyes as she held my wrist in search of a pulse. Externally calm, my mind raced. *My daughter . . . Aimee . . . Here to see me? . . . Why? . . . Why? . . . What does she want? . . . Who's with her?* I finally exhaled the breath I had been holding since the nurse's arrival. My eyes caught her staring at me, but she didn't seem to care. I remember thinking, *How rude.* What was more annoying was that I couldn't gather enough strength to stare back at her. My eyes fell to my lap in defeat. I felt like a sideshow freak.

The hoarseness was from the tubes that were inserted down my throat during surgery; at least that's what the nurse told me as she leaned over to hear my barely audible answer, "I can't see my daughter right now." A flicker of emotion passed over Nurse Stoic, her eyebrow arching as she responded, "Should I tell her to come back in the morning?" My head shook back and forth like some puppet being handled by outside forces. "No?" she verbalized for me. "You don't want your daughter to come back tomorrow?" Somehow I managed to engage the nurse's eyes with mine for just a moment; she wasn't going to make me say any more by way of explanation. It was none of her business.

Yes, I refused to see my daughter. After all, at that point I felt like she had been trying to kill me, and I knew that I had just narrowly escaped death—again. I certainly didn't blame Aimee for the accident, I just thought she'd be happier if I had died. At that stage I still believed she had made everything up about John's abuse. At that stage her father had already tried to put me in jail for missing one child-support check (the court had given him custody of Aimee as long as John and I still lived together). How many months and months had Deed been late with his child support and I never bothered him? But what did I expect? I knew they all wanted to get me. "Paranoid" is a good word to mention here.

I left the hospital in record time considering my injuries, and dedicated myself to healing and getting back to work. There was an *astounding* amount of mail, daily bagsful from all over the world, from fans wishing me well. Their outpouring of love and support absolutely floored me . . . I am at a loss to describe how much their compassion meant to me and I believe their caring was the key to my rapid recovery. I was feeling pretty good in general until a close friend of mine told me I was drugged out of my mind. Why didn't I have a clue? My doctor had given me a boatload of medication when I left the hospital, and I can only suppose the meds did such a great job of rerouting my pain and depression that I didn't even know I was under the influence. (There's the well-dressed, well-mannered enemy in his best disguise.) I immediately called the doctor who had prescribed the medication and confirmed that between the pain pills and massive doses of antidepressants he had put me on for the shock, my lips were stuck together and my mind thought I was happy even though I wasn't.

During this time John wasn't doing very well, because, although he was regularly dipping his hand into my pain-medication, he *wasn't* on antidepressants, and let's face it, everything was pretty depressing. My life had become so outrageous that I sometimes collapsed in gales of laughter, not tears, as I thought about it. Since the shooting had received so much international press, the local district attorney decided to try to make a name for himself and was determined to charge someone with illegal possession of an unregistered weapon. John had said it was his gun when the police arrived with my ambulance, but since his attorney wasn't present at the time, his statement was judged inadmissible. The DA wanted to charge John because, as an ex-felon, John would do hard time for possession of an illegal weapon. Notch-on-belt time for Mr. DA.

John came to me in a panic while I was still in the hospital and begged me to say the gun was mine, because this would result only in a misdemeanor charge for me. I said no. No one would believe it was my gun because of the years I had publicly let it be known that I hated guns. Furthermore, I wasn't going to lie in court. I also said no to the DA, stating I would not testify against my husband. No matter what had happened, I didn't want Reis's father to be in jail. And what was the upshot of this? The DA charged *me* with possession of an unregistered weapon! Any conviction under Mr. DA's belt was better than no conviction at all. I was shot and I was being charged because "the gun was in my hands" . . . *What?* . . .

I was fingerprinted, charged, and taken to court in an attempt to have me turn state's evidence against my husband. After another round of international press coverage and weeks of humiliation beyond description, I was *exonerated,* and all charges were dropped. The DA was also not able to nab John, due to my lack of testimony—a technical victory, although a moral defeat. This experience was an education in criminal and court politics, but unfortunately "the system" was to have its way with me once more in the future. Again I won, but at such a cost. Watch out for the big machines.

It was after court that I told my doctor I was going off all the medication. He advised me to do so in stages, but I made up my mind that I needed to take a hold of my life, I needed a totally clear perspective, and needed this *immediately.* How hard could it be? It had only been weeks since I was shot . . .

Despite all the phenomenal expressions of love and concern I received from the public during this crisis and, for the most part, the responsible reporting about the event, I was not spared the random supermarket-tabloid article—according to which the shooting was everything from an underworld plot against my life to a "stomach fixated" suicide attempt. Thankfully, my support system overrode the vultures. Then, forty-eight hours and several hot baths after I began my withdrawal from the medications, I suffered a seizure in the kitchen. It was in the morning and I was getting some milk. I had two au pair girls working in the house at the time; they found me and called the ambulance. My doctor never warned me that any such thing as a seizure could occur. Advising me to cut back the medication slowly didn't translate to me as risking death if I did it quickly . . . What if I had been out driving with the baby somewhere? . . . It was another big scare in the annals of a lifetime of big scares. Part of Jennifer's ongoing "crash course" through life. I told my press agent I should write a book called *From the Summer of '42 to the Fall of '82* . . . He didn't laugh.

Back in the hospital again, the doctors wanted to reintroduce medication, but I refused and stayed in the hospital for a week with not so much as an aspirin until I was past the risk of another seizure. John never visited me this time, and when I got home, he seemed extremely distant and withdrawn. He was a big coffee drinker and smoker, and when he was stressed for long stretches, he became extremely thin, often vomiting blood and suffering from a bad back . . . Whenever things started to come to a head with us, he seemed to fall ill and all my energy would be rerouted into caring for him. But this time, when the ambulance arrived out of nowhere, John wasn't sick. John had been in the office, I was up at the main house—I was starting to feel I should offer the ambulance drivers permanent garage space as they had been summoned so often to my home in the last three weeks. As it turned out, John had called them for help after he slit his wrists. Obviously he didn't want to die, but he did want some way out from having to deal with the truths that were about to be uncovered. In short, just after John went into the mental institution that day, I found out that I had a total of *seventy-six dollars* in the bank and was deeply in debt.

I am not an unintelligent person, but I was certainly acting like one. I remember thinking of all the war stories I had heard about performers or heiresses losing all of their earnings to con artists or dishonest accountants or lawyers and how ridiculous I thought such people were for being so gullible and flat-out stupid . . . And here I was in the same predicament. Add a few more unsavory adjectives to the description of me and you'll have a picture of what I thought of myself at that time. The hardest part of everything that had happened was dealing with the deception. Not only on the part of John, but from all areas of my life . . . including myself.

I shoved my feelings deep down and locked them up with all my other unwanted experiences and focused on returning to work and getting away from John. Everyone advised me to file for bankruptcy, but as far as I was concerned, that was not an option. But then, when he heard I was shot, the friend who had lent me the $250,000 panicked and called in his loan. Reality smacked me in the face again. This so-called friend wasn't stating a request when he called me into his office, he was making a demand and he had the papers all drawn up for me right then and there to pay off my debt . . . plus. I was to sign my house over to him and there was to be no further discussion . . . Frightened, I did exactly as he said.

Thank God for Sam Pryer, who lived down the street from me. We had a mutual girlfriend who had informed Sam and his wife of my predicament. Before Sam even met me, he offered his legal services for free to help me get back on my feet financially—what a kind and generous act. Frankly, it restored my faith in the human spirit and I will forever be grateful for this man's heart. It took me three years, but I paid everyone back and was finally able to buy another house in 1984.

After losing everything in New York, I went to California; it was only seven weeks after the accident and I still had tubes sticking out of my stomach from my gunshot wound. I was prepared to undertake my first TV series, called *Bare Essence*, believing this was the fastest way to make the money I needed to pay back my debt. Although the role I was cast in was a bit frustrating creatively, I was grateful for the chance to work.

I rented a house near the studio and brought the dogs, cats, Reis, and Rhoda to the coast. Unfortunately, like the proverbial tick on the dog, John was not far behind the pack. It was going to be another year of emotional chess, more lies and more confusion, before I rented John a car, called a lawyer, and got down to the business of ending our marriage. By that time I truly was damaged goods, emotionally speaking.

During this period Aimee and I continued to be locked in an exhausting emotional dialectic of missing and hating each other, often feeling both at the same time. She was ostensibly safe with her father and his family, but her behavior continued to be marked by sexualized expressions of anger and a general lashing-out at others. We finally seemed to have something in common; too bad it wasn't something positive. As always, nothing was understood, grieved, or healed . . . just stored up for more difficulties ahead.

From the time Reis was born, there was such turmoil. I was missing my son in the same way I had missed Aimee. Both of my children were taken care of financially, Rhoda was a doting nanny, but I was not emotionally available to Reis. I was shut down, once again caught up in my own pain and endless neediness. My underlying emotional and spiritual emptiness allowed people and events to throw me totally off track and thereby miss "the best things in life." I had no more contentment, no more peace or sense of security at age thirty-five than I had when I was fourteen, and I was wearing down. After our five-year marriage was over, I knew that John had never loved me. I was just the means to an end for him and I felt a deep loathing for myself. The more I tried to get someone to love me, the more unlovable I felt . . . Trust was not part of my vocabulary anymore, and although most of the time I was controlled, when I drank to quiet the pain, my immense anger and cutting sarcasm would come pouring out. I was inconsolable . . . I was unreasonable.

eighteen

ACROSS A CROWDED ROOM

I DECIDED work was my only option. My life for the next year or so centered on that mission, but despite being busy, I continued to find I was frustrated by the kind of acting roles I was offered. I yearned to work again with the likes of Visconti in Europe, but I had to focus on making money to pay back my debts rather than developing my craft. Since the whole Aimee/John experience, I felt like a badly written script was running my life . . .

After the shooting accident, people seemed to think differently of me though they really knew nothing about me . . . I was a mystery—an unexplained story.

One of the items on my work schedule that year was a Cover Girl shoot in Florida. Reis and Rhoda came along with me and then winged their way to California a day before I did to put Reis in preschool. We were moving again. I was scheduled to star in a TV series for CBS, *Harper and Reynolds,* and had managed to talk the producer into changing its title to *Cover Up.* I thought the connection would make my friends at Cover Girl happy . . . And it did. I always looked for any extras I could for the Cover Girl group because I was so fond of everyone involved with that campaign.

It's hard to imagine an actress being unhappy on the eve of beginning her own prime-time series, but I was coming from another world. To me, TV was still a comedown, and I was yearning to focus on reaching new levels in the feature-film world.

Aimee decided to stay with me for the summer of her eighteenth year. I knew we were both looking to repair our relationship, but we found only more tension, no forgiveness, and a raging battle of wills. No sooner had Aimee arrived in L.A. than she started dating the boss at her new job. Apparently he had a boat that he wanted her to frequent and when I insisted on meeting him, I found him to be much older and sleazy in a major way. I tried to explain to Aimee that I knew what kind of guy he was and that I did not want her alone on a boat with him . . . Besides, she shouldn't be dating her boss. Of course she disagreed, so I fell back on, "This is my house, and if you want to live in it, you go by my rules." Everything escalated from there. It was an old pattern. I had absolutely no control over Aimee and she was determined to make up her own rules about how she ran her life. After all, as she continually reminded me, she was eighteen and legal.

I moved Aimee into a prepaid, furnished motel nearby. Her "independence" had a one-month freebie attached to it and after that, Aimee was on her own. I would literally have hives and stomach cramps when Aimee and I would battle—it seemed any close proximity to each other would set us off. Additionally, nothing had been resolved about the abuse. The more I uncovered about John, the more I realized something may have happened between Aimee and him, but the gray areas remained, which of course tortured Aimee. She needed her mother to believe her and I couldn't. Her promiscuous behavior seemed to me to support the old theory of events and again, it would take a few more years before I understood that abuse can actually trigger the exact behavior I was seeing in her.

And then there was my string of marriages and relationships, which set a less-than-sterling model of behavior for my daughter to follow. I was completely sincere about every attempt I had made at marriage and creating a family—I was never interested in sex for its own sake or felt that that attitude was correct (even when my generation embraced that notion). But I was to realize, once I found my faith and God showed me the truth about love and relationships, that although I had the right idea, I was following the wrong manual. No meaningful, lasting success was to be mine until I got my priorities in order.

Being a lead in a one-hour TV series is a grueling task. When Jon-Erik Hexum and I started to shoot *Cover Up,* we had to cope with the sixteen- to eighteen-hour days that come with the territory— but in Jon-Erik's case, this schedule and the stress it caused was soon to prove fatal.

Lee Majors was shooting *The Fall Guy* on the same lot and was top dog at Twentieth Century-Fox studios. He had been doing TV series for so long, he had every angle down to a science—set hours, apartment on the lot, power. There was no love lost between Lee and me when we had made *Steel* together, and that was largely my doing. I felt that feature films were my arena and I was not happy about working with a lowly "TV actor." Well, Lee was enjoying this payback time watching me try to deal with his world and its downsides.

When *Cover Up* first began to shoot, I would go into the commissary for lunch and there Lee would be holding court at his corner table. One day I went over to see him and he was very pleasant, asking how things were going on my show. I replied with equal pleasantness, "Fine, a piece of cake." It took only one month of filming before I returned to the commissary, found Lee at his table, got down on my knees, and told him, "I take my hat off to you. This is, without question, the toughest work I have ever undertaken and I applaud you for surviving the rigors of TV for so long." I ended with, "I'm sorry I was such a snob about your work, and I invite you to tell me 'I told you so.' " We became good friends after that. I did do another film with him in 1993 called *The Cover Girl Murders* for USA Cable.

Jon-Erik was a terrific guy. We never really spent any time together off the set, but I had a great respect for him. Just one look at Jon-Erik Hexum and you knew this young man had major star potential. He was totally dedicated to his career and did extra press work and travel on weekends to promote the show. He had a larger-than-life personality and would come to the set on Mondays with tales about such things as making a citizen's arrest after following some speeding drunk into the bowels of L.A. Jon lived on the edge in that respect. He was physically fit and very health-minded, but he was also pushing the envelope in his intense drive for success. I thought I was relentless, but in many ways, he was more out of control than I was. He had a sense of his own indestructibility that mirrored the character he played on the show, but on the day he shot himself, there were no retakes.

Jon-Erik had worked all weekend as usual and seemed almost hyperactive from lack of sleep that Monday. He used to get very annoyed with me when I would make everyone check and recheck the prop guns, because, obviously, guns petrified me since I was shot. I used to think how ironic it was that I was playing a character who had to use a gun on almost every show.

I was in my trailer when the commotion and panic spread across the lot like wildfire. Jon-Erik had been shot in the head. The producer was in my trailer within minutes after Jon-Erik was taken to the hospital. Apparently he was doing his last take for the day and was messing around with the gun "Russian roulette" style when he put the weapon to his head and pulled the trigger. The gun was loaded with what we call a "half load," that is, the modified ammunition that causes the jolt and sound when a gun is used in a film scene. It is a totally harmless load when shot in the air, but when Jon-Erik held the gun directly to his temple and pulled the trigger, the close range effect was deadly.

Jon-Erik was already declared brain-dead by the time I got to the hospital. Because he had donated his organs, he was hooked up to all kinds of machines and a respirator. He had no shirt on and was lying in bed so peacefully. I could see his chest rise and fall as breath was forced into his lungs—but he wasn't there anymore . . . Why didn't he wake up! If I could wake up when I was shot, he could. I told him that. I told him he would be okay . . . But he wasn't . . . He was gone . . . He just wasn't there anymore.

There are no words for the incredible loss we all felt. The full impact didn't register on me for quite some time—but it did affect the production team. Within a week the studio was interviewing replacements for Jon-Erik's role. We never shut down production and I worked through the week, including weekends, only days after the accident. I was never able to grieve for his death . . . I couldn't cry because if I did, my eyes would grotesquely swell and I wouldn't be able to shoot. I was told by the producer that so many people who worked on the show and their families were relying on me to keep things rolling so they wouldn't be out of jobs . . .

And so the screen-testing began with several actors and male models who were vying for the role. These tests were particularly difficult since production used the same scene Jon-Erik and I had shot for the very first episode. But when none of the candidates for the role was right for the part, the bigwigs started to panic. I had lost about ten pounds, which I couldn't afford, and was at the end of my strength when the producer called me in to meet Antony Hamilton. He was Australian, handsome, a dancer/actor with great charm. I liked him right off for the part and he was cast on the spot.

Tony was a sweetheart to work with. There was, however, a problem—as with so many dancers who are brilliant on stage these artists can be quite clumsy in normal life: Tony was a total clod on the set. It was regular business for him to be doing a scene with me, walk up to his mark, and stand all over my feet with his giant cowboy boots. We had deep, good laughs about that and about life in general. The studio was pleased with his work, although there was a flurry about Tony's sexual persuasion. What followed was a big hush-hush campaign by the producers about the rumors that he was gay . . . Horribly, Antony died of AIDS only a few years ago. It was a pleasure working with and knowing him, and after the series was canceled because of scheduling problems that next year, Tony and I stayed in touch—and another chapter of my life was closed. How many chapters does a normal life have?

* * *

I met Cheri right after *Cover Up* was canceled. She had a tape-editing company, came highly recommended, and I needed someone to work with me on making an acting tape for my agent's use. An acting tape is a series of clips from an actor's body of work put together in an entertaining fashion to show their talent and range. As a rule, these tapes are used to procure work from casting agents or directors, and should never run longer than ten to fifteen minutes (the industry's attention span).

But what was to happen when Cheri and I compiled my acting tape was more like the making of *Gandhi* or the longest miniseries in history. I had been so frustrated with my acting opportunities since I worked in Europe, I wanted to review my close to one hundred hours of footage, films, TV work, and talk shows. Cheri and I used a lot of my original music to choreograph the opening sequences of my tapes. I had a ball editing because I was in control of the outcome, and for me that was a rare treat. I wanted to see who I was as a performer—what was my essence? . . . Who the heck was I, anyway? I had such a vague self-image. I took over Cheri's facility, importing kids, dogs, and friends through the endless days and nights of round-the-clock editing.

After editing, Cheri and I developed a TV-series concept together called *Business Cards* and sold it to Stephen Cannell Productions. Peter Roth, the company's head of development, joined us to pitch the idea to CBS and was in the middle of describing the two lead women in this sitcom to the network head. These lead characters were based on Cheri's and my personalities and our *I Love Lucy* approach to life in general. During Peter's discourse, Cheri happened to flip her head back as she often did, throwing her hair like a mane; her earring flew off and landed on my chest, sliding down into my cleavage. All eyes followed this unrehearsed stunt, at which point I jumped up and wrestled Cheri to the floor. Recovering her earring, which was now stuck in my bra, I gingerly placed it on her lobe before letting her return to her seat . . . All of this without a word spoken. At that point Peter concluded, "Well, there you have it. Those are our characters."

Cheri and I spent a lot of time laughing; even worst-case scenarios became fodder for our wild imaginations. We would meet at Hamburger Hamlet in L.A., eat the house down, reinvent the wheel, and solve the world's problems since we couldn't seem to make a dent in our own. The little girl in me loved to come out and play with Cheri. The little girl in me was not totally whipped by life—the little girl in me would show up in a burst of freedom as I galloped my horse up a hill in wild abandon. I'd see her in fleeting moments of comedic timing sprinkled into every character I played on screen; I still could find her whimsical flirtations with the snarliest of characters. And then there was my introspective, analytical x-ray vision insight into *everyone*—an instant feel for their barriers and instant breakthroughs for their resolve even if they didn't ask for it.

Yes, life was fun sometimes. Nevertheless, I knew I was going down the same dead-end streets. I could talk circles around almost everyone, but I was not buying my own dialogue. What was wrong? I put so much stock in every new character I played, I never found my own identity. I felt like a leased car. The proverbial "there must be more to life" was taking up permanent residence in my heart. The search was on again, and it wasn't just for my next potential date . . . But I didn't know where to look. I had already studied philosophies and religions and been analyzed ad nauseam, and in the end, man's thoughts felt empty to me . . . especially my own.

Due to the success of *Cover Up,* I was finally able to get out of debt and buy a beautiful home in the flats of L.A. Things seemed to be on an upswing, except that my horses were still boarded out in East L.A. I missed them. Aimee had married, at just nineteen—a local boy who lived near her old high school. I heard the wedding was sweet and simple and I did get to see some pictures later, since I wasn't invited. Deed was, but that's the way things were. Aimee's marriage was tumultuous and lasted only a short while. She was to marry two more times before finding her present happiness.

At the beginning of each new adventure, I'm invariably pumped with anticipation about the people I'll discover and the places I'll visit. I have met some fascinating individuals on airplanes, people who have turned into long-term friends. But it was *after* such a plane flight that I first met Richard, or so he told me later. He was driving for a limo company when he was called for a pickup at LAX. The name was O'Neill . . . My friend Carolyn was gathering me up at the airport with my two dogs and a ton of baggage. Everything was moving fast and a little off center those days. I had no idea I had just met my next husband and the father of my last child. Frankly, I hadn't noticed him.

It wasn't until sometime later that Carolyn asked me if I wanted to go out with a friend of hers, a guy named Richard. By the way, this lady Carolyn ended up being a dear friend of mine for years. She had a heart of gold, a deep throaty laugh, and could dress hair with the best of them. We did several shows together, including *Cover Up,* and she was my spitfire guardian angel with a wilted halo and a loving soul . . .

She set up a date for the three of us to go to a sushi restaurant. And she was right . . . Richard was handsome and "buff." (Again, I didn't recognize him as the limo driver.) "Buff" wasn't my thing, but that's probably because I had never really run into it . . . And I was immediately smitten. This meeting turned into a ten-year odyssey and a lifetime connection by way of our son. I was in trouble with this man because I was so physically attracted to him and he had a kind of "bad boy" personality that was a perfect fit for the codependent part of me. Richard was an ex-marine—Vietnam vet—rodeo cowboy—songwriter—smooth talker—with a low voice and an unusually low regard for women. Especially since he could have any woman he wanted—at least in his mind. When I met him, he was working out regularly at the gym and had aspirations of vying for the "Mr. Forty" title. I had never known anyone who looked in the mirror more than this guy. He was handsome-on-handsome to me, but he was more handsome to himself. He also ended up being the meanest man alive, with a vicious temper and a vocabulary to match.

We twirled, danced, and got married in the throes of passion, despite questions on both our parts as to the wisdom of our decision. But we had this "thing" for each other that wouldn't go away. As I say that, I believe it was more me than him. I believe one person out of a couple always tends to love the other one more, and that can be a real curse for the one that's doing more of the loving. To this day, I don't believe Richard ever really loved me. It would be impossible to believe that he did, given the events that transpired over our next ten years together. (The other possibility is that he's so blocked with old pain he can't love any woman—which may be the case.) But despite all of that, we had Cooper, who is the gift of love to both Richard and me . . . the child we both needed. God gave us this absolutely magical son with a tender soul and a sweet nature so Richard and I would finally have a real shot at parenting—even if we couldn't do it as a team. Cooper was a honeymoon baby, a total surprise to both of us, but a blessing for life.

Richard was the first person who ever talked to me about Jesus Christ. You have no idea how ironic that was given Richard's behavior. I had heard about God on a regular basis through my study of various philosophies, but I hadn't heard any mention of Jesus Christ since I was in Sunday school in Connecticut—the one that stole my weekends and made me yawn. When Richard talked to me about this Jesus person, I became very angry. I wasn't even sure why. I would read Richard's Bible and get really annoyed about details. "So-and-so lived four hundred and fifty years in the Old Testament," I'd say with sarcastic disbelief. "No one can live four hundred and fifty years! Your Bible is a bunch of junk! And what's all this blood-animal-sacrifice stuff? I love animals. Who exactly is this God that wants little lamb's blood? Isn't pointless killing a sin? And immaculate conception? Come *on*!" It's said that the people who protest about the Lord the loudest are probably on their way to him—and I was sniping at every page of the Bible I could put my hands on. A battle for my soul was raging and the enemy wasn't going to give up easily. All the tricks in the book were being used to strengthen connections to my old patterns, ways of thinking, and habits that had held me hostage.

I found every excuse not to hear the truth, starting with Richard himself. As I said, no one has a worse temper. He is volatile and would leave anyone by the side of the road if it suited his needs. (I know, he did it to me when I was pregnant.) I told myself that I was not sure I wanted whatever this "Jesus thing" was if it allowed for such a nasty capacity in him. Of course, if being perfect were the criterion, none of us would have a prayer of salvation— that's why we need forgiveness. And of course, God doesn't make the bad things in us or in the world happen, *we* do—our fallen nature—our choice.

Being pregnant the first year of marriage generally is not the wisest move. A couple needs solid, unencumbered time to settle in and really get to know each other before having children. But in Richard's and my case, that first year probably was the easiest we shared. Richard already had a son in his twenties from his first marriage, whom he had chosen not to see since the boy was three years old. I believe Richard was really looking forward to having another son and another chance at fatherhood—as I was at motherhood. I have never had a single complaint about Richard as a father to Cooper; he loves our boy and spends quality time with him.

Unfortunately, however, Richard showed no interest in my then six-year-old son Reis, who ended up being on the receiving end of Richard's awesome temper too many times. Richard never raised a hand either to Reis or to me, but he could verbally annihilate your very being if you happened to be the object of his fury. Richard described the feeling of his abusive onslaughts as if he were standing in the middle of an artillery cross fire in Vietnam. He said something would just snap when he got angry and it felt to him like his life depended on destroying the person in front of him. Once the rage was over, he experienced relief and never looked back on his victim. The hardest part was, Richard rarely if ever apologized, and worse, he never changed his behavior. And I would just come back for more, much the same as I did with Deed and John. All three of these men kept me off balance and insecure, a view of myself I easily bought into. It was the old pattern: the more I couldn't reach them or hold their affection, the more I wanted them, and the more extreme my behavior became to get their attention.

During the pregnancy with Cooper, I sold my house in L.A. to buy a place Richard found in the mountains of Malibu. Point of View Farm, as I called it, was breathtaking. Twenty-five acres with a small, rustic home offering panoramic views and lots of sprawling land for the horses. There was a six-stall barn and fenced fields already on the property, which we extended to a forty-stall facility. All of this beauty was to be my home for the next ten years. I thought nothing could ever hold a candle to Long Meadow Farm back east, but in a very different style, Malibu captured my heart and imagination as well as my lost home. And actually, I realized my horse dream there better than I could ever have imagined, culminating in a twenty-year breeding program that produced national high-score horses that I bred, raised, trained, and showed. I was in heaven.

Cooper was born two weeks early, just as Reis was, but his delivery went without a hitch, and he was perfectly healthy. Richard did, however, fall asleep while I was in my last stages of labor. It hurt me that he could snooze at such a time. Years later, in therapy, we discussed that very point and Richard explained that when confronted with something he can't handle or fix, he simply removes himself. So, when he saw me in pain and couldn't stop it, he fell asleep. "Besides," he said, "I was tired." I reminded him that I, too, was tired; after all, I was the one having our baby. He, as usual, didn't understand my disappointment.

Richard wrote his best songs about "leaving." Over the ten years we were married on and off, there was a lot of leaving on his part. He would always tell me I told him to go, and technically, except for our final divorce, that was correct. What Richard would do was rage, withdraw affection, and isolate himself from me until I went wild and told him to get out. But through all of our turmoil, something inside me was changing, so this time I didn't lose my relationship with my son Cooper, and I didn't lose myself.

*　　*　　*

I guess the best way to put what happened to me in 1987 is to say that "my time had come." I thought I had tried everything, been everywhere, knew everything, hurt every place, turned to every solution that didn't work. But my time had come to find the real truth instead of inventing my own, because mine didn't work. My time had come to stop my frantic search and accept what had always been mine for the asking. My time had come to shove that addictive need to be loved all the way to hell, where it belonged, and choose a better way, a real love. My time had come to receive the unconditional love that would finally fill the hole in my heart and the sorrow of my spirit. I had worn myself out and was about good for nothing and I knew it deep down in a place that I couldn't argue with. I had almost died so many times, but really, why had I survived? Just to go around the same corner to find the same emptiness? I could feel my heart beat if I put my hand on my chest, but it was only a broken machine, not a dwelling place of love. My time had come to say yes.

You see, I finally asked the Lord Jesus Christ into my heart when Cooper was born. At the time Richard and I dedicated our baby Cooper to the Lord, I was baptized and Richard was rebaptized (the first time occurred in his early twenties). It was a most amazing day, the full impact of which would take me years to really discover and understand and benefit from.

I had been christened as a child and I had both Aimee and Reis christened as infants, but obviously I didn't have a clue what I was really doing, as I was not with the Lord at the time. It was just a ritual one was taught to perform. Today, my deepest concern for Aimee, as her mother and someone who loves her, is that neither her father nor I exposed her to spiritual truth, and although she couldn't be a more spectacular young woman, mother, and wife, with a deep understanding of all the important elements of life, she is without faith in anything beyond her own intellect and emotions . . . And as beautifully as she is doing, it's hard to hold everything on human shoulders. For me, it was impossible. And then, most important, there is the issue of eternal life.

Someone who had interviewed me for a magazine article once asked my mom, "Your daughter is born again. Are you?" My mom replied simply, "Of course not, I've always been a Christian." So many people, even self-proclaimed Christians, don't have any idea what being "born again" really means. So many so-called Christians go to church and have absolutely no personal relationship with Jesus Christ. Being a Christian is not a religion, it's a relationship. The "born again" misconception is not limited to nonbelievers. Being born again is not like AA, where you hit bottom and then (if you're lucky) change. It is not a California cult. Being born again means simply that when you ask Jesus Christ into your life as your Lord and Savior, realizing that He died for your sins and mine—past, present, and future, you receive eternal life, not by your good works, but as a free gift of grace. When you choose Jesus Christ, you die to your old sinful nature and are born again spiritually in Him. From that very moment on, Christ is living on the *inside of you* and you are "indwelled" by the Holy Spirit, a gift from God, as your comforter and guide. It is then that you begin your personal relationship with God, who knows every hair on your head, every one of your needs, large or small. He knows your fears. He will protect you, and never ever desert or abandon you. He loves you unconditionally and will fill you with peace and knowledge beyond understanding. You are God's child because He gave His only begotten Son to die in your place for your sins so that He will present you blameless and washed clean to His Father in heaven. All you have to do is ask Jesus Christ into your heart and you are born again into the body of Christ, forever covered by God's awesome power, love, and individual plan for your life. And all He asks of us is to love righteousness and live our lives with humility and honor to Him . . .

No word is big enough to describe the relief, joy, and excitement that filled me when I accepted Jesus Christ in faith. At long last I was having my first *real* love affair. I now understood what it meant to put God above all else and not feel jealous that my spouse was doing the same. With God at the center of my life, all the needing to be loved and demanding to be filled up by someone else vanished. God was filling me up and He was never going to let me down.

New Christians are a sight to behold—most of the time they don't know how to contain themselves, they're so enthused. They're not unlike a toddler who just made it across the room for the first time without smashing into the furniture. Have you ever seen such an infectious smile? To look at a baby, who would think this giant-headed, fat-cushioned, uncoordinated creature, who can barely complete the simplest task of walking, will one day be running the world? The good news is that no one can tell a toddler he can't accomplish what his instincts have set him out to do.

Every one of us who has learned how to walk has completed a herculean feat by the power of just pressing on . . . Even if the odds are against us.

God loves all His children whether they are young or old, stubborn, early bloomers or late developers, damaged, mean, hurt, scared, slow, even petulant . . . He loves all His children with patience and the ability to bring each one of us home safe and sound. And under the umbrella of commitment made in marriage, God intends for us to share the most blissful, secure, no-holds-barred erotic, tender lovemaking with our partner for life. These are some of the lessons I was finally learning, albeit at a crawl.

From 1987 on, I was on fire for the Lord, but that didn't necessarily mean my life was going to get better. In fact, in some ways it got worse before it got better. But what it did mean is that I'd learned to handle the difficult parts of life better, with more grace and less fear. "Slow and steady" now became my mission, but patience and trust were to come to me at a snail's pace. Don't forget, I was a control freak, so I immediately started to negotiate with God. He says, "Give me all your troubles." I let Him have a few and kept the big ones for me to handle . . . *Why?* . . . Because I had been doing such a bang-up job up till then? Becoming a child of God doesn't mean you still don't act like a child sometimes.

* * *

Richard worked extremely hard on the farm, at times at a super-human pace, building, bulldozing, planning, overseeing, and at other times he lay dormant. Given all the lack of respect and the wild pendulum of love and hate in our relationship, I often succumbed to disillusionment. Richard's dad, in various states of drunkenness, had beat him as a kid, so Richard understandably hated drinking and would vehemently rebuke me for resorting to alcohol (all the while, waving a joint in my face at eight in the morning). Grass smokers are a breed unto themselves. While very few accomplish anything at all at the end of the day, their "buzz" tells them they are the most perceptive, brilliant, creative thinkers on earth. *Mañana* is good enough for them when it comes to getting down to the real business of life. Besides, Richard didn't have to drink in order to break through the inhibitions of his anger; rage and anger came naturally to him.

When Cooper was still a baby, I was hired to star in a film that was to be shot in South Africa. Although I had no way of knowing it, everything about this film was to force me to extremes. Richard's dad, Jack, stayed home with my son Reis while Cooper accompanied Richard and me on location. Baby-sitting for Reis was a selfless gesture of love on Jack's part. Richard's dad was a dear man with an enormous heart. Although, as I have said, he had been abusive to Richard as a child, he had turned into a kind and gentle man by the time I met him. Richard and his dad had a beautiful and unusual relationship that spanned their lifetimes, a relationship that had gone from anger and hate to scale the heights of love and respect. Jack also loved the Lord.

n i n e t e e n

NEVER MORE

$\mathcal{T}$HE South African film was a tough shoot for a multitude of reasons. I say this again because looking back over the thirty films I have appeared in thus far, only a couple have been smooth-sailing productions. Of course, South Africa was fascinating; it gave me a rare opportunity to learn the truth about the political situation in that country ten years ago. I was to return to South Africa again to shoot *The Book of Acts* five years later, and was happy to see firsthand the positive changes that had taken place, at least in the Cape Town area.

Richard landed a small role in the film and I hoped this would make traveling together easier. In addition, we had found a wonderful nanny to watch the baby in Johannesburg. As was the case so many times before, it should have been a good season in our lives, but it wasn't. Richard was never satisfied with me. To try to please him, I had given up alcohol for a full year, but that made no difference. Richard seemed only to find a myriad of other things he didn't like about me, and then he'd start raging about them: Reis bothered him, Rhoda bothered him, my parents bothered him, working on the farm bothered him . . . California bothered him. His songwriting career wasn't going anywhere, and to hear him rant, you'd think I was keeping him from his destiny. Richard had had no career when I met him, but somehow it was still my fault that he wasn't doing what he wanted to do. He would leave, and, as my children often pointed out, would return when he ran out of money. It is the basic imbalance of power at work. When a man isn't the breadwinner, or feeling in control of his family, his innate position and importance are pulled out from under him and he is left only with resentment and anger . . . I became his enemy. God can only heal what you turn over to him, and neither he nor I was using the help available to us as believers. The tail was wagging the dog again.

Our inevitable explosion came at the end of the film. I was sick, hemorrhaging from another miscarriage, and had to go into the hospital for a D&C. This was not a new experience for me; I would miscarry early on and hemorrhage so severely that only surgery could stop the bleeding.

Richard left me in Africa and took Cooper home to the States while I recovered. I followed a week later. Richard's behavior was becoming increasingly hostile and suspicious. At the same time his discomfort with Reis and Rhoda escalated to a point where it seemed we all couldn't stay in the same house. While Richard was looking for reasons to leave, Reis wanted to go live with his dad, who had remarried and had a home in the country a couple of hours away. John's new wife, Cindy, was extremely nice and intelligent; we had all finally found a way to put old hurts aside and focus on letting Reis know John and I were united on his behalf.

Having recently been in counseling (I had gone to work on my relationship with Richard) I took Reis to my therapist to talk about his feelings of living with his dad. I didn't want to make any more mistakes with my children, at least any I could avoid, and I felt I needed a second opinion before making such an important decision. The counselor told me it is very normal for boys to want to spend time with their fathers, especially since Reis and Richard had not bonded. I asked John to come to speak with the counselor and me. He had never actually admitted his abuse of Aimee—though by now I was clear about his offense—and I needed to be reassured that he was no longer in denial and had recovered.

It is difficult to tell you how I felt *then*, particularly in light of what the future held by way of John's next round of abuse. Now

I know this kind of manipulation can continue, even when the abuser is overseen by a therapist. Watch out! I told John in front of the counselor that I was concerned about Reis going to live with him, given what had happened with Aimee. I wasn't worried about him abusing Reis, but I was concerned for and about John's two stepdaughters—not only due to John's history, but also because of Reis, who would be close in age to the girls as he grew up. John had married another time before his marriage to Cindy, his present wife, and the son and a daughter from that marriage were also living with Cindy and her daughters, Melissa and Maryann. Cindy was a loving, stay-at-home mom, who, at this time, was pregnant—so she had four children (her own and two of John's), plus one on the way, and possibly Reis. Quite a handful.

But to Reis they all looked like one big happy family in the country and he wanted to be a part of the troops. John reassured both the counselor and me of his deep and abiding love for all his children and his family and he swore he had finally straightened out his life. As I said before, it is impossible to describe how convincing John was and, I'm sure, will always be. He passed the counselor's scrutiny with flying colors. She felt totally comfortable about Reis moving into his dad's household . . . and therefore, so did I.

Reis was ecstatic when he left for his father's with Rhoda, who was going to stay on for a while during the transition. I was relieved to learn that John's dad was also living with Cindy and John to help out. I knew John's dad well and admired him for his courage in leaving a lucrative advertising job to do community and spiritual work. He was a highly intelligent man and a wonderful influence on his grandson, Reis.

Everything seemed to be in order, although Aimee was worried and dubious about John's apparent recovery. She had undergone a lot of counseling herself for the abuse she had suffered, and wasn't convinced my counselor had made an accurate assessment of John. As it turned out, unfortunately, Aimee was right.

Life at home with just Richard, Cooper, the South African nanny, and me was not proving to be as easy as I had hoped for.

I never lost my hands-on closeness to Cooper, even though there was so much strain between his father and me. (I attribute that directly to my relationship with God, wobbly as it was at that time.) And even when I found out that Richard had been frequenting prostitutes over a long period of time, I didn't curl up and want to die . . . I had known something was going on with him, I could just feel it, although I never imagined anything like *prostitutes*. I was so tired of being told that I was fabricating things, only to find out my suspicions were always well founded. I couldn't stand it anymore: this news, after John's abuse of Aimee, twisted my heart around. When Richard and I divorced, that man owned a piece of me that I couldn't seem to heal—at least for the time being.

I was beginning to consider changing my middle name to "Recovery." I was always recovering from something or someone, but mainly from myself. I had to convince myself that I was better off divorced from Richard, but it wasn't easy as I watched our son emotionally disintegrate, his little heart torn to pieces first with Reis's departure and now his dad's being gone. Forget about all of my garbage—my story of woe had my name inscribed as author on the cover as much as anyone else's . . . But the "Coop" . . . "Mr. DeVille," my baby boy. It killed me to see how sad he was. He missed his dad so much, and I guess I missed the idea of his dad so much. When I would think back to all the hard times Richard and I had, they outweighed the good, but I still couldn't give him up in my heart. I believed Richard and I were *supposed* to make it. Look at our son, I told myself. Look at our blessings.

Everyone said I was different when Richard was around—strained, anxious to make myself into something he wanted. Obviously, if he held me in such low esteem, what value could I possibly have? And that's how I felt for a good, long while. My faith kept me close to my son, working and staying out of a deep depression, but I had so many residual hurts that remained unhealed. So many old hiding places left to uncover. I was one big, fat miserable *work-in-progress*. But the truth is, God never starts a work He doesn't finish, and He had some amazing plans for me as soon as I just chose to proceed.

I had been seeing a Greek psychologist who was only a moral beat or two away from being the most all-encompassing mind I had ever encountered. After he worked with both Richard and me, he concluded, "Jennifer, think of yourself as a magnificent twelve-by-twelve-foot Oriental rug spread across a palace floor, displayed for all to admire and enjoy. Now think of Richard as a twelve-by-twelve-inch finely hewn box sitting over on the nearby table . . . What *you* do"—he paused, his dark eyebrows veiling his stare— "is madly try to stuff your twelve-by-twelve-*foot* dimensions into Richard's twelve-by-twelve-*inch* dimensions. It won't fit." Then he laughed for a moment, exposing the futility of my quest for Richard. *You and Richard don't fit, Jennifer.* It doesn't mean one is better than the other, you're just intrinsically different. A mismatch. I finally agreed about Richard, but disregarded the general advice of this psychologist because, despite his sophistication and intelligence, he did not understand my faith and disagreed with my priorities. If I had followed this man's plan for me, I would have taken on the jet-set world, hooked myself up to the biggest career I could promote, and landed the wealthiest man in town. He challenged me to consider my need for children and family as a hindrance to my otherwise limitless journey—he called it my "quest for the mundane"— and I countered with the virtues and basic values found in God, true love, commitment, and family. He reminded me how unhappy I was. I was confused, but despite his beckoning, and providing me with the best mental chess I had ever played, I was finally out of there on a wing and a prayer. God was on my mind and on my lips, even though I was still floundering in my psychological past with an unconnected heartbeat. I was a baby on milk in my faith—I was still concerned, still vulnerable to despair, and quite capable of bad behavior.

This love affair I started with God at the birth of my last child was not going away . . . It was going deeper and staying longer. It was becoming connected to the very fabric and texture of my needs. In its truth, I would become unswayable amid trying circumstances, if I would just give my pain to God, if I would just *trust* in Him . . . that was not an easy step for this girl to take.

*   *   *

Point of View Farm was my haven, an emotional shelter from the storm of yet another divorce. I threw myself back into my first passion, horses, and hired a young lady named Erin as the "professional" on the farm. I had been breeding horses for years and had come to the painful conclusion that only one out of every three or four foals gets far enough along to see what its socks are stitched with. As big and magnificent as these animals are, they are astoundingly frail. Only inveterate horse owners understand the illogic of an emotional and financial investment in an animal that usually won't come when you call it, can die if it gets a stomachache, can't go in your car on vacations, and costs more than your home.

When I committed to the horses, I did it big time. Erin and I were like the "odd couple," arguing, working all hours, both intent on success and challenging our individual demons. Erin was younger than my daughter, but riding and competing on horses isn't all about chronological age— Erin and I were equal in varying talents as far as the horses went. Unlike most sports, the best riders in international competition run anywhere from sixteen to sixty. Experience counts.

Erin's and my efforts to run an "A" horse-show facility were successful, and then I was offered a huge contract to be the Gucci spokesperson for the next five years. The deal was ground-breaking as far as monies allotted—$6.25 million plus $250,000 a year to support a team of international show horses! Not only was I going to have a prestigious and financially awesome job, I was going to be paid to do my horse thing as well. My thirty years with Cover Girl had just wound down to a natural conclusion, so the Gucci deal was a real windfall.

Contracts were signed with a man named Ed Litwack, agent for Paulo Gucci. I went to Europe to buy the team of horses that was to be on my tab, less expenses. To put such a group of horses together, I sought the help of several professionals and brought in major owners on the strength of the contracted deal with Gucci. And so the team was assembled—a speed horse, a horse off the Swiss Olympic team, and two European Grand Prix horses.

What followed was months and months of lying and deception from the Gucci/Litwack front, which was mentally and emotionally rearranging to me . . . but as usual, it was only the beginning. The horses arrived from Europe based on my credit and the standing of both of the professionals, here in the States and abroad. I personally paid all costs except for the speed horse, and meanwhile received not *one cent* from my contract with Gucci—they were in default from the first payment! My bank and team of lawyers were also taken in by Ed Litwack, who had an answer for everything and nothing to back it up. I was brought up to believe giving your word means something, and here I was, about to embark on an odyssey of deception, with contracts in hand, words of trust, and day-to-day, string-along promises that were never made good on. It is astounding how sophisticated, international businesspeople can charm, lie, deceive, and cheat without even flinching. What a lesson I learned and continue to learn from the dark side of town.

Shortly after I purchased the horses, Paulo Gucci died, leaving his own horses starving on his farm, family members wishing he were still alive so they could nail him, an ex-wife and children vying for whatever lire were left over from his questionable dealings . . . As for Litwack, he failed to respond to the lawsuit I filed against him for his self-proclaimed fraud and breach of contract. The judge handed me a default judgment against him of *eight million dollars plus*. Of course Litwack immediately filed for bankruptcy and I will probably never see a dime. Nonetheless, it felt good to have my damages recognized.

The banks had loaned me whatever I desired to buy the horses, based on my financial history and the (signed) Gucci contract. But due to their default, I had to immediately sell all the horses just to stay afloat. (And then there was the incredible embarrassment of it all.) I was used to working whenever I wanted and in essence making however much money I needed, but this was a staggering financial blow as I had turned down other work in good faith. I had lost everything before, and that was not a place I ever wanted to revisit.

The rules seemed to be changing. After working with Cover

Girl for so long, I assumed other campaigns and individuals would comport themselves in an equally honorable manner. I was wrong. And there were other deals to come that involved equally dishonorable people, but they aren't even worth mentioning. The world was proving to be my worst enemy, and I was in a race to know God better before my circumstances piled me in a corner again.

Around this time I flew to New York to redo (Elle's) apartment I had bought from my parents before they moved out to California to live with me. Mom and Dad have been staying with me on and off since 1990, and I'm happy to say, there has been phenomenal healing between us. I wish I could say the same for my brother, who has chosen for his own reasons to exclude himself from the family.

I was determined to live my life God's way, not to edit His guidance to conform to my own likes and dislikes, but to take in all that I was learning as a complete package able to fulfill every promise within my obedience. But I was having trouble with the "unearned, free gift" part of grace. I was so used to trying to earn love that it was hard for me to accept God's love for me just the way I was, which, as far as I was concerned, was pretty much a mess. I can honestly say that during the times when I wasn't married, not a moment passed when deep down inside I wasn't searching for "my guy for life." It didn't matter how outrageous the past failures had been, I seemed always to refinish my heart with a new veneer of hope and hurl myself into the next commitment with the spunk of an unblemished teenager. I'm not sure whether I was a positive thinker or just plain stupid.

All of which brings me to Neil. Usually, when a man is knockout handsome, he has downsides you wouldn't ever want to mess with, but Neil was truly a terrific guy and as handsome as they come. God was in a good mood when He made Neil. He was brought up in a close, supportive family, by parents who raised their children in a manner we mostly talk about but don't deliver. That is probably why Neil was so down-to-earth.

I met him one night during my redecorating trip to New York

when I was out with friends. We were immediately inseparable. It was important to me that Neil also be a believer, because God says we're not to be "unequally yoked." That makes sense to me; I wouldn't know anymore how to base a life with someone who didn't share the same values and priorities. To this day, my trust for a person is in direct porportion to the strength of their relationship with God. If they hold themselves accountable to God's word, honor, and ways, they have a shot at integrity, but all of us, left to our own devices, are untrustworthy in a Godless condition. Sin is any separation from God, which, of course, is why we all need grace and forgiveness, because we will fall short of His glory on a daily basis. It is so easy for me now to forgive others, because I have been forgiven for so much—every day of my life.

Neil and I married only months after we met—there I was in a hurry again. We did abstain from sex before marriage (which we both believed in) and I was totally convinced that with God's manual in front of our faces every day, our commitment would be solid and lifelong. Neil was absolutely fantastic with Cooper, and Cooper *adored* him—which, of course, was so important to me. This was a good man, it was a happy time, and Neil and I decided we would try to have a baby together. I felt renewed.

But not for long. The moment Neil confessed that he had failed to tell me something of central importance before we were married, I knew we were doomed . . . Not so much because I couldn't understand his withholding of information; I certainly have been caught in a lie or two million in my life . . . It was really because I had such low tolerance about trust issues that I knew I was going to shut down on him emotionally. I didn't hate Neil, but I hated that he failed us in an area that was too hard for me to come back from. He knew all about the deceptions that I had experienced. I told him prior to our marriage that I could handle anything except lies and surprises. Still, I say now that I was wrong to give up on us and I am sorry for that. I sought out as much psychological and spiritual advice as I could find, to bring some balance to my decision, but in the end, our marriage was annulled after six months.

I gave my word that the details of our demise would remain between Neil and me, and that I must honor. The worst part was that Cooper was shattered again.

I was in limbo, numb and lost, when Richard came back into my life as a friend. He had been seeing Cooper all along, but I really hadn't spoken to him in person for a long while. Suddenly we were having lunches together, spending hours just talking about everything—our fears, our losses, our faith, our son, our aspirations. We had never been so close. He had changed somehow. He was gentle and supportive and I thought maybe we were meant to be together after all. The first time I married Richard, I wasn't a believer, but this time I felt we could make it right under God's umbrella. Bottom line, Richard charmed the pants off me again. (I should probably add that Richard married his first wife twice as well.)

I was shooting a film in Mexico when Richard flew down with Cooper and we remarried, with our son present at the ceremony. We told Cooper that he could trust us, that we loved each other and him and we were finally going to be a happy family. We promised that to Cooper, and of course he believed us.

We must have had at least a short period of good times before all hell broke out again, but I'm not really sure; you see, this was the period when it was discovered that John was now molesting his stepdaughter Melissa. I had protected Reis from knowing about his father's abuse of Aimee, believing he shouldn't be told until he was grown and better able to understand his father's problem. Aimee agreed with that approach and we kept the story to ourselves. Everything that surrounded my gunshot wound was also covered in a shroud of secrecy to protect Reis. But now it was not the past, it was the present, and John was destroying lives again like a rabid dog on the loose.

Throughout all the discovery, arrest, and the period before John's hearing, Aimee was an absolute soldier. She was there for Reis, Melissa, and Cindy as well as initiating the entire investigation. When the police first confronted Melissa, she denied that John had abused her, and when Reis was first told about the charges, he didn't believe his father capable of such a thing. I couldn't imagine what it's like to find out something like that about your own father, but I knew that knowledge was going to ravage Reis's life for a long time to come.

twenty

FOREVER

I HAD just finished my study of the New Testament when I
was off to South Africa again to shoot a movie, *The Book
of Acts.* I was becoming more and more imbued with God's Word,
but it was a trip to Jerusalem I took the year before that really
pressed my faith on to another level. I was filled with anticipation
as I made my way to Israel, overwhelmed by the prospect of seeing
where Jesus actually walked. It was, without question, the most
cherished gift I have ever received—other than my faith itself. Just
as God prepares our hearts to hear His truth, He has given us a
tangible place, Jerusalem, to see, feel, and touch—it is an experience that changes one forever.

All the reading I had done, all the Bible study, sprang to life
for me once I found myself at the various locations described in
the Word. The Crucifixion of Jesus Christ was suddenly real, the
pain of all our sins passing through our Lord in His sinless, yet
human form—His teachings, healings, His compassion and grace.
Betrayal was put in perspective for me; fear, evil, and ignorance
took on an almost physical form, which helped define their thievery
of our peace. The line between the enemy's world, with its temporal futility, and the eternal spiritual Kingdom was defined clearly
during my time in Jerusalem . . . Healing waters of mystical depth
and dark blue perfection lapped at the shores of the Sea of Galilee.
Jesus Christ had lived, taught, walked, and died there, and I could

personally feel His presence from then on in a way I had never imagined.

Because I had made a public proclamation of my faith prior to the annulment of my marriage with Neil, I was feeling particularly unworthy of even being called a child of God, let alone being viewed as any kind of example . . . I still feel that way. But just because I'm not perfect doesn't mean that God's Word isn't. Just because I make so many mistakes doesn't mean God is wrong. Just because I was headed for more trials doesn't mean God didn't love me. My pastor put it this way: "Jennifer, God will survive your press." What a relief! When I thought about it, I realized how ridiculous and self-centered it was of me to consider I could make even the most infinitesimal dent in God's perfection. Sometimes I just have to get over myself.

I went on a short trip to Nashville on business and immediately fell in love with the area and the people. Green grass for the horses, a family-minded, spiritually based community, and, of course, music. Since Richard and I remarried, his old complaints about California began, and his wanderlust again took him to Florida, Nashville, and Arizona during his "leaving times." So I had a notion. Since I had a TV series in the works, I talked to Richard about moving lock, stock, parents, kids, and horses to Nashville. I was sure this opportunity would make him happy, especially since it would give him a real shot at working on his music career. And he was happy. I lease-optioned a hundred-and-fifteen-acre estate with lakes, barns, tennis court, and log cabin thirty-five minutes from downtown Nashville. Mom said the grounds reminded her of Hyde Park in London. Boy, I thought, if Richard and I weren't ecstatic here, we should be thrashed—well, time to get the switch.

As it turned out, the TV series was aborted for lack of funds, and I still owned Point of View Farm in Malibu, which I rented out. Three years prior, the farm was on the market for over four million dollars, but the market had suddenly crashed and it was not the time to sell in L.A. Erin left the barn unexpectedly after I moved, and I learned very quickly how hard it is to run a farm long distance. Thankfully, things picked up again with my old ad friends from Cover Girl, who now represented Maybelline. I signed a new contract for a complete line of makeup and we were on our way, having already shot the tests in New York. But suddenly the deal was off because of the L'Oréal/Maybelline merger, causing any old projects to be trashed. Just like that . . . Again. At least this was not a case of breach of contract or any wrongdoing—just wrong *timing*.

While all that was going on, Richard became discontented and angry again. He moved into the log cabin by the lake and said he wanted a divorce in between vicious fights. I was exhausted, simply worn-out. I had to move out of the lease-purchase farm into a much smaller place due to my ongoing string of financial reversals. It was a very scary time . . . everything was collapsing and I couldn't stop it. I decided to buy a home in a neighborhood where the kids would have friends to play with. The horses were going to stay at the Parkers' . . . *Oh, the Parkers*—as much as I was starting to feel abandoned by God, somewhere I knew He had placed this couple in my life as restorers of my heart. Bob and Shirley lived next to my leased farm in Nashville, and we had become great friends—chatting over the fence and having morning coffee together. I fell in love with these two outstanding individuals. They are family to me. Although inseparable as a couple, they open their home and their hearts to whoever happens to be fortunate enough to cross their paths.

Bob and Shirley empathized with me about Richard wanting the divorce and my finding myself with six horses, four dogs, my parents, two boys, and no partner. On top of that, my career was in California and here I was in Nashville. Despite my circumstances, I rallied, believing God could heal anything and anyone. So I committed myself to a twenty-day fast and called everyone in prayer for my marriage. Fasting and prayer, according to the Bible, are a powerful combination for one in need of intercession. God does hear all our prayers, but I was about to learn how He answers them according to His will, not ours. And *His timing*.

While I moved the kids and my parents into the new house, Richard made a deal with the lease-owners to stay in the cabin, even though I objected to them about this. I felt I should have a say since the home was still rented to me. (The owners, by the way, collected over $170,000 for my six-month stay on their property.) It was not that I begrudged Richard the cabin, but since the kids and I had to move, I thought it really wrong to allow him to stay, especially since he never paid one cent for his lodging there. In theory, the owners were entitled to that enormous amount of money for rent because I was no longer in a position to buy the home at the end of the lease. That was our deal; letting Richard stay on was not part of it.

And yet again nothing was making sense to me; I finally went to my pastor to talk to him about Richard's unwavering demand for a divorce. I just didn't know what to do; Richard wouldn't even talk to me and had once more withdrawn into his own world. The cabin by the lake seemed to offer him everything he wanted, and I wasn't any part of it. This went on for months, during which he'd take Cooper for weekends and time off.

My pastor was attentive and kind, and I really appreciated that, since I had been attending the church for only a short while. He suggested I write Richard a letter expressing *all* my feelings. I did just that, and in essence told Richard that he could choose any counselor he wanted, but we needed to begin to work on diligently and prayerfully putting our marriage back together. Cooper was in pain, I was in pain. We missed him and there was nothing that God couldn't heal if we turned it over to Him together. I told Richard that if the separation went on any longer, it would only pull us further apart. I let him know that I loved him very much and we all wanted him to come home, but added that if he was indeed serious about proceeding with the divorce, and nothing I did could dissuade him, he needed to let me go, and Cooper needed to understand that no hope remained for creating the family we had promised him. I sealed the envelope, prayed over it, and left it taped to the cabin door.

I had acquired a terrific friend in Nashville named Sharon, who was set on helping me meet creative businesspeople in the hope of getting me out of my "Richard doldrums." I first met her when she attended a fund-raiser dinner for the New Hope Academy of which I was the host as well as one of the chairpersons. I liked this girl right off, and was happy to make a new acquaintance in foreign territory.

Sharon had arranged a meeting/dinner with some well-respected songwriters, as she had heard my music and thought I might be able to collaborate with some "Music City" notables. I was to meet her at a local landmark at 5:45 P.M., then follow her to our dinner, since I was totally unfamiliar with the downtown Nashville area.

As I drove in from the suburbs that night, I wished I could be somewhere else; all I really wanted to do was roll up and disappear. I caught my reflection in the rearview mirror and thought if one more tear escaped my swollen eyes, I would show up for the meeting looking like a beat-up boxer. I was used to squelching my feelings, but since the call I had received from Richard late that afternoon, I felt out of control well beyond my comfort zone.

Through the phone, Richard's voice was subdued—ominously so. I could all but hear the promise of a lethal explosion if I pushed him . . . But that wasn't going to happen, because I was through begging with this man to stick to a commitment he'd made twice over. He was brief and I could tell he was itching for a fight, but I had no more fight left in me. "Jennifer, I got your letter and . . . Look, it's over, Jennifer. Why don't we just let it go and realize it's never going to work. Let's just be friends and let it go." He paused for a response, but I needed to know only one more thing from him: "Are you telling me that you don't want to work on our marriage? Are you saying you really want a divorce?" He exhaled loudly, then said, "Yes." That was it. I waited for more, but I was fooling myself yet again . . . And once I really realized this, I said, "Fine. But you are not my friend, and if you care even slightly about me, just leave me alone. I don't want to talk to you unless it pertains to our son." I put the phone back in its cradle with a calmness I did not feel. The most important thing anyone can do for a relationship is *stay*. If you leave, there's nothing left to work on.

The evening Sharon had arranged turned out to be filled with good food, good company, and good music. But by the time eleven o'clock rolled around, everyone left the writer's studio to head back home. Sharon and one of the writers followed me to the gas station, where I filled up and was given directions for my journey to the suburbs. Everything was moving right along until I became lost somewhere on the outer loop to the inner loop to wherever and found myself headed forty-five minutes out of my way toward Memphis. (If you know Nashville, you understand my predicament.) I pride myself on my good sense of direction, but somehow that night, even when I drove all the way back into town, traveled the inner-loop/outer-loop nightmare again, I was still lost. I can only attribute this to stupidity on my part; somehow I got the directions turned around in my head. For twenty years I lived north of New York City in the Bedford area. Then, for over ten years, I lived north of L.A. in Malibu. North of cities had always been home to me, but *south* of Nashville was where I needed to go. Obviously, I was heading in the wrong direction.

It didn't matter how logical the reason was for getting lost on the highway, I felt like I was going crazy after circling Nashville one too many times. I was exhausted and I was late, and finally, the floodgates just opened—I can't ever remember crying so hard. Reis was home with Cooper, Mom and Dad were nearby, but I still wasn't comfortable leaving them for so long a time, especially since I was up every morning at six-thirty to take Cooper to school. I had to get home—now!

And then, just about the time I recognized a stretch of expressway not far from my new home, it really hit me: Richard was never coming back. *Never.* God had let me down—*totally.* If God was real, why wouldn't He fix my marriage? I had prayed, I had fasted; I had cried for my boy and for myself. I hated myself. I hated Richard. I hated *God!* I was a joke . . . My life was a farce. My faith was just another invention of my head! I was never going to let another lie take me down. I was suddenly in a terrifying state of fury. I didn't care about anyone or anything.

I heard my voice rise as fast as the speedometer in my car. I was screaming at God and tearing up the road like I was back on the racetrack. The station wagon I was in turned into my old Corvette. I was mad and I didn't give a damn about rules, regulations, or Richard. I was in the midst of renouncing every last bit of faith, love, or good feelings I ever had when the flashing red lights diverted my attention.

Suddenly I found myself in the middle of someone else's short story, trapped in the headlights of a police car piloted by a man with his own agenda. I was nothing less than full-out hysterical when the officer approached my car. I pulled away from the glare of his flashlight; my makeup was gathering in pools under my eyes. The officer was polite at first when he asked me for my license and registration, and if I had had anything to drink that night. I handed him my papers and said, "Yes, a few glasses of wine earlier with dinner." Everything went downhill from there. I have waited with pen in hand for several years to write about all of the injustices and sorry details of this fiasco, but as I sit here now trying to set down in words the real importance of that evening, it's God I want to talk about, not that policeman. The details of what "he did/she did" belong on a bad episode of *In the Heat of the Night* . . . Talk about things escalating out of control. I can tell you this much: it is extremely inadvisable to talk back to an officer, especially one with a bad temper. I might have been screaming at God, but I had just met the enemy wearing a badge and a uniform, and I didn't know when to shut up.

I was charged with speeding and a DUI, and before I was released a few hours later, I was the Southern-fried headline news—and by the end of the day, I was an international news orgy. I listened to the radio report of my DUI charge on the way home from the police station that morning. It took me over a year and a half and *thirteen* postponed court dates (eleven on the court's side) before I got the jury trial I asked for. Meanwhile, local newspapers reported my *home* address on their front pages, printed incorrect information about my divorce from Richard, stating Cooper's full name and age, publicly identified Cooper as an *illegitimate* child because the paper hadn't bothered to learn that Richard and I were married twice . . . Eighteen months of disgrace at the hands of irresponsible press that absolutely cauterized my career. Eighteen months of public humiliation without a forum in which to defend myself. My lawyer would not let me make any statement to the press for that entire year and a half, and I couldn't seem to get my case to trial . . . *Thirteen postponements!* Every time the trial was postponed, the DUI headlines resurfaced all over again all over the world. I had a friend from Europe call and ask me straight out exactly how many times I had been arrested for drunk driving. Actually, I don't know why all this surprised me so much. Remember, I was the one the headline-seeking DA charged with illegal possession of the gun that went off and shot me. I had been in the system before. I should have known.

The jury trial finally took place and after three days in court, requiring a *unanimous* verdict from the jury, I was exonerated . . . *not guilty*, praise God! Prayer works! . . . But on another level, the damage had been done. I was whipped.

Yes, I was definitely speeding down the highway that night screaming at God, but it wasn't about drinking, it was about being lost, not only on the roads around Nashville, but in my life. I was at the end of my rope. *"How could you let me down, God?"* I remember screaming. A wail resounded from the depths of my despair. In my mind I had done all the right things for God and I expected to box Him in with His own promises and insist that He fix what I told Him to fix because I had fashioned the whole thing in His Name. (There you go, Jennifer, trying to control God . . .) I was either going to come closer to my faith after that night, or leave it entirely.

"Times of trials," it's called. God allows things to happen in our lives to help us grow up in Him and to prepare us for the journey He has planned specifically for us. God sees around corners, He knows exactly that we need to learn to handle what is coming up in our lives. God is never out of control. I had to learn to wait on the Lord. I had to realize my complete inability to control any aspect of my life before I could or *would* finally rely on God . . . So I would finally trust in Him and give it up, knowing

He would never let me down. What we think we want may not be what is best for us at all . . . Most of the time it's not.

These last three years have been the toughest of my life, but also the most rewarding. I watched my son Reis hit his teens head-on, full of anger and distrust, mainly because of his father's hideous acts. John taught Reis how to lie, cheat, steal, and con. The year and a half I was waiting for my day in court, Reis was getting in trouble at school with drugs and with the police. My boy was spinning out of control, hating my guts, and I was afraid he literally might not live through the year. He was committing slow-motion suicide, and all I was able to do was stand there and watch him fall. I prayed . . . I really prayed.

I pulled Reis out of school and got him into a medical-wilderness program that I believe saved his life—I liken it to boot camp with doctors, and when Reis came out of this "crash course" *for* life, he had definitely turned a major corner.

Aimee and Reis have always been very close and she took him in for over nine months after he completed the wilderness program. At the time Aimee and her family were living at my farm in Malibu, and although Reis's arrival was on the heels of a difficult time, it also was a healing time for everyone concerned. I love my daughter for her generosity and compassion—for taking Reis on at a very tough stage in his life. She treated him with a beautiful balance of authority and sisterly love that shows, yet again, what a fabulous young woman Aimee is.

For the last few years, Reis has been back home with me and graduated from high school with honors before his eighteenth birthday. I am so unbelievably proud of all three of my children. Aimee and I have made it past most of the pain and are sharing a deep-running love, respect, and friendship for the first time. There *is* a second act in relationships. Reis is a spectacular young man with a big bright future and an even bigger personality; I enjoy him so much and believe we are sharing a miraculous healing. As for my youngest . . . Well, what can I say about this eleven-year-old piece of magic in my life? Cooper is the "Coop," and everyone better fasten their seat belts when he comes to town. I have two marvelous grandsons under three years old—yes, Aimee has been busy lately. My parents live with us and are healthy and a joy to have so close. I have watched them interact with their grand- and great-grandchildren—this family seems to be finally experiencing some of the joys carved out for each of us upon our request. I've learned you have to claim your blessings. I still have a few horses at home that I bred and successfully show. Hey, it sounds like my old pink suede shoes are tapping along to the tune of "The Good Ship Lollipop" . . . Sometimes.

God doesn't promise life will be easy, but He does promise you will never be alone; in Him you can rest, trust, heal, grow, be forgiven, and have eternal life. And "when this old life starts getting you down," just know that it will *always* try to rob you; the difference is, it doesn't *own* you anymore.

And what about my endless quest for love and marriage? Did I mention to you that God has a great sense of humor? Actually he invented it. I met Mervin Louque when I first moved to Nashville. We were working together on an on-line project and were introduced to each other by a mutual friend. Our first round was all business, and after a year of working together, things between us took on a different complexion. Actually, if the truth be known, I had to go and get this man—I couldn't have written a better act III.

I was attending the Nashville Planet Hollywood opening, complete with red carpet. After I walked down to greet the fans and the press in attendance, I left as soon as I had made my solo appearance. On my way home, I swung by Douglas Corner, Mervin's music club, to drop off some contracts. Douglas Corner is *the* club, where everyone from Trisha Yearwood to Garth Brooks started their careers. For the last eleven years it has functioned as a support system and link between many songwriters and performers to the major record labels in Nashville. Mervin, by the way, is highly respected by the music industry, and is a talented writer/producer in his own right.

For all of the above reasons and a few others—he knocks my socks off and puts them back on again—when I went to the club that night, something came over me. Actually, I was as surprised as Mervin when we went into his office to take care of the paperwork, and the next thing I knew, I heard myself saying to him, "You don't get it, do you?" "What?" he looked at me like I was off my nut . . . I gave him a stare that I thought I no longer possessed and said, "We're supposed to be together."

And that, as they say, was that. We've been married for two years now—*amazing grace*. Do we argue? *Sure*. Are we happy? *More than not*. What's our secret? *God*. Will we last? *You bet*. Do we laugh? *More every day*. Do we trust each other? *Implicitly*. Are things easy? *Are you crazy!* . . .

I don't need my husband, or anyone else for that matter, to make me happy or fill me up; God and I finally have that part worked out. And this allows me to fold into my husband's arms, just like in the movies. All my children tell me that I'm a heck of a good mom these days—and my goat voice did not prevail; I just signed a deal for my spiritual vocal group "O'Neill and Company" to release our first album in early 1999. I'm still flying thru the air (hopefully with the greatest of ease) while showing my horses on a regular basis. I'm having a better time than I ever expected to, with a good portion of peace to boot. I recently turned fifty years old and I've figured this much out: life will never be easy, and I will never be perfect, but God is perfect, so I don't have to be. With God's help, I'm surviving myself, and I can't wait to see what He has in store for me next . . .

miracles coming true

We have hearts that beat
Eyes that see
Wounds that mend without thinking
We have deep desires
Sweeping thoughts
Promises worth keeping

We have love—we have laughter
Sun after the rain
Gifts from God to me and you
Miracles coming true—every day

We have birds in the trees
Harmonies
Moments turned into memories
We have babies to make
Mornings to wake to
Higher ground for the taking

We have love—we have laughter
Sun after the rain
Gifts from God to me and you
Miracles coming true—every day

Sunsets and rainbows—are free
Cause God knows—just what we need

We have something deep inside
That doesn't want to lie
Tried and true has meaning
We have a need to believe
A way to be free
Fantasies worth dreaming

We have love—we have laughter
Sun after the rain
Gifts from God to me and you
Miracles coming true—every day